OBSESSED WITH LANGUAGE

A SOCIOLINGUISTIC HISTORY OF QUEBEC

ESSAY SERIES 55

Canada Council **Conseil des Arts**
for the Arts **du Canada**

ONTARIO ARTS COUNCIL
CONSEIL DES ARTS DE L'ONTARIO

Guernica Editions Inc. acknowledges the support of The Canada Council for the Arts.
Guernica Editions Inc. acknowledges the support of the Ontario Arts Council

CHANTAL BOUCHARD

OBSESSED WITH LANGUAGE

A SOCIOLINGUISTIC HISTORY OF QUEBEC

Translated by Luise von Flotow

GUERNICA
TORONTO–BUFFALO–LANCASTER (U.K.)
2008

Luise von Flotow would like to thank the CITL – Centre international de traduction littéraire – in Arles, France, for its support in Summer 2006.

Original title: *La langue et le nombril* (Fides, 1998)
Copyright © 1998, by Éditions Fides.
Translation © 2008, by Luise von Flotow and Guernica Editions Inc.

Antonio D'Alfonso, editor
Guernica Editions Inc.
P.O. Box 117, Station P, Toronto (ON), Canada M5S 2S6
2250 Military Road, Tonawanda, N.Y. 14150-6000 U.S.A.

DISTRIBUTORS
University of Toronto Press Distribution,
5201 Dufferin Street, Toronto (ON), Canada M3H 5T8
Gazelle Book Services, White Cross Mills, High Town, Lancaster LA1 4XS U.K.
Independent Publishers Group,
814 N. Franklin Street, Chicago, Il. 60610 U.S.A.

Typeset by Selina.
Printed in Canada.
First edition.

Legal Deposit — Fourth Quarter
Library of Congress Catalog Card Number: 2008936846
Library and Archives Canada Cataloguing in Publication
Bouchard, Chantal
Obsessed with language : a sociolinguistic history of Quebec /
Chantal Bouchard ; translated by Luise von Flotow.
(Essay series ; 55)
Translation of: La langue et le nombril.
ISBN 978-1-55071-293-3
1. French language–Quebec (Province)–History. 2. French language–Political aspects–Quebec (Province). 3. Sociolinguistics–Quebec (Province). 4. Language awareness–Quebec (Province). 5. Canadians, French-speaking–Québec (Province)–Ethnic identity. I. Von Flotow, Luise, 1951- II. Title. III. Series: Essay series (Toronto, Ont.) ; 55
PC3645.Q8B6813 2008   447'.9714   C2008-902887-2

CONTENTS

PREFACE TO THE SECOND EDITION

Is there such a thing as linguistic security?

The research I began over ten years ago, and that led to the publication of *La langue et le nombril*, was motivated first and foremost by my desire to understand my own relationship to my language. Around 1980, toward the end of my training as a linguist, I had discovered socio-linguistic studies of the roles that social life, power, prestige, recognition and rejection can play in the development of languages. William Labov's concept *linguistic insecurity* – the feeling some people have that they can't speak "well," or are unable to spontaneously use their language in prestigious ways – this concept particularly interested me. Labov's work describes the linguistic community of New York, and shows that the linguistic norm is defined by the upper class, the class that has the power and prestige; other social strata try to conform to it, especially the middle classes who are trying to improve their status. This desire to acquire prestige has all kinds of consequences, notably the tendency to devalue one's own language and assign an exaggerated value to the normalized version. I was particularly interested in Labov's descriptions of this upper class: they were people who seemed to live in utter security, absolutely certain of how they spoke, and I was sure I had never encountered a Quebecois who could be thus described. And so I set off in search of explanations, tracing the collective history of the Quebecois and of their relationship to French.

"On revient de loin: we've come a long way."

Over the past forty years Quebec has experienced considerable social change. As far as the language is concerned, young people today are more detached, less anxious than their parents or grandparents were. Nevertheless, since the first publication of this book in 1998 I have had occasion to note that a certain malaise persists, even though it is less acute. When I discuss this issue with students in class, or at conferences, people are generally shocked to hear what was said about the language in Quebec in the 1940s and 1950s, but they also admit that they sometimes feel torn between wanting to assert their identity on the one hand and being attracted by the linguistic model from France on the other. I have received many comments from friends, family, and acquaintances that my book helped them understand their complex and contradictory feelings toward French. If they were sincere and not just trying to please me, then my work has been useful. But beyond this, we see from the many studies submitted to Quebec's États généraux [Estates General] on language in 2001 that the Quebecois are still far from feeling sure and secure in regard to our language. Though real progress has been made, most people still feel dissatisfied with their knowledge of the language and with the way it is taught at every level. It may well be true that "we've come a long way" as an elderly person said, recalling the intense malaise of the 1950s when she was a young adult. It seems to me that in Quebec society today there is a clear schism between the younger and the older generations, with forty-year-olds making up an intermediary group. The older people, who were adolescents or young adults in the 1950s and 1960s, are still profoundly marked by the identity crisis and the painful linguistic insecurity of those years; they do not seem very aware of the real progress the younger generation has made in mastering linguistic norms, and their comments indicate that they feel standards are declining. This could explain the ongoing pessimistic, even alarmist, discourse in the media, and the repeated references to the États généraux; after all, older people are the ones who tend to write letters to the editor. It will doubtless take a few more decades before a Montreal magazine will carry the fictional headline I imagined when I wrote the introduction to this book five years ago: "The Quebecois have never spoken such good French."

"You say you've only ever heard people in Quebec congratulate each other on their language?"

That is the first question the Belgian interviewer asked me when I arrived in Liège in 1999 to participate in a discussion about the French language. I'd been in Belgium for about two hours, and had had about twenty minutes to chat with the other discussants before the program started, but that was time enough to see that francophone Belgians are facing the same kind of linguistic malaise we are. One of the participants told me, "You Quebecois are pretty lucky!" which took me by surprise. I told the interviewer somewhat hesitantly that I still had some work to do to really understand the situation in Belgium, and I have studied it since. This has confirmed that there is quite a strong feeling of linguistic insecurity in that country which can be attributed to two main factors: the presence of "wallon", a regional dialect, and the role played by the school system that denigrates this dialect in favour of a more or less mythic norm, "bon français"[1] [good French]. Whatever the reasons, it seems that Belgians have a harder time allowing themselves to use their special expressions, perhaps because they are that much closer to France. This does not explain everything, though, since many factors enter into the relationship that societies have with the language they speak.

In France, where I gave several lectures and interviews, and participated in discussions, people were particularly interested in the history of our resistance. This history clarified our allergy to anglicisms, which they tend to see as ethnocentric rigidity or hyper-sensitivity. The most frequent attitudes the French expressed toward us were curiosity and understanding, and sometimes a certain admiration for our vitality and combativeness. That may be the "luck" the Belgians envy us for.

The "nombrile" [navel] . . .

"Nombrile" [navel]. This is how European francophones pronounce the word, whether they are French, Belgian or Swiss; Quebecois only ever say "nombri" – the way people did in Paris and at the French court during the seventeenth century. "Nombrile," a pronunciation based on spelling, established itself in France after the Revolution, under the influence of written texts; in fact, it applies to a whole set of words such as *sourcil* [eyebrow] and *baril* [barrel], both also pronounced with the final "l." Only the word *outil* [tool] has escaped this orthographic remake. From the point of view of the French norm, "nombri" is what is called an archaism; but not from the perspective of Quebec French. If the Quebecois were aware of this difference – and I don't think that most of them are aware – how would they pronounce the word? Would they make an effort to adopt the French version, or would they continue pronouncing it the way they always have? The question is one of legitimacy. While it is not easy to answer this question, I would bet on the second response. It is something to consider, and will doubtless come up for discussion again, if only because thousands of "nombrils" will be showing up in the streets of Montreal in the next heatwave.

. . . and navel-gazing

The navel metaphor I used in the title of the book to represent the notion of identity did not please everybody. Some saw it as ironic, others were disappointed that the critical attitude it had led them to expect didn't materialize. Are the Quebecois navel-gazers, hyper-sensitive, and turned in upon themselves or are they self-assured, open, and secure? Again, I think that Quebec society is developing. The sensitivity, the defensive withdrawal, the fear of other people's judgments that were so strongly present forty years ago have subsided, but new identity structures whose beginnings I have tried to describe are not yet solidly in place. It is no accident that so many studies on identity have appeared in Quebec in recent years.

A *few more comments*

I have taken advantage of this new edition to add a few pages on several other questions, including a short chapter on the language columnists and their relationship to the norm. Since the late nineteenth century in Quebec, these columnists have been a major source for the discourse on language, and have therefore had a great influence on public opinion. It was useful to examine the references they cite, and on which they base their judgments. Further, in the first edition I stated that constant and increasing pressure by the public had caused the Quebec government to get involved in language issues in the 1960s. This edition includes a detailed study of the creation of the Office de la langue française [Office of the French Language] in 1961, the first linguistic institution born of the Quiet Revolution.

INTRODUCTION

*Obsession with language or how talking about your
language means talking about yourself*

The eye-catching cover of a big Montreal news magazine reads, "The Quebecois have never spoken such
good French." Is this fact or fiction? No magazine has
yet made such a bold claim, but it is actually true – provided you specify what you mean by "speaking good
French." There have always been people in Quebec with
a perfect command of standard French. Various social
changes and especially huge advances in education have
increased this number. These people have, in turn, had a
greater influence on the language of all Quebecois than
the small elite that once existed, largely because they are
more present and in daily contact with their compatriots. Moreover, Quebecois today live in an environment
where French is much more present than it was twenty
or thirty years ago. The current language has truly been
"de-anglicized" over the past thirty years, though bilingualism still leads to inevitable interferences. Given this
situation it is appropriate to ask why the Quebec media
continue to publish largely negative views on the question of language-use in Quebec, regardless who is
expressing these views. Do they sell more copy if they
write that French in Quebec is deteriorating? Do journalists, newspaper owners, and editors all share these
opinions? And what exactly do they mean?

They express disquiet, sometimes anxiety, about who we are as a collective and what we are becoming. The state of our language is the measure of our development, and this is so because language has become the central element in our identity. This is a rare, but not unique situation. It is hard to imagine American, French, Italian or German journalists, writers and actors lamenting the degeneration of their culture just because teenagers have coined a special slang, or TV comedians are using popular language to get laughs, or people in 2004 no longer write English, French, Italian or German the way they once did in the nineteenth century. What exactly happened over the course of our history to render this one aspect of our collective identity dominant, and a topic of perpetual concern? And can we get some idea of how this occurred by analyzing what each generation said about language? First, though, we need to establish a clear difference between the evolution of the language in the way linguistic studies might describe this – with reference to changes in pronunciation, syntactic structures, appearance or disappearance of words, semantic modifications – and the evolution of the *perception* that the collective has had of its language. The opinion you hold about your language is entirely determined by social factors, first and foremost by what has been taught as the linguistic model. Thus, for instance, in societies where the linguistic norm is defined and disseminated by the ruling class, the language of certain sub-groups, those who live in regions far from the centre of power, or are members of oppressed social classes will be discussed, and not that of the entire community.

Opinions about language uttered in a certain social context usually reveal the feelings that the person uttering them has about the society to which they belong. Here is a little demonstration of this principle: "Let me congratulate you! You are very articulated" ["Vous êtes très articulée"]. This sentence, which I heard addressed to a woman my age at a party, and which was meant as a compliment, sparked a series of reactions in me that are clearly associated with different aspects of my personality. As I try to write down my reactions today, I have to admit that I cannot place them in any meaningful order. So here they are as I remember them.

Reaction of the professor of translation: now there's a typical anglicism. Articulated, not like a marionette or an architect's lamp, but *articulate*, as you say in English when someone speaks well and presents a logical, well-ordered argument.

Reaction of the sociolinguist: I observe this exchange. The woman, a Montrealer, is visibly flattered that she should be told she speaks well, indeed elegantly. After all, if someone makes a point of telling her, it is because her way of expressing herself must be something out of the ordinary and the man's intention is clearly to flatter her. A Montrealer himself, he is not unaware of the impact of his praise. She thanks him, a little embarrassed.

Another reaction of the sociolinguist: the utterance of this gentleman of a certain age, a member of the Quebec middle-class and a professional, is a perfect example of the idea that members of his social class had thirty years ago about social hierarchy and linguistic prestige. To speak well at that time, to follow the rules of "bon usage" [proper usage] or of "international French," was to prove that you were well-educated and belonged to the social elite.

Reaction of the forty-year-old: what exactly is so special about expressing yourself clearly and correctly? You could say the same about all of my friends, most of the people I know, and most of my students. And yet, I have never seen anyone outside Quebec, congratulate someone else on the quality of their language.

Reaction of the author of *Obsessed with Language*: this is the core of the problem. In five or six words this man has provided a perfect illustration of the idea that people had of French in Quebec thirty years ago. Linguistic competence, judged on the basis of a dictionary and a grammar book, was considered a rare, even exceptional quality and brought those who displayed it unquestionable prestige. Most of my reactions, at least the most spontaneous ones, clearly express the change in mentalities that has occurred since the end of the 1960s. The perceived gap between the language spoken by the majority of Quebecois and that of the miniscule elite who once held linguistic prestige, has been considerably reduced, though not completely eliminated. Quebecois of my generation, however, are still marked by the complex of linguistic inferiority that our parents suffered and that they tried to spare us. As children and adolescents we witnessed the quarrels over *joual*, we took sides in the struggles over the language laws, we demonstrated against some, we defended others, without always understanding their import, moved largely by the conviction that there was something vital there and that our future, stretching out ahead of us, somehow depended on it. And then Zorro arrived, or rather Bill 101, which appeased our anxieties, and let us grow to adulthood with some sense of security, always somewhat fragile, but no less real. That is how I explain my rather contradictory reactions to the compliment paid my neighbour.

Now, let us imagine that a similar compliment had been paid her by a man from France, and not from Quebec. Would she have been even more flattered, or would she have been irritated at his perceived condescension. Maybe both. In other words, the reactions we have when judgments are made about our language can also be analyzed, and can provide information about the idea we have of ourselves. When these judgments and reactions are applied to the whole of a society, they can provide an outline of the image this society has of itself, its collective identity.

Still today, language is a source of concern in Quebec. Whether Quebecois make films, write books, do theatre, devise ads, write songs, or create programs for the internet, they are all confronted with choices. Their situation, an exceptional one worldwide, is that of a small linguistic minority cohabiting with a population spread across an entire continent that uses the most powerful international language, a situation that never lets them forget how precarious their position is. Each time they make contact with strangers, each time another political crisis shakes up their relations with other Canadians, Quebecois are obliged to explain the political choices they make, the attitudes they adopt, and the language laws they pass. But these attitudes, laws and choices can only be explained by the history of this group of people.

You cannot dissociate the question of language from other cultural aspects or from the identity of a group of people. And so, when I set out to study the complex and problematic relations between Quebec society and its language, I also had to search for the elements in its social, political and economic history that make up the society's identity.

Before I start on the history of the language in Quebec, I will provide a brief synthesis of the ideas that various thinkers and researchers have advanced in their work on collective identity and culture, as well as on the role that language plays in the elaboration of these elements and the changes they undergo.

In order to understand the collective consciousness of generation after generation of francophones in Quebec, there was no other way but to analyze the texts they left behind. I made extensive use of the large collection of texts on language that Guy Bouthiller and Jean Meynaud published in *Le choc des langues au Québec 1760-1970*. These texts, written mainly by journalists, public speakers, politicians, and men of the Church, basically represent the discourse of the elite. In order to expand on these sources and acquire a more representative sample of Quebec society, I also used articles that appeared in newspapers such as *La Presse, La Patrie,* and *Le Devoir,* in particular. This corpus includes articles on language as well as reviews, letters to the editor, printed lectures, sermons, conversations, editorials.

Since a detailed study of the discourse on language in Quebec between 1759 and 1850 has already been published by Danièle Noël (*Les questions de langue au Québec, 1759-1850,* Conseil de la langue française, Editeur officiel du Québec, 1990), I focused my efforts on the second half of the nineteenth and on the twentieth centuries, up to 1970. Danièle Noël concludes her analysis with the statement that up to 1850 the *Canadiens* kept trying to *justify* the use of French in political and legal institutions in what was in fact a British colony, and to *resist* English objectives of assimilation: "Thus we believe that the crux of the conflict over language in the colony can be described as follows: the 'question of language' can be understood as primarily a relationship of power between colonizer and colonized, or more precisely between the dominant and the dominated" (Noël, 359).

I have focused more on the metadiscourse on language, on what is said about the language in Quebec rather than on the discourses about language rights, although they are inextricably linked. Danièle Noël showed that the metadiscourse on language appears in magazines and newspapers as early as 1817 in texts by Michel Bibeau, a journalist and writer, and the first person in Quebec to publish a column on the question of language. Still, among all the texts on language, this metadiscourse remained quite marginal. But it became a constant, at times a virtually dominant discourse, from the last decades of the nineteenth century onward.

The analysis of the metadiscourse on language is particularly useful since it at least partially reveals the opinions that the writers have of their own community. What does it mean for Michel Bibeau to criticize the pronunciation "oué" for "oi", or the use of certain anglicisms? The columns on language do not restrict themselves to correcting "mistakes." They also recommend that certain linguistic structures be jettisoned, and thereby reveal the norms their authors adhere to, and what type of divergence from this norm they can accept. In other words, these columns show what the author considers legitimate or illegitimate. Similarly, the letters that readers send to newspapers, to criticize a certain usage, support the views of a columnist, or oppose his opinions, provide considerable information on the linguistic behaviour and the controversies of the period. Lectures and speeches published in the newspapers are also a rich source of material on the attitudes people held at a certain moment. Why are certain words condemned in 1890, but described as "family jewels that need to be carefully preserved" in 1920? What was the change that made the words *weekend* and *shopping* unacceptable in 1930 but preferable to *fin de semaine* and *magasinage* in the 1950s? Which segments of the population are criticized or praised in each era? What kinds of social phenomena underlie the jokes and anecdotes published in the newspapers? What type of metaphor is used to describe borrowings? These various discourses *about* the language reveal the underlying opinions their authors held on the collective of which they were part, and also the image they constructed of their community – its past, its future, and the dangers it was facing.

I have deliberately limited my analyses to the period that precedes 1970 in order, first, to maintain a certain critical distance vis-à-vis my object of study, but also because I personally experienced the events, controversies, and social and ideological changes that marked the following decades. How have Quebecois opinions on their language changed over the past thirty years? First and foremost, one can say that the idea of making one local version of the language – *joual* – the linguistic norm, an idea that moved certain groups in the 1970s, has been abandoned. There are many reasons for this, and this question in itself merits an exhaustive analysis since the choice of a norm determines the direction in which a language evolves. It appears that a majority of Quebecois do not wish to identify with a version of the language that is associated with the conditions of domination, poverty, and ignorance that obtained when this dialect of the working class and urban proletariat emerged. Indeed, in progressively ridding themselves of the characteristics of a dominated people, Quebecois have acquired a higher opinion of who they are and what they are capable of. This overall improvement has had repercussions on the notions they have of the language they speak. Further, more intensive contacts with other French-speaking societies have made them aware of many different ways of speaking French. Today, they see standard French more as a codified reality that serves as a reference for all francophones – in Africa, Europe and elsewhere – than as the once illusory image of a monolithic language spoken in the same way by all the French regardless of social class or place of origin. This is why it now seems more possible to master this norm: it no longer means giving up every regional characteristic. If you can speak excellent French with an accent from Switzerland, Belgium, Marseille, or the Ivory Coast, why could you not speak it with a Quebec or Acadian accent? The same goes for the vocabulary: younger generations of Quebecois are more able to differentiate between words specific to Quebec and those in general use in francophone countries, and are thus better able to adjust the use of these words to the contexts or the interlocutors in question.

To sum up, a number of the characteristics of French as it is spoken in Quebec have become much more legitimate for Quebecois than they were thirty years ago. But it still remains a fact that the linguistic norm, a codified system, must be learnt, in this country as anywhere else, and that this learning demands time and effort. The recurrent polemics around the teaching of French seem to indicate that Quebec schools have not met citizens' demands in this regard. The long story of insecurity about language in Quebec puts a heavy burden on the school system, doubtless heavier than elsewhere, but it is a burden that the schools and the state must assume since it has been assigned to them.

A few remarks on the corpus

I have restricted my study to the French-speaking community that lives in Quebec, the centre of French-Canadian culture, and from which the Franco-American group that lives in New England derives. It is a relatively recent phenomenon to identify francophones with Quebec territory, but I have imposed this restriction upon myself for practical reasons. The texts studied come from Quebec newspapers. I cannot, therefore, apply my results to other francophone communities in North America who, at times, lived under very different social, political, and economic conditions than did Quebecois.

The texts written before World War II come from a very small section of the population. This is one of the limitations inherent to this type of study. We will never know the opinions of those who were illiterate or members of the working class who hardly leave a trace in the archives, except for baptisms, marriages, and burials.

The opinions that women may have held account for another great gap in this corpus. Among the one hundred and nineteen documents that Bouthiller and Meynaud collected for the period 1760-1970 only one is signed by a woman, Madeleine Huguenin (Anne-Marie Gleason-Huguenin), a journalist and woman of letters, and founder of the *Revue moderne*. It is the text of a talk given at the first Congress on the French language in 1912. In my own corpus, there are a few more texts written by women, especially after 1945, but the number is still very small and they are mainly letters to the editor. Only about forty years ago did women in Quebec begin to participate in discussions on the mother tongue and other questions that moved society. But they played determining roles in transmitting the language to their children, teaching it in the schools and the convents, taking an active part in all sorts of movements. A good number of the speeches, articles, and sermons that are concerned with the question of language contain passages addressed directly to women, especially to mothers, to whom the mission of transmitting not only language but love of language is assigned. Today we can say that generation after generation of women fulfilled this task. In the post-war years, when they became more present in the magazines, as journalists or as readers who comment on current affairs, their discourse is not very different from that of the men, at least on the question of language. We must keep these limitations to the corpus in mind as we begin our study.

CHAPTER I

Culture, Language, Identity

What is culture?

What is it that allows a group of humans to identify as a community? This question usually gets the following responses: a certain number of common characteristics, customs and shared interests; the fact of living in the same territory; the ability to communicate among members of the group; the identification of the individuals with the collective. But culture cannot be summed up as the shared beliefs and customs of a group of people; it constitutes an actual code of meanings that allows each individual to interpret the world in which he or she lives, and to define themselves in this world. This code of meanings is shared by all the members of a community; it is acquired little by little, like language, as a result of living in the group, and at the same time it conditions the perceptions and the understanding individuals have of the events and things that surround them. The sociologist Carmel Camilleri defines the role that culture plays in human relations and their environment as follows:

> Culture plays a fundamental role in human life: it supplies the units of meaning or the *significations* that inevitably mediate our access to reality. No stimulus acts upon us "directly"; there is always an intermediary meaning within which – consciously or unconsciously – it is packaged.[2]

This rapport between culture and the individual is the basis of life in society. In the same way as communication is possible because speakers of a language agree to allot the same meaning to a certain word, so the sharing of cultural meaning makes life in society possible. For Camilleri, culture acts upon mental states, behaviour, knowledge (including language, technology, etc), on the products this knowledge brings forth, and finally on the institutions that organize collective life.[3] While culture has the function of creating coherence within a community, it creates difference in regard to other cultures. It allows an individual to identify as a member of a group to the exclusion of every other group. Of course, a culture may consist of a number of sub-groups that correspond to differences in the environment, or the living conditions (rural or urban sub-cultures), but these sub-cultures share most of the units of meaning that make up the global culture.

This set of meanings develops over the course of centuries of a society's shared experience. This is why the idea of culture is always associated with heritage and knowledge transmitted by generations. And yet, the set of meanings is not immutable or fixed forever; if it were, no social change or adaptation would be possible. Indeed, changes that take place in a society and adjustments to changing conditions are directed by the culture. In a study on the relations between the cultural and the political, Bertrand Badie argues that culture influences the choices that present themselves to a society in which material conditions are changing:

> Social change is constrained and conditioned by the development of the resources to which a society has access; economic changes will trigger or demand innovation, but such innovation is in turn elaborated and developed according to the cultural traditions that characterize a society.[4]

In the face of any kind of change in its conditions of life, a society will thus for some time be subject to contra-dictory forces: those who resist cultural change since they accord value to the transmission of the defining cultural heritage, those who seek to adapt to the new state of affairs. With time, the cultural code will be modified to address the changes, but always in a manner that conforms to this code.

Despite the interpretive constraints that culture may impose, there is always a certain flexibility of action. While two members of the same culture may disagree on the action to be taken in response to some event, they will agree on how to interpret the event. The clearest example of this is found in language. The group of people that shares one particular language agrees on the meanings of words, on syntactic structures, etc. Language is the code that everyone shares. Nevertheless, every speaker uses this code in their own way, and every language is sub-divided into a great number of dialects, sociolects, and an endless number of idiolects.

In regard to language, we can say that the more complex a society is, the more the language will sub-divide into regional and social varieties. Similarly, the more diversified a society is, the more sub-cultures will appear. In a traditional society, where there are few differences, where the division of labour is minimal and the conditions of life are similar for most of the members, most people will share the one culture. Conversely, modern industrial societies that maximize the division of labour and multiply the conditions of life of their members create forms of culture that are more flexible, and where the network of meanings is less dense and less generally shared by the individuals:

[. . .] there is reason to believe that the unity of contemporary industrialized societies is less a result of a shared heritage transmitted by earlier generations than of conventions based on reason, will, planning, and engagement that would be interesting to identify. In other words, today's large societies are founded more on the wish to stay together *despite the differences* than on some common "already-established basis," whether this refers to objective "content" or structure.[5]

What is identity?

Culture, the system of meanings that organizes reality and facilitates its interpretation, is also a code that allows individuals to define their universe. It supplies categories of thought within which they can situate themselves in relation to others and thanks to which they can construct their identities. As a result, culture and identity are closely related. From the elements that make up a culture individuals choose those with which they identify more or less directly: race, religion, language, clan, family, etc. Some of these elements function at a primary level, others at a secondary level, and they make up a hierarchical structure.

The series of identity structures allow the individual to take on defining characteristics; this is the ontological function of the structure. However, identity is constructed at the heart of a complex environment that is susceptible to change. An individual must thus be able to adapt to the changing conditions of their milieu and smoothly adjust their self-image. This is the pragmatic function of identity structures. In constructing their image, individuals tend to give themselves a certain value, both with reference to an ideal self and with reference to others.[6]

The identity of an individual, elaborated over time and constructed from elements the culture supplies, is a function of the milieu and of otherness. An excessively radical change in the milieu, to which the individual cannot adjust their identity without destroying their self-image, will set off an identity crisis. Similarly, if there is too great a gap between a person's self-identity and value and the image that others reflect back to that person, this endangers the stability and coherence of this identity and can also set off an identity crisis. An aggressive attack on a person's identity may cause them to develop a negative self-image.

Identity crises and strategies to cope with threats

There are many situations that can seriously threaten the identity of an individual, but I do not intend to study them here. Certain contemporary situations have triggered research that casts an interesting light on this topic. In a study of immigrant children, for instance, Hanna Malewska-Peyre presents a classification of strategies of identification that she observed in troubled adolescents:

> A negative self-image results in large part from the negative judgments of others. Several research projects have shown that loss of self-image is closely linked to negative opinions that parents and teachers have uttered about the individual during their socialization. Such negative judgments are often the mark of children who commit more criminal acts than others as adolescents.[7]

The author notes two strategies that are used in the face of threats to identity posed by such negative judgments: internal strategies, or strategies that have to do with the psychological reactions to these threats, and external strategies, actions or other manifestations directed outward, against others.

At the psychological level, there are three types of reactions. First, the individual rejects the negative judgments of others, denies them, and refuses to see them in order not to suffer. This negation of the self causes anxiety in the individual. On the other hand, internalizing the negative image expressed by others can cause victim behaviour:

> The other reaction that is dangerous for the construction of the self is the internalization of the negative image received from society. It implies submission, and even guilt, about being what one is. The usual strategy is to "not draw attention, not make a fuss, not make demands".[8]

Yet, in the face of such attacks on their identity, individuals may also resort to aggression, an aggression that brings on self-destructive behaviour if it is turned against themselves. Aggressive behaviour directed toward others, and considered healthier for the individual, "externalizes the problem and allows them to maintain their dignity," but such behaviour is usually met with immediate sanctions from society.

Externalizing strategies may be individual, or they may be collective, when people are devalorized for belonging to a certain social group. The first strategy, which is similar to suppression, consists of assimilating as completely as possible into the group that is uttering the negative judgments. This strategy both rejects the original culture and identity of the individual, and is often a vain attempt to faithfully copy the dominant group. It may lead the individual to deny their origins and display even more contempt toward them than does the group into which they want to assimilate. At the other end of the spectrum, the strategy to revalorize their identity will cause the individual to "demand respect for their difference." This can lead to the idealization of their own group, and a sometimes ferocious critique of the other, that rejects or scorns them:

> The strategy of valorizing collective identity can lead to people participating in collective, social movements. Once the problem of inferiority concerns a group, the strategies become collective.[9]

Malewska-Peyre also notes intermediary strategies that consist in people searching for resemblances between the cultures concerned and valorizing these, thereby minimizing but not renouncing their own specificity – a weak form of acculturation. Finally, strategies of compensation, such as showy behaviour, can allow a more positive self-image to develop. These strategies, which consist in facing the challenge of difference, may have negative outcomes, such as delinquency, or positive results such as sports or artistic activities, but in all of them there is an undercurrent of aggression.

As we can see from this brief exposé, threats targeting an individual's identity may have to do with that person belonging to a social group that is regarded with contempt. The study I cite deals with the adolescent children of immigrants, confronted with the racism of the "host" society, a term that in this context has a particularly cynical tinge.

Once the threat has been defined as social, we need to ask what the collective identity of the maligned group might be and what strategies the group adopts to face this threat.

Collective identity and identity crises

Any group of humans whose members share certain characteristics which each member values in defining their own identity may feel like forming a separate entity, different from all the others. The nature of such characteristics may vary considerably from one group to the next, much like the values they are assigned. For example, sharing the same territory may be part of the identity of one collective, but this territorial aspect is not always necessary. Certain communities, Roma for example, have a collective identity in which the territory plays no role. In other cases, this characteristic is no more than secondary when compared to more powerful ones. For someone from the Maghreb, it may well be more important to identify as Arabic and Muslim than as Tunisian or Moroccan, though that would have to be verified. A collective identity cannot be reduced to a mere list of shared characteristics, but must be seen as a set of hierarchical characteristics whose role and respective value are defined by each community.

Members of a society will choose certain values from this set of cultural characteristics, and organize them hierarchically, thereby constructing their collective identity. Among these cultural elements some play a central, determining role: race, religion, and language. In his study of inter-ethnic relations, Selim Abou notes:

> [...] three basic factors – race, religion, and language – are the most powerful among the possible elements that make up ethnic identity; language, because even though it is one element among all the others, it transcends them all with its power to name them, express them, and carry them onward; religion, because even though it is part of a given cultural system, it transcends this system by including a greater vision of the world and a corresponding set of val-

ues; race, because even though it may be hard to determine, it symbolizes shared origins, and through fantasy mobilizes the dark forces of instinct, sexuality, and blood.[10]

A collective identity is generally seen to exist when the members of a group *give themselves a name*, a name that shows they belong to this group. This power to name is never deployed needlessly. Because the need is there, because the concept exists, a name is required. Every human being obviously belongs to numerous different collectives, all of them somehow linked. It is possible to be a native of Strasbourg, Alsace, France and Europe all at the same time, but some of these defining identifications are more important or more determining than others. It is rather unlikely, for example, that when this person moves from Strasbourg to another city in France they would continue to refer to themselves as a native of Strasbourg, though they may always identify as being from Alsace, or, if they live abroad, never stop being French.

The name a person assumes is a translation of the strength of their attachment to a certain collective; among the various communities we can identify with, the ethnic community is one of the most central because it is founded on the basic characteristics of the culture.

As we have seen, certain cultural factors that make up one's ethnic identity are more important than others. I am not concerned here with all the possible combinations. Instead, let me simply assert that in the collective identity of a particular group the factors that distinguish it from neighbouring groups are generally the most important. Abou explains why:

The problem of identity only comes up where difference appears. One needs to identify oneself only in regard to the other, and this affirmation of identity is first and foremost carried out in self-defence since difference is always perceived at first as a threat. If there is no ethnic consciousness in isolated primitive societies, this is because the feeling of security that cultural adherence to the group supplies is not threatened or even disturbed.[11]

There are few human societies that live in total isolation, and so the stability of a human collective can only be ensured if the adjoining societies do not exert pressures that are perceived as threats. Further, the geographic, political, and economic conditions in which a society lives have an important influence on its culture, and on its identity structure. From the moment when pressure from others, or pressure resulting from socio-economic change begins to be felt, to the moment the culture transforms and adapts to the changes in its own particular way, between these two moments, a society may undergo a more or less prolonged period of destabilization, or an identity crisis set off by these pressures. For example, many different peoples experienced colonization, and then decolonization, and they suffered serious identity crises as a result, whose negative effects are still being felt. Similarly, the sudden industrialization or urbanization of certain regions has sometimes been traumatic for groups ill-prepared for such changes.

An identity crisis can manifest itself in different ways, although these usually parallel the strategies of identification. Every collective, every society must be studied separately in order to determine which factors play a role in the collective consciousness. In the case where several collectives exist within the same country, Abou writes:

When analysing the ethnic identity of a given group, it does not suffice to objectively list the racial and cultural elements that differentiate this group from the rest of the nation; you have to know to what extent these differentiating elements mobilize collective consciousness and demands for a specific collective identity. Such demands and the ideology within which they are formulated can only be understood if you know the history of how this group became part of the nation (is it a history of colonization, nationalism, immigration?), and the psychological conditions of its integration into the nation (is it valued or viewed with contempt, recognized, or rejected?).[12]

Thus, to understand the history of a collective, you have to know how its collective identity was formed and how this identity adapted to the changes and pressures it underwent.

The cultural aspects of ethnic identity: Language

Located at the very centre of collective life and culture, language is as the most powerful factor organizing thought and social integration. It supplies humans with all the conceptual elements on which lexical meaning is based, and offers the child learning it a system that orders the universe and conditions its perception of this universe. When a child hears a word for the first time, it has no idea what this sound might comprise. It may think that the word names a specific object, or that this word designates an object with a specific characteristic, and that therefore all objects with this characteristic can be named with the same word. Through repetition of the word in its context, a child learns to grasp the meaning and apply it correctly to the objects adults name with it. This repetition helps the child understand that within the category of objects that the word may apply to, only certain types of objects are admissible while others are excluded. For a child raised in other conditions, in a culture where this type of object is not used, for instance, the concept does not exist, nor does it have a name. The same thing applies to abstract concepts that translate the philosophy of each culture into its language. The syntax and morphology of any given language also condition thought, providing a human being, from birth, with a way to organize concepts that produce meaning, modes of expression outside of which communication is impossible, or chaotic and unpredictable. It is due to these semantic, morphological and syntactic structures, specific to each language, that it is impossible to completely translate one language into another. In the same way a language is loaded with the social history of the people who speak it, culture is also partially determined by the language that underlies it. The point is not to deny the richness of cultural and linguistic exchanges, which have always taken place between human societies, but to simply show the determining influence that the maternal language has on perception. The same event can be interpreted differently by people with different languages, and from different cultures.

At another level, language is a primordial factor in social integration. Language, the mode of communication upon which all other modes of communication are based, allows for the exchange of information that is necessary for life in society. Through it emotions and knowledge are expressed, and becomes collective action possible. It is thus the foundation of every institution.

Religion

The relationship that humans maintain with "the beyond" plays a major role in the establishment and development of social institutions. Societies devise and construct their political institutions according to the place assigned to transcendence in the imaginary world. For Bertrand Badie, for example:

By distinguishing between the transcendent order and the terrestrial order, the big religions, the Judaeo-Christian tradition and Islam, as well as Confucianism, Hinduism and Buddhism, provided a highly significant innovation, freeing up human action, making it possible to think of legitimacy as autonomous, and thus giving birth to ideology.[13]

According to Badie, in monotheistic religions the terrestrial, and thus the political order, must be constructed to conform to the divine laws. But here too, different societies define their worlds in very different ways, depending on whether they separate religious power from secular power. The historical conditions that brought forth Christianity and the religions deriving from it powerfully affected the solutions adopted by each of the societies involved:

The meeting between an Empire already organized on the basis of its culture (the Roman Empire) and a religion from elsewhere helps explain the rise in secessionist practices that make the Christian cultural code so original.

Roman Christianity imposed itself little by little as a cultural code that was not only distinct from nascent Islam but also from eastern Christianity, a form that remained closely linked to the Empire.

Using the same evangelical message, eastern Christianity however promoted a culture that fused the religious with the political, which later hampered the establishment of secular states in Eastern Europe.[14]
In the West, the idea of the state developed over the course of the Middle Ages, as a result of tensions between secular powers, represented by nobility, and religious powers, represented by the Pope. After the Reformation, the concept of the state changed again in those societies that adopted this change in religion:

the Church-as-institution, perfectly incarnated by Roman Christianity, and characterized by its management of mercy and the sacraments, became a bureaucracy that presented arguments for a logical organization of the cosmos and thus for natural law, and finally moved toward an alliance or compromise with the state that complemented its organization of society. A sect, however, is more flexibly organized; it calls for individuals to live ascetic lives, scorns secular law in favour of divine law, and rejects all division of labour with the state. The Reformation, with its doctrine and the directions these took, clearly manifested the behaviour of a sect; its relevance extended well beyond the religious domain and shook up the entire political culture of the state, which was at the time in full development.[15]

By profoundly changing the concept of the state and its role in organizing society, the Reformation transformed the cultures that grew out of the diverse forms of Protestantism and made them different from those that remained Catholic. Even if Western cultures have become considerably more secular over the course of the twentieth century, the form of Christianity they practiced for centuries has continued to profoundly mark their political and social organization.

From here on in, the Reformation and the Counter-Reformation can no longer be analyzed as religious phenomena, not even as mere episodes in the history of ideas; as a result of social practices, they have become actual cultural models, that do not so much support antagonistic *ideologies* as uphold and diffuse different *ways of understanding* the main categories upon which social action is based.[16]

Relations between the law, the state, the Church, and God differ profoundly for Catholics and Protestants. For Catholics, the rapport with God is mediated by the Church, which consists of hierarchic power structures.

The secular power structures of such societies mimic those of the Church, and tend to be centralized, using a strong and highly diversified bureaucracy to manage society.

For Protestants, only divine law is legitimate, and the rapport with God is direct; there is no intermediary. Under such conditions,

> power does not derive from relations that constrain the individual, but implies knowledge of the law and everyone's obligation to comply with it. The law is legitimate in that it is an expression of collective conscience, and it creates a culture and a type of social control that relies on the self-regulation of civil society and on limited state powers.[17]

The notion of salvation is also very different in these two forms of Christianity. Catholics have to accept the clergy as intermediaries in order to be forgiven for the sins they commit against divine law. Since this mediation is human, and therefore fallible, it can be contested. For Protestants, salvation comes through strict obedience to divine law, and only the conscience of each individual can indicate by which path to interpret this law. This approach forces Protestants to constantly examine their consciences. Since they cannot be cleared by confession, individuals must subject themselves to severe and constant self-censorship. It seems clear that relations between the individual and human law are powerfully conditioned by the religion that is practised. Social behaviours and the perception of institutions differ profoundly depending on whether censure is meted out by a power outside the individual or if individuals impose it upon themselves. This in turn orients collective behaviour in very different ways.

Race

The notion of race has changed considerably over the last century. For the case we are concerned with, a very nuanced approach is necessary. Fifty to sixty years ago it was still believed that living in different parts of the world produced identifiable external differences – skin colour, shape of skull, eyes, structure of face, etc. These differences divided humans into distinct groups, which were called races. The research on differences even went so far as to identify a British race, a French race, a Polish race. Many different events, and in particular the systematic extermination of the Jews in the Nazi death camps as well as the supremacist ideology that underlay these massacres, completely overthrew these ideas which consisted more of prejudices than scientific truths. Since that time, progress in genetics has shown that it is impossible to draw clear lines between groups of humans. Nevertheless, advances in science may attenuate, but they do not completely invalidate, the feeling of difference, especially in cases where communities with different physical characteristics are in contact.

For the French who arrived in Canada in the seventeenth century, the Amerindians doubtless belonged to a different race, or several different races. At first, this difference seems not to have presented an insurmountable obstacle between the communities since an entire Metis people sprang up as a result of these contacts, some of whom were integrated into Canadian society during the French regime. Basically, the Amerindians had to assimilate culturally to the French community in order to become part of it.

While the French and the *Canadiens* of New France fought certain Amerindian nations for political reasons and alliances, other nations were their allies. After New France was ceded to England, the English had quite a different approach to the Amerindians, whom they tried to keep as separate from White society as possible, an attitude that led to the creation of reserves at the end of the nineteenth century.

In relation to the English, or perhaps in opposition to them, the concept of the *French-Canadian race* and its particular mission in North America existed for a long time. This use of the term "race," which is in line with its use throughout the West in that period, has no particular importance and should be understood as referring to ethnicity – language and religion, institutions, history, and shared customs. Like everywhere else in the West, this usage became outdated after 1945 for the reasons mentioned above.

The formation and transformation of Quebec identity

No one would now contest the fact that the French language is central to Quebec identity. While this may be an intuitive assertion, it is also supported by observation. For over thirty years the French language has held a constant place at the centre of debates; indeed, collective political action was initiated in order to protect and develop it. For as Fernand Dumont and Guy Rocher wrote in 1961, "For most French-Canadians, Canada is a legal entity; it is not a real country."[18]

How was the collective identity of today's Quebecois formed? To find out, it is necessary to study their history, reconstitute the image they created of themselves, and study the transformations this image underwent. What role did the French language play in this history? Was this role always as important as it is today? What do Quebecois think of their language? What was their opinion thirty, or one hundred, years ago, and how did this opinion affect their collective identity? In order to explore these questions and propose some answers it is necessary to study the society as completely as possible; every aspect counts, whether it be economic, social, institutional, experiential, or psychological. Relations with other groups – English Canadians, English, French, Amerindians, Americans – count as well. Since the question of language is at the very centre of my study, before I explore the idea successive generations have had of their language, I will have to study the origins and objective transformations of the French language in Quebec since the seventeenth century.

colonists. Not much is known about the languages of the various French provinces in the early seventeenth century; more information is available on the later part of the century due to the extensive research conducted by Abbé Grégoire during the French Revolution. Without going into more detail,[3] I will simply note that by the time of the Revolution, French, which was the dialect of the Île-de-France (Paris) area as well as the national language, had begun spreading far beyond its original boundaries, and had become the language of about one fifth of the entire population of France. Other mother tongues spoken on French territory were Provençal, Occitan, Breton, Alsatian, northern dialects closely related to French, such as Norman, Champenois, or Picard, and patois that developed out of them. The term "patois" normally designates a linguistic variant that is used in a very limited area, sometimes in only a few villages; it does not normally have a written form, and comes from a dialect or language whose importance is decreasing in relation to a language that has become dominant. Because the territorial origins of the French colonists are so distinct – there were hardly any from Brittany, Occitania or the Basque country among them - almost all other languages except those belonging to the northern regions can be set side. On the other hand, the western and northwestern dialects of these regions were heavily represented. Barbaud estimates that about one-third of the colonists spoke French as their mother tongue, one-third spoke some patois of the northwest and west, and one-third was bilingual in French and patois. There is considerable dispute among linguists over these figures, especially in regard to the proportion of colonists who allegedly spoke only patois when they arrived in America.[4] Some assert that many of the colonists came from towns or small cities where French had arrived before spreading to the rural areas. Further, those who left their province in order to go to America had to first go to La Rochelle or Nantes, one of the ports of embarkation, and sometimes wait there for several months before making the long journey. Since patois was hardly useful beyond the immediate limits of their restricted regions, these emigrants would have been forced to learn enough French to survive, so that by the time they arrived in Quebec, the number of people speaking only patois was probably very small. Whatever the outcome of these discussions, which may never be resolved due to the lack of first hand documents, specialists concur with Philippe Barbaud on one point, and that is the linguistic unification of New France, which gave French the upper hand and caused the various patois to disappear quickly. They could not be maintained for long or transmitted to later generations for a number of reasons: the great distances between those who spoke the same patois did not allow homogenous groups to form; marriages between couples of different linguistic groups, with a much larger proportion of the women than the men speaking French, undermined patois, and finally, French was the language of all of the colony's administrators. According to Barbaud, in only a few generations, by the end of the seventeenth or latest, at the beginning of the eighteenth century, the mother tongue of all the colonists was French and there was linguistic unity.

Which French?

So patois had disappeared completely. But which variety of French was spoken on the banks of the St. Lawrence? To get some idea, we have to examine the origins of those who brought the language to North America in more details. The colonists who came from the Île-de-France or its surroundings, an area that was already

French in the seventeenth century, as well as those from bilingual regions, were almost all craftsmen or peasants. To this we add the soldiers who stayed in New France, the "Filles du Roy" [King's Daughters] who were penniless orphan girls and wards of the state, sailors, and others. Thus, the vast majority of the first settlers in New France were from the lower social classes. They would have spoken popular French. While administrators, officers and other dignitaries came from France, most of these returned after the territory was ceded to England or even before, since many only spent a few years in the colony. The only representatives of the educated classes who stayed in any numbers were those in the church – priests and nuns. For the most part, the seigneurs were not members of the aristocracy, but colonists who had grown wealthy and were assigned territory to administer. Given this situation, it is likely that the French spoken in Quebec in 1756 was very close to that of the working classes in the Île-de-France and its immediate surroundings, although there is some evidence that certain elements of higher levels of French entered everyday language.[5] The various forms of patois that part of the population brought with it also left their traces in the structure of the language. A number of studies have shown that in terms of pronunciation there are traces of old dialects and patois,[6] and that in the eighteenth century variations in pronunciation could still be attributed to them. A certain number of words and expressions that came from these dialects have survived and been integrated into French. Not much is known about the syntax of the spoken language, except that it must have been very close to that used in popular French of the period. On the whole, then, the French spoken in Quebec in the mid eighteenth century was probably not very different from that used by lower social classes in the French-speaking parts of France, in particular in the northwest. Travellers' accounts further confirm this assumption.[7]

Subsequent developments

What are the reasons for the gap that developed between Quebec French and so-called standard French? First, we must note that standard French is a normalized, codified form of the language, and that the grammarians of the sixteenth and seventeenth centuries who established its norms and codes referred exclusively to the language spoken by the upper social class of the Paris region, the aristocracy, the court, and the scholars of the time. It is a recurrent phenomenon in the history of languages that the particular version chosen among all others as the language of instruction, of official communication, and literature, is the version spoken by the social class that is in power and comes from the region where this power is exercised. Because of its association with the royal court, Francien, the dialect of the Île-de-France in the Middle Ages, progressively replaced all the other dialectal variations, some of which, such as Picard and Champenois, had developed a sophisticated literature, and it slowly imposed itself across the entire territory of France. After the demise of Latin as the language of administration with the decree of Villers-Cotterêt, and the literary movements of the sixteenth century that sought to *illustrate* the French language, the need for a more precise codification and normalization of the language became pressing, as much for the requirements of printing as for teaching. This task occupied the rest of the seventeenth century and carried on into the eighteenth. The first dictionaries and grammar books appeared illustrating the usage of "the most educated part of the court and current writers."[8]

The Cession of Quebec occurred at precisely this point, just as modern French was emerging, and severed virtually all the connections between the colony and France. Trade between France, the Antilles, and Canada stopped, putting an end to French immigration to Canada and to direct exchange with France. Some individuals still made the journey, in one direction or the other, but these contacts were far too rare to have much linguistic influence. When the administrators of the colony and the elite returned to France after the treaty ceding Canada to the British Crown was signed, they left behind the working classes and the clergy, turning the latter into the only teachers able to transmit the codified forms of the written language. From this point on, the French language evolved differently in Quebec and in France. Two phenomena developed that contributed to further separate the two versions of the language. On the one hand, different types of transformations appeared in each version of French, especially at the level of phonetics and the lexicon; on the other, certain forms that were once common to both only disappeared in one. This is why certain pronunciations in Quebec French are forms that were the norm in France in the seventeenth century; the well-known "oué" for anything written "oi," for instance, was simply conserved in Quebec, while it disappeared in France. In relation to standard French, this is considered an archaism. A much more recent example is the pronunciation of *un*, which in France is becoming the same as the pronunciation of *in*, while in Quebec there is still a clear distinction of the two sounds. Almost all pronunciation considered typical of Quebec can be ascribed either to provincial origins or to this type of conservatism.

At the level of the lexicon, the question is somewhat more complex. There are, of course, many archaisms and regionalisms in Quebec French. However, other phenomena also play a role. The new environment brought with it new words to name plants and animals that resembled those of France but were not completely the same, thus causing some semantic variations in these names – the French *chevreuil* [deer] is not the same animal as the Quebec *chevreuil*, which bears the name *cerf de Virginie* [Virginia deer] in standard French.[9] The adaptation to new climatic conditions also caused neologisms to form. Further, there was much borrowing from Amerindian languages in the early years. But progressive borrowings from English are the most important aspect of Quebec French.

After the Renaissance, during which French adopted terms mainly from Italian and Dutch, the language was widely imported into other languages, but by the eighteenth century it was also taking in English words. This phenomenon, which expanded significantly over the nineteenth and twentieth centuries, began well before French Canada was ceded to England. In Quebec, however, once the connections with France were severed, technical as well as institutional innovations came via the English, and later the Americans. The result was that certain domains were quickly anglicized, specifically legal and political institutions, since these were copies of English institutions, and also business, which was taken over by British merchants who replaced the French network in place when they arrived with their own English and American networks. This was the status quo until the mid-nineteenth century. Anglicization became more intense as the population moved from the country into the cities and contact with speakers of English became more widespread. The gap between Quebec French and standard French thus grew wider, because, not only were different words borrowed on either side of the Atlantic, but borrowings were much more common in Quebec.

Another phenomenon that played an important role was the relative impoverishment of Quebec vocabulary. Several factors were involved and it is hard to determine their respective importance. First, most of the colonists who came to Quebec were between fifteen and twenty-five years old. Not many of them can have been extremely skilled in their craft, or in the technical vocabulary pertaining to it. Further, the conditions in the colony in the seventeenth century made superfluous a number of the skills and crafts associated to more diversified lifestyles or to luxury. Studies of the inventories left by deceased metalworkers in the eighteenth century, for example, reveal a very limited and undifferentiated terminology for the tools that are listed. They also show how multivalent the craftsmen were, doing the work of coppersmiths, blacksmiths, armorers, crafts that were specialized in France.[10] Finally, since education was very limited for many generations, vocabulary was largely transmitted orally, with all the limitations that this imposes.

If Quebec's isolation had lasted much longer, a different language might perhaps have emerged. After all, the various Romance languages – Spanish, Italian, and Romanian – developed in similar ways. They have the same origins, yet developed in isolation, and were later influenced by various other languages. However, such conjecture leaves out the phenomenal development of systems of communication. Contacts with France were taken up again toward the middle of the nineteenth century. While they were rare and superficial at first, and affected only the educated class, they became more intense. The educated class resolutely adopted standard French as a model and ensured its diffusion through education, later through the print media – newpapers, journals, literature –, and finally through radio, television and film. Further, personal contacts have expanded over the past fifty years, largely due to travel, affecting ever larger sections of the Quebec population. And in each generation, education has become available to an ever greater number of Quebecois. The sum total of these phenomena has had the effect of decreasing a good number of the characteristics of Quebec French, and even causing them to disappear, both at the level of pronunciation and the lexicon. Most of the Amerindian terms, for example, disappeared from Quebec usage by the beginning of the twentieth century.

Anglicization, which had made considerable progress until the 1960s, began to decrease as a result of the contacts with France and the efforts of the Quebec government in establishing the *Office de la langue française* [Office of the French Language], thus providing the province with the necessary terms to gallicize business, signage and labelling, and the technical and general vocabulary that most people only knew in English.

It can be said that the reversal of the process that separated Quebec French from standard French was something that the Quebecois wanted, and that it is the result of a deliberate choice, even if some sectors of the population may not have been fully conscious of this. For there were other options: further development of an independent dialect, the emergence of a hybrid language, or pure and simple assimilation by English. I will be investigating the reasons for this choice.

CHAPTER III

The Habitants: 1760-1867

The society that developed during the French regime in New France was organized around trade with France. Indeed, France at first put all its efforts into founding and developing trading posts and missions, and only later made the decision to establish a colony. Nonetheless, the system of land division was quickly established, and maintained until after the Treaty of Paris. This profoundly affected the social structures of French Canada. The trading posts turned into villages, and then into towns, with colonists beginning to occupy land nearby. The system of land distribution was based on the principle of the seigneury. Land was assigned by royal decree to a seigneur who was charged with settling colonists to work it. If he did not comply, the land could be taken away and assigned to another seigneur. Since waterways were the only systems of communication, the colonists settled along these, with each family allotted an area of about the same size, a narrow elongated piece, with one of the narrow sides fronting on the water. The houses constructed along the waterway were built relatively close together allowing social contact as much for mutual help as for leisure. Once the banks of the St. Lawrence and its main tributaries were occupied, another section of land – a "rang" – was opened up behind the first cleared section, with a road that ran parallel to the waterway to provide access. As time went on, the houses dating from the first settlement were moved from the water's edge to the road, and so the roadways ended up lined with houses on each side.

This type of settlement was not conducive to villages or towns developing quickly. Once a territory had a sufficiently large population, a church was built to serve this group of people. A number of businesses or artisans' shops would spring up around it and professionals such as lawyers, doctors, notaries, and others would arrive.

It is estimated that at the end of the French regime in 1759-1760 one quarter of the population was settled in the towns of Montréal, Québec and Trois-Rivières. However, by 1825, only twelve per cent of the population was living in an urban environment, and this included the English-speakers who arrived later. In other words the English regime brought with it considerable social transformations, as sociologist Marcel Rioux explains:

> The Conquest hastened the transformation from a feudal to a rural society. [. . .] it led not only to the exodus of those members of the middle class that had been administrators, but also to the replacement of the merchants by their English rivals. The English substituted the business networks that already existed between England and America for the French business system that had been disrupted by the war, and thus succeeded in gaining complete control of local business. The Conquest sounded the knell for both the feudal and the merchant societies.[1]

The departure of the French urban middle-class that had run the administrative and business affairs of a rather diversified society made up of several classes, and centred around towns and extensive commerce, was an abrupt change. The society became radically simplified, and essentially rural. As a further consequence, the only remaining elite in the countryside was the clergy, the only educated group able to organize and lead a people consisting primarily of farmers and spread out over a vast territory. Under the military government, the seigneurs managed to maintain the system of land distribution that ensured their income, but they lost much of their importance and influence once they had lost access to political power.

At the time of the French regime, the clergy had to some extent competed with the merchant and administrative class whose views and interests it did not share. For a long time after the end of the regime, the clergy found itself in a position where it could decide on the direction society should take. This is how the sociologist Hubert Guindon describes the situation:

> the military victory of the English brought with it the triumph of clerical ideas about how society should be organized in French Canada. Things were simplified and oriented toward rural development to the exclusion of every other type of social development.[2]

Other phenomena besides the ideology of the clergy, which saw rural development as the way to preserve and reinforce religious and family values, had the effect of keeping French-Canadians of the late eighteenth century out of the cities. After the Treaty of Paris, English merchants and administrators settled in the colony, then under military government. They sought to apply British laws, including those that required "any person fulfilling ecclesiastical functions and any layperson holding a post of any kind or rendering service to the Crown, as well as any person leasing Crown lands to pledge allegiance to the Queen and her successors, under pain of losing his goods and charges [. . .][3]; in other words, they applied the Test Acts. For Catholics, this pledge meant renouncing their religion; its effect was to prevent the French-

Canadians from exercising any administrative or legal function. The Quebec Act, adopted in 1774, abolished this pledge as a requirement for public service and re-established French civil law, leading to the development of a class of lawyers, notaries, solicitors, doctors and judges, who formed the basis of middle-class society and played a considerable role in the following decades. Before the Act, however, the unacceptable pledge required by the Test Acts had caused the last remaining members of the urban middle-class to take refuge in the country.

From the end of the eighteenth century, a rural society, characterized by great social uniformity, thus developed along the banks of the St. Lawrence. Every colonist owned a parcel of land of approximately the same size, with access to the waterway or the road. This land and its produce as well as its woodlots allowed a farming family to be virtually autonomous, though at subsistence level, since only enough could be produced to fulfill the needs of the family. The sale of any little surplus allowed people to buy the few things they could not produce themselves. It was almost impossible to accumulate capital.

While this system of inheritance and of establishing one's children ensured the stability of this way of life for many generations, it also brought about its total collapse toward the middle of the nineteenth century. At the end of the eighteenth century, the few colonists inhabited only a small part of the territory that could potentially be cleared and worked. Instead of dividing the land between the children when the father died, as was the custom in Europe, a custom that would not have allowed the population to survive in Canada, the land was passed on intact to one son, often the youngest. When the other sons reached the age at which they could establish themselves, their father helped them buy a new piece of land to clear. This system required high birth rates because workers were needed to clear the land and to work it; the children's futures were clearly laid out. During the same period in Europe, the scarcity of land and its division between heirs led, instead, to fewer births.

Rural society was thus closely structured around several basic units: the family as the unit of production, the "rang" as the social unit, and the parish as the administrative and religious unit. In fact, the parish, the territory served by a church, rather than the village, soon became the centre of collective life. The priest held such high moral authority that he played the main role in decisions ranging from civil administration to religious questions. The identity of the habitant in the eighteenth century was thus defined by his adherence to these different units, as Jean-Charles Falardeau writes:

> He [the habitant] quickly forgot the name of his seigneur, and identified himself as an individual, spontaneously adding the name of his "rang" and his parish to his last name.[4]

The social structure of the parish was simple. At the top were the clergy, the priest and the curates; then came the professionals, the notary, the doctor and their families whose status was based on education; and next came the farmers and their families who were by far the most numerous. The farmer's lifestyle and independence were valorized by the community. Gérald Fortin, a specialist on the rural parishes, explains the status of the farmer as follows:

> The priest, who was himself the son of a farmer, valorized agriculture and the rural way of life and saw this as a way to ensure the practice of Christian virtues.[5]

The status of artisans and merchants was lower than that of farmers. Lower still, were the farm labourers and itinerants.

Given this context, an education system took a long time developing. There were local primary schools here and there, but since the farmers needed workers at home, their sons only attended school until the age of twelve while the girls often got a better education than their brothers. Secondary studies were only for those boys who were physically weak or destined for the priesthood since this involved high costs for the family. It is difficult to assess the educational level of the population in general. We know that the first generations subject to the English regime were largely illiterate, and that efforts were undertaken from 1830 onward to expand education. This caused conflicts between the government and the clergy, which were settled largely in favour of the clergy. The Catholic church thus maintained its control over public education and consolidated its position as leader.

In the cities, where institutions of higher education were located and the assemblies that resulted from successive constitutional acts were held, immigration caused the population of British origin to grow quickly. Business and industry were completely in British hands. French society, made up of middle-class professionals, artisans, workers, clergy, and students in educational institutions, developed slowly. A few newspapers were founded in Montreal and Quebec, immediately claiming to represent the French-Canadians and their interests. In 1831, according to Alexis de Toqueville, "all the French papers take an oppositional stance; all the English papers are pro-government, with the exception of *The Vindicator* in Montreal; but it too was founded by French-Canadians."[6]

The political situation

For the French colonists who were ceded to England along with the territory and their descendants, the first century of British rule (1763-1867) was characterized by constant struggle. Throughout this period the colonists demanded that their rights to their own culture, language, and religion be recognized, since these rights had been inscribed in the official texts. After they succeeded in having the Test Acts abolished and French civil law reinstituted by the Quebec Act in 1774, they focussed their efforts on proving that applying French civil law meant using the French language. Until the constitution of 1791 was adopted, the French-Canadians formed such a majority in the country that the question of language came up only in regard to the courts. But once Canada was divided into Upper and Lower Canada, political and demographic questions grew more important for their future. This division had the effect of limiting the territorial expansion of the French population by creating an administrative area, namely Upper Canada, where they were not in the majority. What with new immigrants arriving from the United Kingdom and joining the population of American Loyalists, the colonists of French origin in Upper Canada quickly found themselves outnumbered. From that point on, their fate was linked to Lower Canada, the only territory where they could exercise their political will, the territory that became the province of Quebec in 1867.

In 1837, exasperated after decades of trouble with English merchants and colonists who behaved like occupation forces, the Patriots staged a rebellion in hope of shaking off English control. The revolt was severely suppressed by the British army and its leaders were executed or exiled. In 1841, after these troubles and the civil unrest that followed, the British parliament, acting on the advice of Lord Durham, adopted the Union Act of Upper and Lower Canada. Durham's stated objective was to ensure that the French-Canadians (he was one of the first to use this term) become a minority:

> If the population of Upper Canada is rightly estimated at 400,000, the English inhabitants of Lower Canada at 150,000, and the French at 450,000, the union of the two provinces would not only give a clear English majority, but one which would be increased every year by the influence of English emigration; and I have little doubt that the French, when once placed, by the legitimate course of events and the working of natural causes, in a minority, would abandon their vain hopes of nationality.[7]

Durham attributed the ongoing ethnic tensions to the very unstable situation that had developed in Canada, but at the same time he recognized that the arrogance and contempt displayed by the English, as well as their monopoly of the economy and public services, had provoked animosity and set off the rebellion. Taking note of the conditions of inferiority imposed on the French Canadians, Durham did not propose giving them equal opportunities, but rather focused on assimilating them, linguistically and culturally, as quickly as possible. By joining Upper and Lower Canada and making English the only official language of government, the 1840 Union Act pursued exactly this logic. Only in 1848 was Article 40, which proscribed the use of French in the legislature, repealed. Meanwhile in Lower Canada, those French-Canadians living in the countryside with hardly any contact to the English did not feel that their way of life was being threatened; in the cities, however, the unilateral bilingualism that would become the rule a few decades later was beginning to develop. In the middle of the nineteenth century, 55% of the population of Montreal was English, and so was 40% of Quebec City.

During the first half of the nineteenth century the two communities lived almost entirely separate from each other, with the exception of the upper class of French-Canadians, who seem to have consorted with the English from the beginning of the British regime. However, these contacts were reduced to a minimum in the period of the revolts between 1837 and 1839. Durham writes: "There has never been any social life between the two races except in the upper classes; this has now almost completely disappeared."[8]

The English monopoly of business and early industry created conditions that, over the last third of the nineteenth century, caused a radical deterioration of the social position of French-Canadians. Well before the processes of urbanization, industrialization, and proletarization of French-Canadian society began, the traditional image of the "habitant" had developed and been consolidated in people's minds. It was maintained until well after the lifestyle it denoted had ceased being that of the majority.

The identity of the Canadiens

How did the British citizens of French origin living in Canada between 1763 and 1867 see the identity of the *Canadien*? Although they sometimes defined themselves as French, in reference to their language and ethnic origin, they usually used the term *Canadien*, already employed by the colonists born in New France. This expressed the feeling of having a territory, albeit with rather unclear boundaries, that their ancestors had colonized and that they continued to log and clear. They inhabited this land, they were the *habitants*. The merchants, the colonists, the English-speaking administrators, whether from England, Scotland, Ireland, or the

United States, would only ever be *les Anglais*. Besides referring to their recent arrival, this term was justified by the fact that the new immigrants did not change allegiances by coming to a new territory; they remained subjects of the British Crown and did not feel they had changed nationality. It took several generations for them to see themselves differently.

The *Canadiens*, on the other hand, felt they were part of a nation; that is, they were conscious of having a culture of their own that might be indebted to the original culture of France but also had its own traditions and lifestyles. Two elements were central to this culture: the French language and the Catholic religion. All the political struggles of the first century of the British regime had to do either with language or with religion, most often with both at the same time. While religious freedom was acquired very early on, the proximity of Protestants and their political and social dominance were always seen as a threat to religious integrity. Further, the clergy, whom historical circumstances had placed at the top of the social pyramid, saw to it that religion was a constant preoccupation of French-Canadian society. Conscious of the fact that linguistic and cultural differences seriously hampered access to Protestant ideas, the clergy always defended French language rights. The French language, which was the only communicative tool for most people, the symbol of their ethnic origins, and the link with ancestors and traditions, thus quickly acquired a dominant position in the identity of the *Canadiens*, for one thing because of the constant threats and direct attacks it had been subjected to ever since the English took control of the economy and politics. The need to constantly re-assert that French had every right to exist in Canada made the language the symbol of the *Canadien*, particularly in the face of the assimilative intentions the English openly expressed at the time.

The *Canadiens* were thus Catholic and French-speaking, and they were country people. Their way of life, which was virtually autonomous, made them independent, proud, and strongly attached to family values. All descriptions of the *habitants* concur in presenting them as conservative, with little sense of enterprise, although there were the occasional adventurers, *coureurs de bois,* sailors, or colonists setting out in search of new land to clear. But these were physical adventures rather than business ventures. The *Canadiens* had what was necessary to live and eat well, but they lived modestly without any luxuries. They generally had little education, and were respectful of those who did, and of authority in general. From their French ancestry they drew the easy-going, pleasure-loving and social characteristics. This is the somewhat clichéd portrait that can be drawn of the *habitants*, a portrait based on the realities of the first half of the nineteenth century.

Linguistic awareness

The language spoken by the *Canadiens* at the end of the eighteenth century was a popular variety of French marked by certain local terms; it cannot have been completely uniform. During the war and after the Cession of the territory to England when the influx of French colonists stopped, the language developed in a limited space, with very few, if any, contacts to France. While the French Revolution in the last decade of the century caused a number of non-conformist priests to go into exile in Canada, they probably had little influence on the language. However, their violent rejection of the Revolution and its ideas certainly created an even greater distance between the *Canadiens* and France, which had become an atheist republic. In regard to language, this distance cut the *Canadiens* off from the transformations taking place in France. The Revolution, which completely upset the social structures of France, shifting the prestige of the aristocracy to the bourgeoisie, caused hundreds of new words to be coined. These changes were not shared by the *Canadiens*, and this widened the gap between the two versions of the language. Further, in the towns where business was run by English merchants and administrators, linguistic contacts worked from the top downward. The upper class was the first to learn English. After the pledge of allegiance was abolished, the parliamentary delegates and especially the lawyers had to work partly in English. Retail business also put the two linguistic groups in touch. Nonetheless, in the countryside, French unilingualism remained the rule.

In the towns, linguistic contact began to cause linguistic interference. In the early part of the nineteenth century, only fifty years after the Cession, travellers already remarked on the numerous anglicisms in use:

> The intercourse between the French and English has occasioned the former to ingraft many anglicisms in their language, which to a stranger arriving from England, and speaking only boarding-school French, is at first rather puzzling. The Canadians have had the character of speaking the purest French; but I question whether they deserve it at the present day.[9]

The same author noted that the *Canadiens* used numerous "antiquated phrases." Twenty years later, Alexis de Toqueville remarked that while French was heard on the streets of Quebec, all the signs were in English, the style of the newspapers was "common, filled with anglicisms and strange expressions," court hearings were bilingual and Quebec lawyers "speak French with the accent of the Norman middle class. Their style is vulgar, mixed with foreign expressions and English phrases," while the clergy "speak pure French."[10]

The *Canadiens* themselves seemed to be unaware of the linguistic differences developing between them and France, for only in the middle of the nineteenth century did the first expressions of anxiety appear. From the very beginning, these anxieties focused on English interferences. The other differences – phonetic and semantic – were either not recognized (this is the case for most of them), or considered unimportant, perhaps even legitimate. In 1810, for instance, Jacques Viger, mayor of Montreal, began work on a *Néologie canadienne* that was finally published in the early twentieth century, and lists words that have taken on a particular meaning in Canada or a slightly different pronunciation, some Amerindian expressions, and a few anglicisms. Unlike the long series of corrective manuals of which the first was the *Manuel des difficultés les plus communes de la langue française*, published by the priest Thomas Maguire in 1841, Viger's listing does not set out to correct the language of his contemporaries or condemn it, but rather point out its particularities. Later, books such as the *Dictionnaire de nos fautes*, self-help corrective books, and other lists of anglicisms to be banished or nasty expressions to be eradicated appeared, but in the early 1800s, the *Canadiens* seemed to be living in an atmosphere of linguistic security, that is they did not have negative feelings about the language they were speaking. Documents dating from before 1850 hardly address this question, which is in itself a useful hint. If no one finds it necessary to address the question, it is obviously not one that moves people. When issues of language were addressed, it was to defend one's right to speak French and not to criticize differences from the norm.

The interferences due to contact with English, which began in the early nineteenth century, were what sparked the first anxieties. These showed up in educated people, who also had the most contact with English. The language of the courts and the parliament, which adopted much of the vocabulary of the British institutions when the English took them over, was the first to suffer hybridization. This comes out clearly in the following quatrain published by Michel Bibeau, in the first collection of poetry published in Quebec in 1830:

> Très souvent, au milieu d'une phrase française
> [Very often in the middle of a French sentence]
> Nous plaçons sans façon une tournure anglaise:
> [We casually insert an English phrase.]
> "Presentment, indictment, impeachment, foreman,
> Sheriff, writ, verdict, bill, roast-beef, warrant,
>   watchman."[11]

With the exception of *roast beef,* all the English used here is taken from the language of the courts or the institutions. However, while educated people were the first to be disturbed by the interferences, the real criticism came from outside. By the end of the century, the French-Canadians noted, with some surprise, that the English and the Americans felt they did not speak "real French," but only a patois. If we accept an anecdote reported by Emmanuel Blain de Saint-Aubin, the English were already subscribing to this negative prejudice around 1860. He recounts that he was hired by Lady Monk to teach her children French, and reports her saying, "I assume you speak Parisian French; I have to ask this question since I have heard that the French-Canadians speak a terrible patois."[12] From this point on, the English of North America seemed to contrast "Parisian French" with the so-called Canadian patois, although they never asked whether they themselves spoke Oxford English. The term "patois" is obviously derogatory, if only because it is accompanied by the adjective "terrible." Blain de Saint-Aubin explained to Lady Monk that the French-Canadians speak French as well as their peers in France, and that the Canadian farmers speak better French than French farmers because they have had a better education. He added that the French spoken in Paris "is more defective than the language spoken in all other parts of France." With this little story the myth of French-Canadian Patois entered the consciousness of Quebec, along with all the ingredients that characterized the debates it set off: the contempt expressed by the English, Parisian French as the reference, the rejection of "Parisian French" as the norm, and praise for the language spoken by the Canadian farmers. One element disappeared, however, and that was the assertion that the French Canadians spoke a language that was just as correct as that of the French. A constantly deteriorating image of the French-Canadians systematically seeped into the late nineteenth century, and grew worse with each generation over the next century. But for the time before 1867, one can say that with the exception of a few educated people who travelled to France, the population of French Canada did not feel at all insecure in regard to the quality of their language.

From the early nineteenth century onward, and perhaps from even earlier, the *Canadiens* vigorously rejected English attempts to assimilate them. Those who gave in to English pressure were taxed with betraying their nationality. In what was already perceived as a struggle for survival, those who were attracted by the prestige of English and the economic and political power associated with it, and who adopted the English language and lifestyle, were viewed as traitors. On the other hand, the increasingly important place that English took in business, commerce, politics and the courts made parents demand that their children be taught English. Toward the end of the nineteenth century, certain educated people or clergy began to express a certain anxiety at what they perceived to be a threat to the position and the quality of the French language. While the teaching of English was considered necessary for those destined for the liberal professions, commerce, or industry, it was felt to be of no use for the majority:

> Over the course of a long lifetime of study, one can hardly learn to write one's mother tongue properly, and now we are sacrificing this important and difficult area of study to a foreign language that is relatively useless. This is worse than nonsense, worse than bizarre; it is a direct attack on our nationality.[13]

It is noteworthy that learning to write French was presented as an arduous task, a constantly recurring aspect of the discourse on language in Quebec. The great fear was that general education in English would push more and more *Canadiens* into assimilation, a fear that was mainly justified by the difference in social prestige between the two languages. If French had been the language that was necessary for improving one's social position, there would have been no reason to fear the disintegration of the French-Canadian nation in the face of English. By the last quarter of the nineteenth century, however, the prestige factor began to have a strong negative influence on French, and to touch a much broader section of the population. Why else would there be talk of sadness and shame?

> Our language. This word, dear compatriots, will doubtless cause your souls to be penetrated with patriotic feelings, mixed with joy and with sadness [. . .] Everywhere, in our public places, our streets, our offices, our living rooms, you hear the invasive sound of a foreign language. Alas! the genie of this jealous language lies in wait at the cradles of our children, forming them after its own rigidity. [...]

And what has demanded all these sacrifices of us? Justice? No. Charity? No. Politeness? Not either. What is it then? It is the contempt and the shame in which we hold our race; it is the preference and the honour we extend toward a foreign race. Oh, treacherous deserter of our language, beggar before a foreign life, go hence, you are not seemly for our life as a nation.[14]

In 1865, the year this speech was held, Arthur Buies published a series of articles in the Montreal newspaper *Le pays* that criticized the "barbarisms of the *Canadien*," with some humour. His list, obviously drawn up for purposes of correction, contained archaisms or provincialisms as well as anglicisms. The years 1860-1870 thus saw the development of a change in mentalities on the subject of the French language in Quebec. Up until that point, a certain security in regard to the quality of the language was in place. Yet even if by this point the English grip on business, industry and politics was obvious, the vast majority of those *Canadiens* who lived in the rural areas did not experience this as a limitation. The need to learn English was only a requirement for the urban middle-class, a very small group that apparently submitted without too much complaint. The threat of assimilation or of linguistic interference had not yet entered the consciousness of the *Canadiens*. The linguistic battle was still being played out at the political level, in the need to ensure the right to use French for the laws and their application. All this changed after 1860-1870; the *Canadiens* became French-Canadians and entered a period of crisis that lasted a century.

Social changes

From the beginning of settlement in New France, lands had been passed on in a way that ensured that most of the children of a family could become farmers. This had the effect of keeping most of the *Canadiens* in the rural areas, since they were not attracted by the towns, where the English ruled. From 1830 onward, however, the farmers' sons who did not inherit the family land – and this affected most of them, because families were large – found it increasingly difficult to establish themselves. And from generation to generation it got worse. Population growth had been so strong since the beginning of the settlement that people had to go farther and farther afield to find land to clear. Indeed, territorial expansion was limited by the fact that all arable land in Quebec had been claimed. And finally, politics intervened to keep the French-Canadians within the boundaries of Quebec. The division of the colony into Upper and Lower Canada in 1791 had given the English control of the institutions in Upper Canada, and these discouraged the French-Canadians from settling farther west. Instead, the government chose to open up these territories to immigrants from Great Britain. These policies were hardly modified by the Union Act of 1840. The constitution of 1867, which increased the number of provincial governments where French-Canadians were hardly, or not at all represented, ensured that the English dominated politics everywhere, except in Quebec. And they quickly used provincial laws to limit the rights of French-Canadians, mainly through educational restrictions. New Brunswick took this type of action in 1871. Manitoba, which entered confederation in 1870 with a linguistic status much like Quebec's, implemented a series of anti-French measures with similar goals in 1890. Ontario followed suit in 1912, with Regulation

17. Thus, French-Canadians in search of new lands were largely kept within the bounds of Quebec, and immigration westward, which could have offered a solution to the lack of agricultural land, remained quite small. Young people had little option but to go to the cities and work in industry. In the last third of the nineteenth century, this migration was constant:

> We see that from 1871 onward the exodus from rural Quebec is never lower than 50% of the natural increase in population, sometimes it is even 80%. The rural population of Quebec therefore remains constant, due to emigration that is not a recent or sporadic phenomenon but ancient and established.[2]

Thus more than one half and sometimes up to 80% of each generation were forced to leave their native environment to join the growing class of labourers in the cities. The fact that these young people had no other choice but to become industrial labourers was due to several factors. On the one hand, hardly any of them were educated. The political economy was based on farmers' almost complete autonomy, and they produced what was essential for the lives of their families. However, this economy hardly produced surpluses, and so there was no money with which to educate the children. Most of the young people who thus arrived in the cities had no qualifications whatsoever, as Jean-Charles Falardeau has described:

> It is generally accepted that most of the French-Canadians arrived in the industrial marketplace at the lowest level of non-specialized labourers. They had to learn and master new techniques on the job, slowly and laboriously. Technical schools and vocational schools were created later, relatively recently, in order to provide specialized education for their children.[3]

In 1881 the rural population of Quebec represented 77% of the total population; in 1931 it was no more than 37%, and decreasing rapidly. Over the course of this half-century the conditions of life and socialization of most French-Canadians changed radically. The period from the end of the nineteenth century to the 1930s also saw many French-Canadians leave Quebec to find work in the industries on the American east coast. This emigration is estimated at 800,000.[4] But another phenomenon also had an important effect on the Quebec society: the economy of North America underwent profound changes from 1911 onward. Up until that point this economy had been based on trade, centred in the coastal cities of the east, with wood as the main product, and Quebec was fully and actively involved in this continental economy. However, the steel industry began to develop in the United States and the location of the economy moved toward the centre of the country, as Albert Faucher and Maurice Lamontagne observe:

> The most important factor for the move from trade to industry occurred without any doubt when steel replaced wood as the basis of the industry. [. . .] From that moment onward, only the regions that had coal experienced rapid economic growth.[5]

Until 1939 Quebec thus experienced a period of decline during which both industrial and commercial employment were rare. Surplus labour found no work in industry, and the economic crisis that hit all of North America at the end of the 1920s aggravated this situation:

> After all further urban employment came to an end – it is still very limited today – attempts were made to open up new territories for the excess rural population. [. . .] This was evidently only a short-term solution.[6]

A ruralist ideology began to emerge among the clergy and the liberal middle classes, a back-to-the-land ideology of colonization. Throughout the 1920s and 1930s attempts were made to open up new agricultural lands – in Abitibi and Temiscaming – as had been done in Lac-Saint-Jean at the turn of the century, in order to absorb the excess rural population. However, the difficult living conditions and the sparse returns from the land defeated these attempts, and from 1939, when industry in Quebec regained strength, the urbanization process accelerated even more. The figures given by Faucher and Lamontagne are very clear on this:

> In one century, from 1839 to 1939, employment in the manufacturing industry increased by little more than 200,000 people. During the short period from 1939-1950 the same number of people entered industrial employment in Quebec. Growth in these eleven years was ten times more rapid than it had been over the hundred preceding years.[7]

Until 1960, the industrialization and urbanization of French-Canadians brought with it a considerable deterioration in social status. They arrived in the cities without education, without qualifications, and their only resource was work at the lowest levels in industry. They moved from a farming situation in which they had led modest but independent lives as valued members of society to being unskilled labourers, dependent on skimpy salaries and with precarious employment security.

This phenomenon of proletarization of the peasant class as a result of urbanization and industrialization is not unique to Quebec. It has occurred in many countries, and continues to affect regions where industrialization came late, especially in least developed countries. What is more specific, though not exclusive to Quebec, is that the peasants who went to work in industry found themselves subject to bosses who belonged to another culture and spoke another language.

The English had taken over business from the beginning of their regime. All through the nineteenth century they developed and consolidated their networks, and began founding industries. The ideological discourse of the French-Canadian clergy that contrasted materialist and mercantile English-Protestant values with the spiritual values of family and the conservative French-Catholic tradition certainly contributed to the rigid positioning of each community in its own camp. The clergy had, after all, gained considerable influence over the French-Canadians, and had been fully in charge of education since 1838. They systematically oriented young people toward the liberal professions and did not encourage commercial or technical training. As time went on, a kind of tacit agreement between the French-Canadian clergy and the English capitalists developed, an agreement that assured each party that their respective interests would be respected. Hubert Guindon explains:

> The people looking for work in the cities were not forced to come. The capitalists offered the excess population coming from the country both employment and a place to live. In exchange, those who held power locally allowed the capitalists to dictate the rules of the industrial game. They were the masters of industry, and they drove out intrusive unions. Moreover, their participation in local society had a very specific purpose. They sought the greatest return and were not at all interested in political and religious matters or in urban expansion, and this fit very well with the demands the local powers continued to impose upon the foreign invaders.[8]

And so the French-Canadians at work found themselves subject to bosses and foremen from a different culture who did not speak their language. They were often forced to learn English in order to carry out unskilled and poorly-paid work. Having left a highly structured environment, they found themselves in cities whose rapid, unplanned development hardly made it easy to integrate. Jean-Charles Falardeau writes:

> In their move from fields to factories, the rural inhabitants were transplanted into environments that had no character, and were often quite unstructured. There was no solid urban culture around them that might have helped them integrate. Their only recourse was to cling to institutions and models of behaviour that were dominated by the values of the past.[9]

Generation after generation, from the end of the nineteenth century, an increasing number of French-Canadians thus suffered systematic loss of social status. The frustrations and bitterness that this situation engendered took long to manifest themselves openly. And it also took a few decades for the traditional image of the French Canadian to adjust to the new realities. Meanwhile, the image was deteriorating as proletarization affected the community, and English domination did not let up.

While the two communities had been content to live side by side during the first century of the English regime, avoiding contact, and dividing up the roles and territory between them, the situation changed radically once the processes of urbanization set in. By taking jobs in industry, the French-Canadians became the employees of the English- Canadians. English political domination, which had been strengthened by the Union Act and Confederation, was now reinforced by social domination and by economic domination, which made the French-Canadians dependent. They began to associate their collective identity with the conditions into which a series of circumstances had placed them. The move to the cities had brutal psychological effects, and was one of the main reasons for the identity crisis, whose effects are still perceptible in contemporary Quebec society.

The minority status of French Canada

Demographically, until about 1830, the French-Canadians were in the majority. The Union Act of 1840 that united Upper and Lower Canada made them a minority. However, the formula adopted by this Act gave each of the two provinces the same political weight. The Confederation of 1867 changed this state of affairs by joining together four provinces, as well as Manitoba in 1870, a group among which only Quebec had a French-speaking majority. The francophone population that had settled west of Ontario was rapidly outnumbered by continuous immigration from Great Britain and the United States. Thus, the French-Canadians who, in the first decades of the English regime, had constantly defended their French language rights with the argument that they were in the majority, now had to inscribe these rights in the federal constitution as a condition of their joining Confederation. From here on in, they had to refer to the notion of "a founding people" to ensure the respect of the central government. Since no such safeguards could be established at provincial level, the French-Canadians living outside Quebec were refused the right to exercise most of these rights until late in the twentieth century. At the end of the nineteenth century then, the French-Canadians knew that they were the core of a minority, which, though still relatively strong and with exceptionally high birth rates, would progressively decline because of assimilation, emigration to the United States, and a constant increase in the number of

English. The "revenge of the cradle" was a response to attacks and a first battle lost. But in the face of the evidence, hopes of winning the demographic battle could not be maintained. Minority status thus entered the French-Canadian identity, little by little, with all that implies in regard to political powerlessness in a system where the majority governs.

A *deteriorating identity*

The traditional image of the French-Canadian farmer, which developed over the course of the nineteenth century, had less and less to do with reality. The social, economic, and political changes that began in the last third of the century radically changed the conditions of life of most of the former *habitants*. Nevertheless, Léon Guérin, writing in 1932, described the typical French-Canadian family as follows:

> How do we select a typical Canadien family to serve as an example? The first condition is that the family live in the country, for French-Canadians are true country people. Second, and this is related to the first condition, the rural area where we set up our observation point, has hardly felt the effects of the urban centres or business and industrial development.[10]

When Guérin held this talk, 63% of the population of Quebec was already living in the cities. Furthermore, only a small minority of the population would have been living in regions far enough away from cities to fit his description, and were thus hardly representative of the whole. Why did this traditional image persist in the discourse of the French-Canadians about themselves, and long after it had ceased to be a reasonable representation of reality? For almost half a century, there was an enormous gap between this image, that continued to be widely disseminated, and the new, very negative, identity that was developing and would not be expressed or represented until after the Second World War in the first urban novels by Gabrielle Roy and Roger Lemelin. In the meantime, however, this (negative) identity that one could describe as repressed, made its way into the collective consciousness of the French-Canadians and conditioned their behaviour.

The repressed image: mediocrity

The image that was repressed was that of a dominated people, a minority that was powerless to change its status, that was poor and ignorant, and whose ethnic status alone determined its mediocre position, a people dispossessed of its country, its past, its culture, and even its language. Although one finds few explicit traces of this negative identity before the 1950s, when intellectuals and writers, the new elites of Quebec society began to enter into battle against it, one does find copious implicit references to this condition in the discourse of the traditional elites, from the nineteenth century onward. Take, for example, the way people were exhorted to be proud of their origins, language, culture, and nation when these things are normally self-evident. What is the use of such talk? With the exception of patriotic discourse at the time of war, when it becomes necessary to artificially inflate national pride so that the people agree to the sacrifices demanded of them, you hardly find such sentiments – except in societies that are dominated, or in decline. Thus, when you see these appeals for people to be proud, you can be sure that precisely this pride is under threat. In Quebec, from the 1860s onward, there is no end to such appeals for people to be proud – in the sermons, the speeches, the talks, the articles – as well as reproaches against those whose behaviour reveals that they are ashamed of what they are. Earlier, people had been content to say, "We are proud of our culture;" henceforth, they said, "Let's be proud of our culture." In a speech for Saint-Jean-Baptiste in 1866, for instance, Monseigneur Laflèche criticized those who assigned too much prestige to English:

> Since language is the primary element of a nation, the primary duty of every citizen is to speak this language, to respect it and preserve it. Now, putting our hands on our hearts, let us ask ourselves if we have always and faithfully fulfilled this sacred duty. Have there not been moments when men who once gloried in being Canadiens blushed at this name, renounced it, and thus sought to erase this primary aspect of our national character?[10]

The more the actual situation of the French-Canadians deteriorated and English domination made itself felt, the more appeals of this kind took on urgent tones, and the more the traditional image of the *habitant* was presented as the "official image" with which to exorcise the progressively negative self-image of the French-Canadians.

In actual fact, an entire defensive ideology, associated with the traditional image, was being constructed at the end of the nineteenth century. Not only were people supposed to be proud of their culture because it descended from one of the most brilliant cultures in the history of mankind – no reason to blush, therefore –, but destiny (or God) had assigned the French-Canadians a particular mission in North America, and that was to disseminate the wisdom of the French spirit and the Catholic religion. The more the situation deteriorated, the more lyrical the discourse became, as this passage from a speech by Oscar Dunn, held in 1870, shows:

To be French, is to found a lineage, a new family; it is to represent France and Catholicism. France! that noble land that marches at the head of civilization and that generous minds have never found indifferent. France! eldest daughter of the Catholic religion, the religious truth. What a position for us, a position worthy of the world's respect and which gives to our existence such high purpose! What a mission is ours to continue the role that France plays in Europe on this side of the seas![12]

Taken up a few years later by Jules-Paul Tardivel,[13] this idea of the spiritual and intellectual mission of the French-Canadians receded little by little to make way for another discourse that was similar but not quite as megalomanic; it focused on "the language as guardian of the faith." Around the turn of the twentieth century the hope of having any kind of influence on the English who were more and more numerous and triumphant, was abandoned. This second discourse, which was more defensive than masterful, had actually appeared at the same time as the other, and had also been used by Tardivel;[14] it soon replaced the other. The exaltation of the spiritual and intellectual values of French-Canadian society in actual fact masked its defeat at the political and economic level. Virtue became a necessity. Tardivel wrote:

A newspaper in this country recently told French-Canadians: you must, in your own interest, give up your language. We shall not listen to such perfidious counsel. Even though our faithfulness to our language condemn us to relative poverty, even though it hinder us from marching as quickly as we might wish along the path of material progress, we must not hesitate even for one moment in the face of our duty.[15]

The elites, led by the clergy, thus spent several decades trying to convince the French-Canadians that their poverty was a virtue, their culture was on a higher intellectual and spiritual plane than that of the English, and the preservation of their language protected them from excessive contact with the English-Protestants and thus assured them of continued moral superiority. It is noteworthy that while the first version of this ideology, that of a mission, had expansionist objectives, the second version from the very start expressed the awareness of a threat poised over French-Canadian culture. After all, there is no need to engage a guard to protect goods that are not endangered. From the early twentieth century, this threat became so clear that there was talk of *survival*. However, despite all these efforts, it is obvious that, in the 1920s and 1930s, the French-Canadians felt they had lost ground as movements to "refranciser," to restore French, developed; there was talk of renaissance, of recovering the position that was due to French. Esdras Minville, an economist, expressed these feelings in an article from 1934:

> If the people we belong to is to survive, let it be known that it will do so through its intelligence. All the rest – the economic restoration and social restoration which are supposed to lift it out of the abject position it is slipping into – is subordinate to this intellectual restoration.[16]

While some continued to go on about the moral superiority of the French-Canadians, others, like Esdras Minville, considered that it was not enough to maintain French-Canadian culture, and expressed the idea that French-Canadians must take over the economy in order to achieve prosperity; poverty, far from being a virtue, was more certain to render them extinct than any other factor. The general prosperity that developed after the First World War provided the opportunity for French-Canadians to begin to struggle out of the web of poverty in which they were entangled. In the meantime, however, the negative image had made considerable progress and the traditional identity, which no longer corresponded to reality, could not serve as a resource. There was talk of defeatist mentality, of servility, of colonized behaviour. The discouragement the French-Canadians felt as they faced the constant erosion of their position and the apparent continuity of an oppressive social structure, made them reproach themselves for this decline. This had important consequences in that they began to have negative views, not only about themselves, but about everything they produced. The years 1940-1960 produced the blackest opinions ever about the French that was being spoken. Socially, the position of French clearly deteriorated between 1867 and 1960, regardless of all the speeches held in its honour.

The position of French

In the towns of the early nineteenth century, the language used on public signs was mainly English, as Alexis de Toqueville remarked. However, since the majority of French-Canadians did not live in the towns, this hardly moved them. Again, the urbanization that took place at the end of the century changed this situation.

The position of a language is evaluated according to the different domains of life where it is used: in private life, in education, at work, in public life (politics, courts, business, media), in religious life, in the arts and leisure activities (theatre, cinema, literature).

At the end of the nineteenth century, French may not have held a dominant position in all spheres of life, but it did play an important role for most of the francophone population of Quebec. The majority of those who lived in the countryside knew no other language, and those who did speak English rarely had the chance to use it. In the towns, however, English held the dominant position; it was the language of business and commerce, and those who worked in these areas, as well as in industry, had to have at least a rudimentary knowledge of it. To practice law and pursue politics, a more refined knowledge of English was required. Everywhere in the province, French was used in teaching, though there was education in English as well, and French was the language of worship. Nevertheless, the strong position of English in business caused parents to increasingly demand education in English for their children. At the end of the nineteenth century, some teachers objected to this pressure:

> We willingly admit that the circumstances in which the French race in this country finds itself obliges those who work in the liberal professions, especially in the towns, and those engaged in business, to learn English. We also admit that to achieve this end higher schools are virtually forced to teach their students English. We also believe it appropriate for industrial colleges and academies to follow the example set by the classical colleges in this regard. But we find it absolutely ridiculous that all our model schools and even our elementary schools should be required to teach English.[17]

In 1922, research done by the Association catholique de la jeunesse canadienne-française (ACJC) [Catholic Association of French-Canadian Youth] revealed that English had penetrated almost all the social milieus and most activities. Indeed, the way the survey questions are formulated shows that the researchers already had a pretty clear idea of the situation and very few illusions:

> What kind of anglicizing influences are there in the *pharmacy*, the *store*, and the *grocery store*? Are the announce-

ments and the labels on the products French, English or bilingual? Are French-Canadian products for sale, and do you choose these over others? Have you done any research on this question? Give figures. *Should there not be a campaign to remedy this problem? Do you propose to organize such a reaction?*[18]

The results of this survey showed that 95% of all labeling, and most signs, were in English. In 1915, 77% of small retail businesses were owned by French-Canadians; this decreased to 43% in 1935.[19] Industry and commerce remained English. The division of roles had apparently not changed much. However, one fundamental change had occurred: English had become the working language for a large part of the population, and the language of the daily environment, since this was now predominantly urban. French may have gained some space in the public service sector due to the Lavergne law of 1910, which made bilingualism obligatory in this area, but it lost everywhere else. More and more, English was perceived as necessary, and French became a "luxury language," to cite Adélard Desjardins.[20] A part of the population established itself with the two languages, with French relegated to private life. Even education was no longer as uniformly French as it once had been; the business schools, for example, taught certain subjects such as bookkeeping, arithmetic, and correspondence in English only.[21]

In the 1930s, a strong reaction began to develop against the bilingualism that some wanted to see expand – a reaction by people like Esdras Minville and Lionel Groulx –, and all kinds of groups formed in order to "restore French" in Quebec, but the forces locked in struggle were rather lopsided. The fact that the English occupied almost the entire economic domain meant that English was necessary for work and this pushed French into the private sphere. Early in the twentieth century some influential people had seen the unilateral bilingualism of the French-Canadians as an advantage since access to both languages was useful, but by 1930 it had become clear that this was not the case. The English continued to prefer their own for any management jobs, even when all of the personnel was francophone. Bilingualism on the part of the French-Canadians only gave them access to subaltern positions. At the federal level, the civil service used only English, and francophones who worked there could not use their French. From 1867 until the 1960s, the history of French in Canada was marked by small symbolic victories – bilingual postage stamps and money (1927 and 1936), and epic battles that often ended in francophones who were living in other provinces losing language rights – in schools in New Brunswick and Manitoba (1871, 1890-97) and Ontario (1912). On the whole, this period marked a continuing decline in the position of French in increasingly diverse and important sectors of life. Further, over the course of the century, the image of the language deteriorated in the minds of the French-Canadians themselves, a direct consequence of the degradation of their self-image.

The deteriorating image of French

The decade 1860-1870 saw the first manifestations of linguistic insecurity that in the 1940s swelled to enormous proportions. Men of letters such as Arthur Buies, Louis Fréchette, and Jules-Paul Tardivel were the first to raise the alarm. They all addressed anglicisms as a major problem, though most of them also wanted the French of their compatriots modernized, rid of regionalisms and archaisms, and adapted to the norms of standard French. In 1888, Buies wrote:

Twenty-three years ago already (just imagine!) I opened fire in *Le Pays*, the Montreal paper, with a series of articles entitled "Barbarismes canadiens" [*Canadien* barbarisms]. Hubert La Rue also addressed the subject, and after him Tardivel in his little opus that threatened excommunication!, then Oscar Dunn in his "Glossaire francocanadien," published in 1881, and finally, four years ago, Fréchette, Lusignan and I took up the struggle again with furious energy, determined to strike the death blow against those shapeless, monstrous, unnameable things, neither expressions nor phrases nor parts of sentences, that are proliferating in our language to such an extent that all structure disappears.[22]

The targets for Buies as well as Tardivel were above all the politicians, the lawyers, and the journalists. In daily contact with English and obliged to translate and work with English, they were the ones who introduced all kinds of borrowings and calques into French. Only later did general criticism of the French of all the urban classes set in, for some time using that of the peasant farmers as an example to follow. In the late nineteenth century, however, this stigmatization hardly touched the majority of French-Canadians, if it even reached them. What affected them more, and reached the entire population, was the prejudice against patois.

The first mentions of French-Canadian patois also date from 1860, but the newspapers which reached a wide readership only picked up on it around 1910. The French-Canadians once refuted such attacks by simply shrugging their shoulders; then they took to denying them more energetically, and finally began, little by little, to reproach themselves for being guilty of patois, or to convince themselves that they really did speak it. The contempt expressed by the English towards them and the language they spoke evolved along the downward spiral of their self-esteem, which, as we have seen, declined in direct correlation to their socio-economic status over the same period.

The extremely negative idea of French in Quebec culminated toward the end of the 1950s, and in the first years of the 1960s, over the course of which it seems that most French-Canadians were convinced they spoke a vulgar and extremely dislocated language. The question arose about whether it might not be better to give this language another name rather than continue to call it French, when everyone seemed to think it was no longer French. The term *joual* appeared, and produced an extraordinary shock-wave in the population of Quebec. If it was really no longer possible to talk of *French*, what was the point of all those battles fought over the past two centuries in the name of the language? Only at the end of the 1970s was this question resolved on the side of French, in other words, when the idea that *joual* be set up as the national language was completely abandoned, though in the meantime, the Quebecois had vociferously aired their differences on the topic.

CHAPTER V

The "Canayen" and the Anglicism: 1867-1910

The first phase in the deterioration of the image of the French language occurred in the years 1867 to 1910. Throughout this period the main issue was anglicisms. A few men had noted the interferences in Canadian French earlier, among them Ernest Gagnon, who wrote in 1802:

> There are two things that characterize the language we speak: *archaisms* that we should preserve like family jewels, and *anglicisms* that we should systematically get rid of.[1]

For Gagnon, the working class in the towns was most affected, since these people worked for the English and adopted their vocabulary without much thought. But Gagnon also criticized borrowings from France in this text, especially those relating to the railways, and he asserted that the *Canadiens* did not want them.

At the end of the century, the attitudes of the men of letters who energetically pursued the question of language in numerous campaigns in the press and other publications had changed significantly. Their tone was vengeful. They violently attacked the politicians, lawyers and journalists. Buies, writing in *L'Électeur,* said:

> It is obvious that I am not talking about the truly educated people here, but rather about those who think they belong

to this class, professionals who are only professional in name and as ignorant as a plough, and who introduce the most grotesque barbarisms into official and legal language; I am talking particularly about those whose repeated and regular contributions to the bulk of daily publishing bring with them a deluge that will soon drown us all, us as well as our language, if we do not immediately set up a solid dike to stop this. [2]

Louis Fréchette, Jules-Paul Tardivel, and Oscar Dunn went for the same targets and were no less aggressive. Their texts expressed an anxiety that Ernest Gagnon's text had not. This anxiety was focused on the fear that the French-Canadians would end up changing their language to such a point that it would no longer be recognized as French. The fear was that they would thereby lose one of the most efficient arguments in their possession to defend their collective rights: the claim that they were part of a prestigious international culture. If they lost their French, they would be nothing more than a small impoverished people, isolated, dominated, and awaiting imminent extinction. Arthur Buies wrote:

I ask the reader to consider just one thing, and that is to reflect on the real formidable dangers inherent in this situation, to realize that the gibberish we speak defiles us, or rather makes us quite indefinable among other peoples, and that if we do not make up our minds to finally speak French the way it is generally spoken in other parts of the world, and to make our thoughts intelligible, giving them clear, rational expression, we can only expect contempt, and cruel blows to our self-esteem. [3]

The newspapers started printing regular columns on language. Some of these came across as lessons in French. For a long time the column in *La Patrie* was written by Louis Fréchette, from a position very close to Arthur Buies, and in a similarly aggressive tone. Tardivel, who published a pamphlet in 1880 with a title that would become a slogan, *L'anglicisme, voilà l'ennemi!* [Anglicisms. They are the enemy!], responded as follows to a journalist from *La Minerve* who accused him of exaggerating the problem:

> My wise colleague thinks I exaggerate the situation. Let him be assured of one thing, he is not the only one who thinks that way. Ninety-nine out of a hundred people who write in are deeply convinced that our language leaves hardly anything to be desired. [4]

Indeed, in 1880, few people were aware of the interference from English, but the campaign unleashed by Buies, Fréchette, Tardivel and Lusignan soon awakened a response in the population, and by the end of the century the "monster" they were attacking was not vanquished, but they had at least succeeded in communicating their anxiety to a larger segment of the population. In this first phase of the struggle against anglicisms, the main focus was vocabulary, formal borrowings, semantic anglicisms, and expressions that were calques of English.

The vernacular

For the period before 1910, the vernacular was still the rural language. Since it was not particularly affected by English, it was hardly criticized. However, Buies and Fréchette wanted this vernacular to be modernized, and to give up the archaisms that Ernest Gagnon had wanted to preserve. Both writers wanted the French-Canadians to bring their language as much in line as possible with the norms of standard French, which is why they did not like idiosyncratic pronunciation or vocabulary, even if these had their origins in the French of the seventeenth century, the "Grand Siècle." Fréchette responded with cutting sarcasm to those of his readers who criticized him, claiming that the French of the *Canadiens* needed no correction since it was the language of Bossuet and Racine. For instance, he published in its entirety the letter of one reader, signed *Vieux Castor* [Old Beaver], and his defence of the French used at the time of Louis XIV, italicizing all the mistakes in it, all the anglicisms it used. Elsewhere, he coined the term *canayen* to designate the vernacular language, and he made it clear that he meant this pejoratively. His aggressive attitude toward the vernacular in use may have been part of a fierce resistance against a widespread notion of the time that French-Canadians had preserved the pure French of the seventeenth century, the classical French, and that their language was thus better than that used in France:

> If from time to time I allude to the "canayen of Louis XIV," I do so not out of contempt for a century that gave French literature so many masterpieces, but to show how ridiculous it is for those among us who are bloated with their own crass ignorance and who couldn't produce a single correct sentence in French, to criticize those who wish to learn, especially as they then mask their stupidity by saying that if they don't speak French the way it is spoken in France, this is because modern French has been corrupted, while we have preserved the true French, the French of the grand siècle![5]

The view that Fréchette made fun of here, and that remained in vogue for a few decades more, did in the end grow weaker. Those, like Tardivel in 1912, who continued to defend it, used it to legitimate the vernacular; they felt that while there was no reason to feel ashamed of it, it should not be preserved totally either.

They also argued for aligning with modern French, while maintaining a few distinctive little archaisms. This position reveals two things. On the one hand, it shows that French-Canadians had become aware of the gap that had developed between their language and the French spoken in France, a gap in part due to their isolation after the Cession of Canada and the upheavals caused by the French Revolution. On the other hand, it translates the extent to which the Revolution had made the French-Canadians suspicious of French morality. Encouraged by the clergy to feel superior, at least at this level, they extolled the virtues of the literature of the seventeenth century, the classical period, and some authors of the eighteenth century, but suspected that the literary movements of the nineteenth century were morally corrupt and pernicious, and even reflected negatively on the language they used. To prefer the language of the seventeenth century to that of the nineteenth or the twentieth centuries was a step that many took. Henri Bourassa, for instance. Nevertheless, until 1910, the vernacular, the language of the peasant farmers, was not particularly under attack. Some found it excessively archaic, others said the archaisms made it special, but the disputes were not particularly heated, and the main target remained the urban middle-class, because of its anglicization.

The myth of French-Canadian patois

While the French-Canadians were still in the throes of deciding whether to keep the archaic aspects of their language or get rid of them, the English in North America had formulated a much more radical judgment. As we saw, the different French patois had disappeared in Quebec, even before the English arrived. However, toward the middle of the nineteenth century, the *Canadiens* noted, with some surprise, that the Americans and the English-Canadians believed they did not speak French, but rather a patois that was as incomprehensible for the French as it was for foreigners. The journalist Louis Tesson wrote:

> During our travels abroad we could not help noting the very unfavourable opinion people have of the French spoken in Canada. Moved by feelings of justice and patriotic solidarity, we always made it our duty to advise those we spoke to of the true state of affairs.[6]

A few years later Tardivel added:

> In certain milieus, especially in the United States, people are under the impression that the French spoken in Canada is not real French but a miserable patois. Some of our neighbours proclaim their contempt for *Canadian French,* which they perceive as very different from the real *French as spoken in France.*[7]

Already in 1903 Edouard Fabre-Surveyer described the prejudice regarding patois as an "old question." He wrote:

> Let us not forget that one of the reasons, and not the least important, why the English are indifferent to our language, is the widespread opinion that we speak a patois, as they say, and not even properly.[8]

The first reactions, such as Blain de Saint-Aubin's in 1862, were relatively quiet. The authors who took note of these comments refuted them, often nuancing their responses in regard to archaic or anglicized French, as Louis Tesson did. But their texts also reveal the beginnings of a certain anxiety that this reputation might cast contempt and disdain upon the French-Canadians. At this point, *Parisian French* was only used as a point of comparison, forming the basis of comments from the English. The conclusions drawn by those who discussed the problem were generally to encourage their compatriots to develop better French teaching, which, by normalizing the language, would cause the myth to disappear by itself. But this was to set aside the very persistent and negative national stereotypes, which were reinforced by certain events. In 1897, William Henry Drummond published a book entitled *The Habitant*, which focused on French-Canadian peasants. Drummond, who had lived in Quebec for a few months, had his characters speak a poor version of English interspersed with French words. Here is an extract:

De fader of me, he was a habitant farmer
Ma grand'fader too, an'hees fader also
Dey don't mak no money, but dat isn't fonny
For it's not easy get ev'ryt'ing you mus'know.[9]

This book, oddly enough with a preface by Louis Fréchette who saw it as a friendly, realistic portrait of the French-Canadian peasant, was a huge success, and reprinted several times. Its author, who pursued only this one theme, published numerous poems in English-Canadian newspapers and a number of other books, which were sold throughout North America. These works, of which imitations were produced and that generally represented the French-Canadian as illiterate, poor, modest, and big-hearted, certainly contributed to constructing the myth of the *French Canadian Patois* and reinforced the traditional image of the *habitant*. It is hard to evaluate whether the English of America believed that the mix of English-French that Drummond concocted was the language of the French-Canadians or whether they believed there was a patois that originated in France. The fact remains that the French-Canadians suddenly saw themselves confronted with this bad reputation that was being imputed to their language. By 1910 this had been going on for half a century, and finally a campaign to refute this perception was set in motion.

To summarize, during this first period in which the image of the French language in Canada deteriorated, men of letters attacked the middle classes of the cities for their anglicization, while the more archaic French of the countryside was valorized by some (as the French of the "Grand Siècle"), and denigrated by others (as the "canayen of Louis XIV"). In the end, the contemptuous opinion of the English began to spread. Most of the French-Canadians were probably not aware of the arguments and discussions between the men of letters, and not affected by them either. It was in the last third of the nineteenth century, in the middle-class, and particularly the urban middle-class, that the history of the French-Canadian complex around language began. Up until that point, the language had been a positive aspect of the collective identity, but its value would progressively deteriorate.

1867-1910: Identity under threat: arguments and reactions

Between the moment when Canada was ceded to England in 1763 and the Union Act in 1840 questions of language were basically political. The seigneurs, and later the liberal middle class, sought to ensure their participation in the governmental and judicial power structures. Their insistence on the use of French in the Assembly and the law courts opened up these domains for the *Canadiens*, and ensured that any offenders would be dealt with by institutions they could actually participate in; excluding French would, after all, also have meant excluding them. However, factors such as the Union Act, with its clause specifying the exclusive use of English in Parliament, the years of obvious anglicization policies of the British authorities, and the change in the status of the *Canadiens* from majority to minority, put the *Canadiens* on the defensive. They became aware that the exercise of their rights depended upon institutions they did not control, even if they participated in them. Their discourse on their language changed. The arguments based on ethics, history and politics which had supported their demands, were now expanded by two additional elements: the claim that French was the language of a great civilization and culture, and the concept of the language as a barrier against moral and religious corruption. In regard to the first point, Danièle Noël has pointed out that this was not a completely new position in 1840, but it became a particularly recurrent argument.[10] As for the argument that the language was "the guardian of the faith," this idea was first formulated in a text by Étienne Parent, dated 1842:

> As for religion, we cannot conceive of the clergy easily agreeing to a change [anglicization] which would provide the spirit of proselytism with a means of action it has so far not had, fortunately for the peace and happiness of their flocks.[11]

The very formulation of this citation shows to what point the clergy held power in *Canadien* society at that time. Over the years, between 1867 and 1910, the discourse on the universality of the French language violently collided with the prejudice about patois. And indeed, it makes little sense to evoke the beauty, wealth, and widespread use of the French language if this is not, in fact, the language being used; if, instead, only a vulgar and incomprehensible patois is in use, as the English claimed. That is how the discourse about language progressively changed from being political to being metalinguistic. From here on in, it became necessary to demonstrate that it was actually French that was spoken in Quebec. While the demands for language rights remained firm, especially as they were constantly under attack, and particularly so in the area of education in the anglophone provinces of the new Confederation, it is still true to say that since the condition of the language itself was being criticized – both from within, in regard to interferences, and from without, in regard to the prejudices concerning patois – it finally became necessary to look at how it was being used. In other words, linguistic assimilation began to seriously worry the French-Canadians, for such assimilation would decrease their political and social clout and undermine their rights even more.

Faced with this threat to their identity because of the prejudice against patois, the first reaction of the French-Canadians was to simply deny it, firmly and calmly. In 1862, the campaigns against interferences had not yet commenced. In 1901, however, Tardivel, one of the most impassioned critics of anglicisms, demonstrated a clear awareness of patois as a threat to French-Canadian identity when he commented as follows:

> Basically it doesn't matter what others think of the French the *Canadiens* speak. What counts is that we don't share their low opinion of our language. Isn't it obvious that if we felt contempt for our language, we would stop loving it, stop defending it, and would end up abandoning it? That would be the beginning of the end; and our assimilation, our disappearance into the abyss of *great big* Anglo-America would follow. So let us take care as we work

ceaselessly to purify our language; let us make sure not to give any credit to the idea that we speak a contemptible jargon.[12]

The danger, as Tardivel pointed out, was that the French-Canadians might come to feel such contempt for their language that they would choose assimilation over a negative and stigmatized identity. The disappearance into the abyss of great big Anglo-America now became the nightmare that underpinned all the discourse on language. The language was not just the guardian of the faith, it was, and it became even more, the central element of French-Canadian identity, and the guardian of their nationality. This is why the prejudice against patois was not just a little episode; it was, in actual fact, a violent attack on the very identity of the French-Canadians. If they only spoke patois, it was not worth fighting for something that downgraded them; their language did not deserve an official status and it did not deserve to be taught or maintained. Their culture and their very existence as a nation were, thus, put in doubt and viewed from outside as an anachronistic fragment from a distant past, doomed to imminent extinction. And so, at the end of the nineteenth century, there began a huge ideological project to legitimate the French language of Canada, first in the eyes of strangers, and then in the eyes of the French-Canadians themselves. The first strategy was to refute negative judgments, by simply claiming they were wrong – as Blain de Saint-Aubin had done, and Faucher de Saint-Maurice did as well, when he wrote in 1892:

In a lecture entitled "La langue que nous parlons" [the language we speak], Napoléon Legendre proved that patois does not exist in French Canada. This patois that is ascribed to us by little *snobs* or weighty *cockneys* on vacation from their regiments or under family guardianship needs to be discussed, and that is what we will do.

In Canada and in Acadia, the language is spoken just as well if not better than the language used by the peasants in France.[13]

It is noteworthy that Faucher de Saint-Maurice accompanied his rejection of the criticisms with hostile comments toward those who formulated them. The ideological strategy that would develop over the following decades was inaugurated with his book, which sought to link Canadian French to Norman French, and show that *English* was nothing more than a "derived patois;" it was supported by the thesis written by Napoléon Legendre[14] that defended the rights and particularities of French in Canada. The response to attacks was a discourse that valorized and legitimated Canadian French by linking it to its historical source. Since the socio-political and economic situation of the French-Canadians was not very prestigious at that point, prestige was sought in the past. There are hardly any texts available from this period that argue for assimilation into English, a strategy that would have negated French-Canadian identity and promoted the acquisition of the other, more valorized, one. From the reproachful tones that some authors used against their compatriots, we know, however, that some people adopted this solution, especially in the urban business class. Albert Lefaivre, a French diplomat, wrote in 1877:

> Some of them [the French-Canadians] have made nice little fortunes in business and industry; but among those favoured by Plutus, a certain number are weak enough to anglicize themselves, as though they were ashamed of their origins. Although they hold first place in their own society, they prefer to be admitted to that of their former persecutors. Some of them put on stiff British airs and pretend they have forgotten their mother tongue.[15]

This marks the beginning of a major break within the French-Canadian middle class which Alexis de Toqueville had already felt during his stay in 1831:

> The people's instincts are turned against the English, but many of the *Canadiens* who belong to the educated class did not strike us as being as devoted as we might expect to keeping intact traces of their origins, and becoming a separate people. Some seemed ready to melt into the English if they adopted the interests of the country.[16]

In the educated class then, there were some who decided to benefit fully from the activities of industry and commerce, entirely controlled by the English, and they gave in to this domination by more or less assimilating or acculturating. The others, who refused to give up their culture and rejected the inferior status assigned them, sought to defend all aspects of French-Canadian culture, and especially the language. The former adopted a discourse they described as pragmatic: since English is the language of the economy and of power, let us speak English so that we will acquire power, wealth, and prestige. The latter invoked morality: the language is the core of our nationality, carrying moral, religious, and spiritual values; it has been transmitted by our ancestors and it is our duty to be proud of it and defend its rights. The newspapers were dominated by this second discourse of the defenders of the French language, with the journalists, writers, clergy, lawyers and doctors who were publishing there almost all subscribing to it. But the discourse of the pragmatists is there too – between the lines of those refuting it. While this was going on between two opposing factions in the middle-class, the nationalistic defenders of language soon turned to the other classes for support, to those who, so far, had not been much involved. This is when the press campaigns with the metalinguistic discourse on legitimizing Canadian French and the political discourse demanding its rights came together. The stakes were sizeable; it was a matter of saving the *Canadien* nation from dissolving "in the abyss of great big Anglo-America." In the eyes of those who led the struggle, the people had to be be made aware of the risks, and not let themselves be swayed and pushed into assimilation by powerful socio-economic pressures.

Bilingualism

During the first century of the English regime, bilingualism slowly established itself in the political and legal institutions of Quebec, though many battles were fought over this. With Confederation came the proclamation that the federal government was officially bilingual, although this did not affect the public service. In reality, not many individuals practiced bilingualism. While it was mandatory and unilateral in the political and legal sectors, and while it was necessary for anyone who wanted to do business in the cities or rise in industry, most *Canadiens'* bilingualism was quite limited since they still largely lived in the countryside. With urbanization and industrialization at the end of the nineteenth century, bilingualism suddenly seemed a necessity for a much larger part of the population because this determined their chances for social promotion. Different discourses developed. Writers such as Monseigneur Laflèche considered bilingualism a form of bondage, and wanted it limited to the absolutely necessary:

> Brothers, I will not hide my thoughts; the heaviest tax the Conquest imposed upon us was the need to speak English. I admit it is appropriate that some know how to speak

English, but this tax should only be paid as far as it is strictly necessary.[17]

Others, like Pierre-Joseph-Olivier Chauveau, considered
bilingualism an intellectual advantage, especially as both
languages stemmed from great cultures.[18] Those, like
Arthur Buies, who thought that the use of both languages would cause confusion and interference were
more numerous:

> We are so used to the two languages being mixed that we
> no longer make a difference, or see the character, the sep-
> arate nature of each one.[19]

True, by the end of the nineteenth century, the alarm had
been raised against anglicisms and the struggle was well
on its way. The defenders of French, men such as Tardivel and Henri Bourassa, felt that bilingualism might be
necessary for a certain governing elite and for business
people, but that generalized bilingualism for the mass of
the population would pose a severe danger for the survival of the French-Canadian nation:

> Some of our people would like to make the French-Canadi-
> ans *bilingual*. How powerful we would be, they say, if all the
> French-Canadians talked English as well as French! Let us be
> careful! This is a trap; a gilded trap, perhaps, but still a trap.
> Do you know many bilingual peoples? I know of none. But
> I do know a people that lost its national language because it
> was forced to learn another language. Let us not, voluntari-
> ly, venture into such a dangerous experience.[20]

And then there were those, like Fabre-Surveyer, who
thought that besides the socio-economic advantages, the
study of English would also offer people the possibility
of avoiding the unconscious interference of English in
French. The argument is worth citing:

At the risk of appearing paradoxical, I insist on voicing my opinion: the only remedy against anglicisms is English. We have to study more English and spend time with English people who know French in order to learn from them how to avoid mixing the two languages when we try to speak ours.[21]

This kind of argument, which is indeed rather paradoxical, is the sign of a situation where the diglossia of a part of the population – of lawyers, journalists, clerks, etc. –, caused numerous borrowings and calques to spread throughout the population, of which the majority was unilingual. It also translates a feeling of dispossession: people no longer possessed the spirit of their maternal language, and had to study a foreign language in order to locate it *by contrast*. Later, such arguments appeared from the pen of men like François Hertel. Whatever the opinion advanced on the topic of bilingualism, it was always accompanied by comments about the teaching of French in the schools and colleges. Fréchette complained bitterly of this in his columns in *La Patrie*; Buies was adamant in his criticism. Indeed, the calls for reform and for the reinforcement of this teaching are so constant in the history of Quebec that one must assume that the French-Canadians always hoped that teaching would improve their language, and that their hopes in this regard were always dashed.

At the level of practical measures, an important step was taken in 1910 when Louis Lavergne, after failing in Ottawa, had the Legislative Assembly of Quebec adopt a law that made bilingualism mandatory in the public services: in transport, electricity, and gas companies. English unilingualism had been the rule up to that point, and so the French-Canadians perceived this law as a victory. It was also the very first legislation on language in Quebec, and it marked the beginning of a period of militancy in regard to language. There are, for example, numerous letters to the editor reporting infringements of this law. In the first years of the twentieth century an organism that played an important role in the next decades was also founded: the Société du parler français au Canada [Society for French spoken in Canada]. Created in 1902, the objective of this society was to defend the French language by producing scientific studies of the specific characteristics of the French language in Canada, of its history, and the conditions in which it existed. The society was also concerned with pinpointing the threats against the language, and finding ways to counter them. From the founding text of the society, we see that the signatories were aware of the changes affecting French-Canadian society as it was urbanizing, and thus considerably increasing its contacts with the English, and we also see a desire to adapt and modernize the language in order to respond to new needs. This society produced the first scientific research on the origins and the development of the language of French-Canada; it organized conferences on the French language, the first of which was held in 1912, and in 1930 it published the *Glossaire du parler français au Canada* [Glossary of the French Spoken in Canada]. The society, whose founding members included such indefatigable defenders of French as Adjutor Rivard, Jules-Paul Tardivel and Monseigneur Camille Roy, was very active and very present over the following decades, and the ideas expressed by its members dominated public debates. It is noteworthy that the name this society gave itself used the terms "le parler français au Canada" [the French spoken in Canada], and not "le français" [French], or "la langue française" [the French language]. This translates not only as an awareness of dialectal difference, but also as a desire to emphasize the specificity of the language, a direction that can be found in all of its works.

CHAPTER VI

The Peasants' Hour of Glory: 1910-1940

Most of the factors leading to the growing tension about identity that marked the period 1910-1940 originated in the last decades of the nineteenth century. However, in the year 1910, the threat was aggravated, at least in the perception of the French-Canadians. That year, the Lavergne Law was adopted in Quebec, after several years of struggle, and after a failed attempt in Ottawa. The language question thus returned to the centre of the debate, and the resistance that this law caused, reinforced francophones' feeling of being second-class citizens. The feeling had already sprung up in the years when French was under attack in provincial schools in New Brunswick (1870), in Manitoba (1890-97), and in Ontario (1912). Then, a speech by Monseigneur Bourne at Notre-Dame Basilica made tensions rise. In this speech, Monseigneur Bourne, an English prelate, committed the Catholic Church in Canada to a process of anglicization in order to allow the religion to spread more widely throughout North America. Henri Bourassa responded with a speech that has become famous, and in which he presented a major theme in defence of French – the theme of the language as the guardian of the faith. This idea had already been in circulation for a few decades, but Bourassa proffered it to the general public. *Le Devoir,* the newspaper he had just founded, would contribute powerfully to its further propagation.

In fact, this paper continued to play a very active role in the defence of French. The edition of June 24, 1912, for example, which came out to mark Saint Jean Baptiste Day, was almost entirely focused on questions of language; it reviewed the struggles over language, reproduced the comments made by foreigners and French-Canadians on the language spoken in Quebec, and included a long speech by Tardivel from 1901, as well as poems on the glory of French.

Socio-economic status and identity

The urbanization process was well underway by 1910, the period when the urban population began to outnumber that of the rural areas. While the rural areas did not become depopulated, all of the natural growth of the population occurred in the cities where young people went to find work. Many were hired at the lowest level in industry. These were people who left an environment into which they were perfectly integrated and then found themselves in a world that offered no support. The economy of Quebec was going through a difficult period, passing from the mercantile to the industrial era, and was finding it difficult to adapt to these changes because of its unfavourable geographic location. The vast surplus in labour could not be absorbed as easily as had once been possible. Faced with this situation, the traditional elites and the clergy reissued calls for colonization in attempts to keep as much of the workforce as possible in the country. This was the ideal solution for the clergy who disliked the cities, where their influence was less solid. For the government of Quebec, colonization was a way to combat unemployment. And so, the agriculturalist discourse of the earlier century was rekindled, a discourse that sought to persuade French-Canadians that their vocation was to clear the land and protect themselves from the vile influences of the cities and the English Protestants. This discourse held up until the end of the Second World War, despite the increasing gap between it and social reality. The novel *Maria Chapdelaine*, by Louis Hémon, which dates from this period and describes the peasants' hard lives, served, paradoxically, to vindicate traditional values and praise colonization. Ideologically, the peasant became the repository of all the virtues of the race. One may well ask how the thousands of men and women felt, who, for lack of employment, went to work in industry and live in the cities whose corrupting influences they were constantly being warned about. They left no trace of their feelings, but we can imagine a sense of dispossession, a drop in social status, and an alienation that must have grown worse as city life and work in industry offered only a meager salary and little hope of promotion because they spoke French and were uneducated. Wedged between an elite that kept singing the glories of a past that no longer existed and English bosses that kept expanding their sphere of influence, and living in cities where their language was a mark of inferiority, the French-Canadians began to internalize the negative judgments they heard about themselves. While they doubtless wanted to believe in the glorious background and mission of their people, they could hardly help feeling bitter at their cramped situation. French-Canadians of the years between 1910 and 1940 were Catholics – this was the period when the clergy held them in the tightest ideological and social grip –, and they were French-speaking (a source of discrimination they could never ignore); they were poor and they were dominated. Nevertheless, very quietly and slowly, a small middle-class began to develop in the cities that within a few decades became the motor for change, but it had to wait until the end of the Second World War and the strong economic growth that followed to develop more fully.

During this entire period the dominant ideological discourse remained the same; and it took no account of the changes in social realities. There were certain practical purposes underlying this discourse, and also reasons for its divorce from reality. From the time of Confederation, domination by the English had grown stronger and so had their distrust and contempt. When the French-Canadians made demands about the use of French, the English responded with the myth of the French-Canadian patois in order to justify limiting concessions as much as possible. French-Canadian men of letters who, for thirty years, had been criticizing the liberal middle-class for its anglicization, and decrying the linguistic contamination of the working class, had no other resources but the peasants and their glorious origins with which to legitimate their language and justify their demands.

From 1910 onward, there was thus a huge initiative to rehabilitate the peasant class, and especially its language, an initiative that was led by men of letters whose objective was apparently to combat the deteriorating image the French-Canadians had of themselves. While the scathing discourse of writers such as Buies and Fréchette did not continue, this was not because the problems they addressed had disappeared; on the contrary, linguistic contamination was constantly increasing. However, the threats from outside the community were so immediate, and the social deterioration was so glaring, that it became urgent to give up self-criticism and consolidate, or rather, reconstruct, a positive image. The fact that these elites did not try to persuade the French-Canadians to take their future in hand, by whatever means possible at the time, improving their education, and taking over the means of production and business, this fact says a lot about their feelings of powerlessness. There were, nonetheless, a few exceptions, such as Albert Lévesque, who wrote the following in 1934:

> The survival, and even more so, the expansion of the national character of the French-Canadians will remain an illusion as long as their material well-being depends on the goodwill of the nations who control them. One of the main elements that consolidates the existence of a people is the collective possession of a territory whose destiny it controls. National security is not only threatened by a military force that seizes territory by firing its cannons. It is also threatened, and perhaps more seriously threatened, by the invasion of a foreign economic power that monopolizes its natural resources, organizes economic life according to its own egotistical interests, sets in motion and dominates, according to its requirements, policies that create ridiculous scenes where plutocrats agree to let a few puppets dance in order to appease the last shreds of resistance of the national soul.[1]

On the whole, however, the intellectuals gave up the economic domain to the English, and insisted on the spiritual values of the French-Canadian culture, often also declaring their contempt for the ungodly materialism of the Americans and the English-Canadians. In the 1930s, a certain economic nationalism emerged, developing from movements such as the ACJC (Association catholique de la jeunesse canadienne-française) and thinkers like Lionel Groulx. French-Canadians were encouraged to deploy their economic power on behalf of their own, to "buy from our own." Lionel Groulx, for instance, declared during an evening on the "restoration of French":

> Because we bought from the others, we increased their enormous fortunes, and nothing, or almost nothing has come back to us. [. . .] At the same time, we have con-

tributed to the English appearance of our towns, our countryside, our province; we have increased the feelings of inferiority in our people and their victim mentality; we have increased the mass of resigned workers [. . .]; we have taught the French-Canadians exaggerated respect for the English language; we have anglicized our schools; we have endangered the pre-eminence of the French language, and perhaps compromised the way it is taught.[2]

Still, the intellectual elite basically worked to supply the French-Canadian people with reasons to be proud, and these reasons were historical. Suddenly, the mission of the French-Canadians was not to prepare a better future for their descendants, but to transmit intact their moral, spiritual, cultural and linguistic heritage. The discourse of this period was dominated solely by the idea of survival, and since territory had been lost, the idea of regaining this territory was also ever-present: hence the conferences on *refrancisation* [restoring French], and hence also, terms such as *recouvrer* [to recover], *patrimoine* [patrimony], *héritage* [heritage], *richesse léguée* [inherited wealth], that are found throughout these texts.

The arrival of thousands of French-Canadians in the towns and cities changed nothing in regard to public and commercial signage in their language. According to the surveys carried out by the ACJC and the many commentaries on this question, English was visible everywhere, and even bilingualism was rare:

The parish of Saint-Pierre has fourteen merchants with signs in poor French, thirty-three French-Canadians with signs written in English only [. . .] three French-Canadians who have announcements in both languages but who have indicated a preference for English, and fifty-one Jewish businesses. It is not enough to simply describe this situation; a remedy must be found. To this end, 244 personal letters have been sent out to invite merchants, industrialists, and French-Canadian businessmen of the parish of Saint-Pierre to attend a special meeting where presentations will demonstrate the best methods our people can implement to conserve the French appearance of the parish of Saint-Pierre.[3]

It is noteworthy that the organizers of these campaigns to restore French expected nothing of non-francophone businesses since they addressed only French-Canadians with their circulars; moreover, English seems to have been so strongly tied to commerce in peoples' minds that a majority of French-Canadian merchants did not even think of using French for commercial purposes, even in a neighbourhood like Saint-Pierre that had a huge majority of French speakers, and still does today. The conditioning was very powerful and no amount of militant action could produce satisfactory results.

Activism

The period from 1910 to the beginning of the Second World War saw the birth in Quebec of a large number of organisms, papers and journals whose purpose was to defend the French-Canadian nation and its language. Besides the ACJC and *Le Devoir*, *L'Action* was founded by Jules Fournier in 1911; then the "Ligue des droits du français" [League for the Rights of French] was founded by Father Joseph Papin-Archambault in 1913, and its name changed to "Ligue d'action française" [League for French Action] in 1921. This organism of which Lionel Groulx was one of the main leaders launched *L'Action française* in 1917. After a few years' interval, between 1928 and 1933, the league took up its activities again under the name of "Ligue d'action nationale" [League for National Action] and launched the journal *Revue d'action nationale.* In 1923, Jules Masse founded the Société du bon parler français [Society for speaking good French] in Montreal. The Société du parler français au Canada [Society for French spoken in Canada], based in Quebec City, had already organized a first conference on the French language in 1912. A second conference was held in 1937. During this second conference, a standing committee on the survival of French was formed, and its report *Pour survivre* [In order to survive] was launched two years later. Meanwhile the ACJC was increasing its surveys and its campaigns for the restoration of French.

In the political domain, the French-Canadians fought extensive battles and had a few, largely symbolic, victories. In 1912, Ontario had adopted Regulation 17, which restricted the use of French in separate schools; that is, in the bilingual schools that had taught some of their classes in French to francophone students. It took fifteen years to get this regulation repealed, fifteen years during which the Quebecois very actively supported the struggles of the French in Ontario, by lobbying Ottawa, holding public events, and organizing more concrete activities such as running campaigns to raise money or shipping French textbooks. At the federal level, great importance was accorded to the struggle over symbols. In 1927, the federal government issued the first bilingual postage stamps. A few years later, a campaign on behalf of bilingual currency was also undertaken. On this topic Omer Héroux wrote in *Le Devoir*:

> The bilingual banknote, especially if it is issued by the Bank of Canada, will attest everywhere it goes to the fact that our country is a bilingual country; that even though the sons of the pioneers may have changed allegiances, they have not lost their own character, and still count in the country. It will do this, eloquently, and frequently, – like the postage stamps do now [. . .] In all of the

provinces, it will proclaim that Canada is a bilingual country, and that French is not the language of a pariah or of second-class citizens.[4]

In 1934 a similar campaign was launched to have cheques issued by the federal government made out in both languages. Such militancy began to affect more people than ever before. Popular movements such as the ACJC and large scale events such as the conference on the French language were widely reported in the newspapers. The activities in support of the French in Ontario attracted large numbers of people, as the following article from 1916 reveals:

We have described elsewhere the main aspects of yesterday's event. It was certainly one of the most beautiful – and most meaningful – to take place in Montreal. First, in regard to attendance. There was not an inch of space left unoccupied in the room, and from eight o'clock on, hundreds and hundreds of people had to give up trying to get into the hall, much to their regret. Then, in regard to the spirit of the event the harmonization of thoughts and hearts was perfect. All the calls for resistance were acclaimed, the more precise and the clearer they were, the clearer too, was the applause.[5]

In this case, the event was held to protest Regulation 17 in Ontario, perceived as a direct attack on French-Canadian nationality, against its "right to live." The use of the term "resistance" is noteworthy; the attitude was defensive rather than offensive, as another passage from the same article confirms:

This energetic desire to struggle is not just a useless quarrel for its own sake. We are on the defensive, ready to fend off all the attacks, ready also for any kinds of legal arrangements.

This is a good summary of the French-Canadians' political position during this period; all they wanted was to live in peace on condition that the institutions they deemed necessary for the perpetuation of their culture not be attacked. A relatively modest desire, it would seem, yet one that was perpetually left unfulfilled. It is true that their exceptionally high birthrate made the English fearful that they might extend their grip all across Canadian territory, which could have eventually brought on a much more real form of bilingualism than the wholly theoretical version the federal government practised, limited as that was to the parliamentary institutions then in operation. Regulation 17, like the anti-French laws of Manitoba and New Brunswick, sought, on the one hand, to limit the expansion of French-Canadians and to confine them to Quebec and, on the other, to assimilate the francophone communities that were already established. More than ever before the Quebec elites managed to mobilize the population on these points, which were viewed as vital. The many social actions of the period, ranging from the surveys of the ACJC to the conferences on the French language, the campaigns to revive French on public signs, the foundation of leagues to defend the language and other such activities, were conceived and carried out with constant threats in the background. And the entire discourse on language, even its metalinguistic aspects, must be understood as a reaction to these threats, as a clearly expressed and constantly reiterated refusal to melt away into "the abyss of great big Anglo-America," in spite of all the forces to the contrary.

This militant stance was basically defensive. The measures it supported aimed to ward off the immediate threats, get Regulation 17 repealed, demand French from the merchants. These measures did not address the sources of the problem, which were the growing socio-political weakness of the French-Canadian nation, its proletarization, and its resulting lack of prestige.

Toward the end of the 1930s, the activism slowly let up. Its last manifestations took place at the conference on language in 1937, which wrapped up with rather pessimistic assessments of the situation of the French language and its quality. In the following year the Duplessis government adopted a law that assigned primacy to the French version of the Civil Code. This law was hotly contested by the anglophones, and withdrawn the year after. The beginning of the Second World War and a new conscription crisis put linguistic and nationalist preoccupations on hold for a few years. The strong economic growth that North America experienced while Europe was being laid waste, and the new push toward industrialization and urbanization that followed, placed the French-Canadians into a situation after the war where they could no longer define themselves as a people consisting largely of peasants.

Strategies for affirming identity

During the period from 1910 to 1940, those who spoke on behalf of French-Canadian identity adopted the strategy of valorizing, and sometimes exaggerating, everything that made French-Canadian culture different from other cultures. Obviously, the language, under attack by the myth of *French Canadian Patois*, was at the centre of the operation, but this did not exclude other aspects of the culture from the discussion. In spite of the brutal social transformations underway in these years, the elites clung to the traditional image of the *habitants*, their glorious origins, their fervent Catholicism, the language of the seventeenth century, their cultural heritage, in other words, anything that in their eyes made French-

Canadians wholesome, moral, and proud beings. Though the question of pride was rather delicate, since this had to be constantly reiterated and proven, morality was apparently a sure thing. The traditional culture was thus turned into a fetish, and a reactive identity was constructed whose first objective was to allow the French-Canadians to resist the erosion of their culture. For this purpose, French-Canadian Catholicism, the shared, distinctive, and apparently most solid component of the culture which was not under attack by the English, was mobilized.

It is rather peculiar that a large part of the defence of the language was based on the concept of "the language as guardian of the faith," especially when that very language was under attack and losing ground. There were several good reasons. First, those who put forward this argument obviously had no doubts about the French-Canadians' attachment to their religion, and they exploited this fervour on behalf of the language. Further, since freedom of religion had been in place since the Cession, this was a principle the English could not undermine without openly and explicitly breaking all the treaties. Finally, while transitional bilingualism could, over time, soften the erosion of one language to the advantage of another, prolonging the change and even rendering it unconscious, it is impossible to practice two religions at the same time. Hence, a loss or a change of religion is a much more brutal and visible social fact. The defense of French-Canadian culture was thus organized around Catholicism, its most stable element, and apparently the least endangered. However, in order to encourage the people to consolidate all the weaker aspects of their culture, the discourse claimed that religion *was*, in fact, in danger.

Indeed, the whole of the culture, as a system of understanding and analyzing the world, was in question.

Such a concept of culture, in which all the elements are linked, necessarily led to questions about the relations between the cultures of France and French-Canada. The writers in Quebec were fully aware that Catholicism might still be the dominant religion in France, but they also knew it no longer played the central role in France that it did in Quebec. So, depending on the importance they accorded to religion, the response was either that Quebec participated in French culture and had to find sustenance there, or that Quebec preserved "true French culture." This latter approach implied that by pushing Catholicism into the background, France had corrupted its culture. In 1918 Henri Bourassa wrote:

> Separated from the France of the Encyclopedia and of Voltaire, from the licentious France of the Revolution, from imperial and enslaved France, we have remained the children of Catholic France, the loving brothers of the priests of Christ, and the admirable nuns, of all the Catholics of France, who in continuous struggle on all the fields of battle and action seek to save the soul of France, to bring back and protect its true grandeur.[6]

And further on in the text:

> We speak the good, old, and wholesome language of the France that upheld the Church, of the France that had more children, for God, the Church, and the fatherland.

Thus, claims were made that the French-Canadians were part of French culture, but that anything contrary to Catholic dogma was to be rejected, which is why pre-revolutionary French literature and God-fearing authors were privileged. This was also why the archaic aspects of the French language in Canada were valorized. In the first decades of the twentieth century, no one called for the need to modernize the language as Buies and

Fréchette had done at the end of the preceding century. Still, although the ideology linking language and religion clearly held a dominant position until the Second World War, and even beyond, a few voices were raised objecting to the clergy's hold over the life of the nation. Among these, Olivar Asselin was especially noteworthy:

> If one is absolutely set on tying the language to the faith, then this must be done without detriment to the language. The Société du parler français could have done much to promote French in English Canada; we know what influenced it to become the Société du parler catholique et français [Society for speaking Catholic and French]. In order to comply with the narrow objectives of Monseigneur Roy and a few others, it has alienated not only those *Canadiens* who are Protestants and who could have supported its efforts, but also the huge army of Catholic French-Canadians who do not share the vocation for religious propaganda, and who feel in some confused way that in this marriage of language and faith, decreed for reasons of the State, or rather for reasons of the Church, faith will not be the one to lose out [. . .]
>
> [. . .] by all accounts only closer intellectual exchanges with France could provide us with the French esprit as well as the strength we now lack to expand our influence; [. . .] however, for fear of "irreligion," and in spite of all the beautiful speeches, those who could bring about a rapprochement with France behave as though they want to keep us separate from France. The day the French-Canadian clergy no longer attach conditions to their defence of French, they will conquer the hearts of those for whom the French language is also a religion.[7]

Nothing could be clearer. For Olivar Asselin, linking the language to the faith cut the French-Canadians off from contacts with French culture, which made them inward-looking and threatened to suffocate their culture. Few dared to criticize the clergy so overtly since it held considerable power. After this article appeared, the student paper, *L'Étudiant*, was, in fact, closed down. The newspapers, on the other hand, first among them *Le Devoir*, continued to develop this concept of "the language as guardian of the faith." The conferences on the French language also served as occasions to repeat the idea, but as time passed, its use decreased. Regulation 17, which had originally set off the use of the concept as a major argument, was repealed in 1927. Then, with the economic situation of the French-Canadians deteriorating, there was an increasing tendency in the late 1930s to set aside the discourse that extolled spiritual values to place emphasis instead on what Olivar Asselin had already expressed in 1915: "[. . .] never has a people with low economic standards held any prestige nor exercised any influence beyond its own borders."[8]

The discourse adopted by the elites in defence of French-Canadian culture thus ended up being eroded and rejected, for lack of realism. After the Second World War, the overall situation of the French-Canadians was evaluated in all its difficult reality, and there was a clear recognition of the fact that the culture of the urban labourer had little to do with that of the traditional habitant whose virtues had been lauded for the past thirty years.

The discourse on language 1910-1940

In the years from 1910-1940, two problems were closely linked in the discourse about language: anglicization, on the one hand, and the myth of *French-Canadian Patois* on the other. In other words, the discourse was concerned with the more or less dialectal aspects of the French spoken in Quebec. We have seen how the middle of the nineteenth century marked the point when men of letters began to criticize interferences from English, in particular in the urban middle class, in the language of the lawyers and journalists. They wanted to modernize the language, and align it with the French spoken and written in France. The campaign they waged with considerable vigour, however, abruptly changed course in the face of the very negative prejudices expressed by English Canadians in regard to Canadian French. Further, factors such as the precarious position of French in the Confederation, the dangers of assimilation hanging over the minorities outside Quebec, the deterioration of the socio-economic position of the French-Canadians, and the end of their rural isolation forced the men of letters to revise their positions. While they continued to criticize anglicisms, they tried to avoid providing fodder for any of the negative opinions uttered by the English.

On the topic of archaisms and canadianisms, the discourse changed completely. The myth about patois had overtly put the quality of the language in question, and so the thesis of the "language of the "Grand Siècle" [the seventeenth century], that Fréchette had already mocked, was recycled. Tardivel, among others, enthusiastically exploited it in a lecture held in 1901 that was republished in the special issue of *Le Devoir* for Saint-Jean-Baptiste Day in 1912. He cited numerous examples taken from French grammarians of the seventeenth century and from travel writing. In the same breath, he declared, however, that while it was important to recognize the legitimate status of this language he did not advocate teaching it:

> Should we try to re-establish this old-fashioned pronunciation in our colleges and convents, and teach our studious young people to say, *i zaiment* for "ils aiment" [they love]; *note curé* for "notre curé" [our priest]; *quèque chose* and *quèqu'un* for "quelque chose" [something] and "quelqu'un" [someone]; *su la table* for "sur la table" [on the table]; *gloère, crère, devoère,* ["gloire" [glory], croire"

[believe], "devoir" [duty] etc. Certainly not. But we should not laugh at these archaic pronunciations, nor should we admit that they are expressions of patois, and even less, corrupted pronunciation.[9]

This idea, which was heard often between 1910 and 1940, always came with the same two reservations: this is not a language that is useful for the modern world, and, while it should not be taught in schools, its most colourful words and most imaged expressions should be conserved. The Société du parler français au Canada, of which Tardivel was a member, and which was particularly active in these years, produced this kind of argument. The Society had correspondents all over Quebec, mainly located in the colleges, and was engaged in collecting canadianisms, determining their origins, and if possible, proving their derivation from varieties of provincial or seventeenth century French. By organizing conferences on the French language, it disseminated the ideas of influential members such as Monseigneur Camille Roy. The Society did the first scientific work on the French language in Quebec, taking the lead from Romance philology, then in full expansion in Europe. In 1930, this Society published the *Glossaire du parler français au Canada* [Glossary of French Spoken in Canada], edited by Adjutor Rivard and Louis-Philippe Geoffrion. However, as Olivar Asselin's text cited above shows,[10] the clergy held important positions in the province and the Society actively contributed to the idea of the "language as guardian of the faith." The need to bring that in line with "the language of the Grand Siècle" which was used constantly to counter the prejudice about patois, sometimes created rather fantastical interpretations. In 1928, for example, on the occasion of a French theatre company performing Corneille's *Le Cid* in Montreal, a journalist wrote:

Despite the old-fashioned forms of the classical line, despite the many words whose meanings have changed since 1636, the piece had an extraordinary success that cannot be attributed only to the actors' performances. Indeed, few of those who applauded could probably claim to have read the play since they left the convent or the college. For the spectators to have acclaimed it the way they did, they must have understood the sense of every line which, meaningful and dense, always contains an idea.

Perhaps we should seek out the reason for this astonishing success in the fact that our vocabulary which is studded with archaisms and is more limited than that of the French today, is, in fact, closer to the language of Corneille.[11]

Establishing a relationship between French-Canadian French and the French of the seventeenth century or its provincial versions is one thing; claiming that the French-Canadians speak a better version of the language than the French, because it is more classical, is another. But many people happily confused these two points during this period. The thesis of the "Grand Siècle" was indeed powerful, but from time to time it was contested by writers who were alarmed by the level of interference from English which seemed to be growing, despite all the efforts. In an article in 1930, Léon Lorrain commented approvingly on the opinions of a teacher, Father Gustave Lamarche, who wrote:

I hope there is no longer anyone who thinks we speak a normal language, and that we have nothing to be envious of in the language written or spoken by other peoples.

Léon Lorrain continued:

I wish to God it were so! If people didn't refuse to see the shameful condition of French in Canada, we could institute the necessary reforms. But we need time and patience to disillusion those who go around repeating that we speak the French of Louis XIV, and those who take seriously the certifications that we speak good French politely issued to us by the occasional visiting Frenchman, often against their better judgment, after they have spent an hour talking to a few *Canadiens* who were, in any case, speaking their Sunday best.[12]

There are many columnists who wavered back and forth between these two extremes, criticizing anglicisms, glorifying archaisms, and alternating between defensive and offensive positions when the question of patois came up or when they suddenly judged that a reform was urgently necessary. They clearly suffered from the fear of providing ammunition for those who claimed that French in Quebec was nothing but a vulgar patois. At the same time, they felt that if certain reforms were not undertaken, the language would truly become an incomprehensible jargon, "a little language just for us," as Léon Lorrain put it. This ambivalence carried on, at least in the newspapers, until the quarrel over patois died out. Writing in 1927, this journalist clearly presents the dilemma that men of letters found themselves in:

> We agree with our colleague from *Canada* that under the pretext of defending our speech against unjust attacks we have become so chauvinistic that we claim our French is purer than modern French. This claim is not only ridiculous, it also has the great weakness of hindering the development of a linguistic culture in young *Canadiens*.[13]

The same article paints a black picture of the situation, but as always the language of the peasants is excluded:

> On the subject of how *Canadiens* speak we think there should be some differentiation. Some of the peasant population has maintained a form of French that is full of colourful language and charm. They probably speak the

language of our ancestors better than most peasants in France do. But those of our peasants who have traveled usually return home with a suitcase full of barbarisms that are far from ordinary. As for the people living in the cities, their language is generally abominable. The intellectual elite, educated women, and the small number that has had the advantage of spending time in France speak more or less correctly and without accent. But there are a considerable number of men in the professions, and especially in public office, whose language is studded with every mistake in the book.

Few escape criticism. In 1927, peasants made up 35 or 40% of the total population of Quebec, and the proportion of those living in cities who avoided censure was very slim. Despite the initial intentions to legitimate the language of the French-Canadians, the discourse that extolled only the virtues of the peasants' French thus turned against the great majority of the population, and became a discourse that violently stigmatized them. Hardly ever was mention made of the working class, then in full expansion. While it is true that the peasant origins of most of the working class were still very recent, Quebec society was undergoing rapid diversification; but it was still not conscious of class, a phenomenon that was quite late in developing. In the discourse on language, this translated into the constantly reiterated opposition between the language of the country and that of the cities, without any further distinctions being made. But what was developing was an ethnic consciousness, with the French-Canadians growing increasingly aware of the social obstacles the English owners of the means of production were erecting against them.

In a study on the social classes of French Canada, Jacques Dofny and Marcel Rioux wrote:

In all the political crises, this ethnic "we" prevailed and masked the development of any awareness of social class in French Canada. Ethnic consciousness prevailed, whether in regard to Riel, the Boer War, conscription in 1918, the economic crisis of the 1930s or the plebiscite of 1942.[14]

Dofny and Rioux believed class awareness took hold in 1945, and that before this date, the discourse on language simply absorbed the lower classes into the peasant class, the symbolic representative of the nation, in spite of all the facts to the contrary.

The peasants and the others

What exactly was being said about the peasants? They don't use a patois, their language is not full of interferences from English; it is colourful, inventive, full of images, and descends directly from classical French and provincial varieties:

> I think there is nowhere in the world where less patois is used than in Canada. [. . .] I would even add, without exaggerating or being chauvinistic, that the differences between our vernacular and that of peasants in France, when such differences even come up, are generally to the advantage of our people.[15]

Note here the equation: vernacular language = language of the peasants.

> All the residents of Saint-Irénée speak French, and purer French than is normally spoken in the countryside of France. [. . .] The pronunciation is like that of Lower Normandy. The French spoken in the country is perhaps purer than that of the cities, especially Montreal, where the interferences from English are constant.[16]

Here, the anglicization of the urban class is indirectly addressed. Other writers, such as Édouard Montpetit, focused on origins:

> We tend to confuse inherited archaisms with dialects from the provinces because we are not used to distinguishing what comes from the mother country; it is enough to trace one of our words back to somewhere in France, in order to feel pleasure and recognize it as French.[17]

The methods of Adjutor Rivard and Louis-Philippe Geoffrion, and more generally, of the Société du parler français au Canada were clearly at work here; they had assigned themselves the task of establishing the links between the French spoken in Canada and the French from France. By positing the mix of French and various provincial dialects they could show that a large number of terms specific to Canadian French were not the result of interference from English. They were happy to be able to prove, as Montpetit did in his speech accepting his nomination to the Royal Academy of Belgium, in 1924, that the use of words such as "clairer" [clear] or "mouver" [move] could not be attributed to interference but rather to the conservation of words that were originally from Normandy, or the regions of Poitou and Picardie. The issue became somewhat more delicate on the topic of patois, since a number of these words originated from the different patois of northwestern France. As Geoffrion, among others, argued, there might be traces of patois, but its roots were French vernacular:

> Our people speak the French vernacular in common use in the north of France, but they add archaic forms, patois and regionalisms as well as some foreign elements. Which is quite acceptable. It is true there are some rough aspects to the French-Canadian language, and it is not worthy of

being taken fully into our literature. But there is also something quite cheery about a few of its terms, and some of its expressions.[18]

Such reservations on the use of Canadian French in literary texts show that even those who most ardently defended the legitimacy of the peasants' language considered it too crude to be used in the most refined forms of national culture. They supported the careful selection of certain examples of "family jewels" for use as local colour rather than a faithful transcription of the spoken language. Authors, such as Claude-Henri Grignon, who tried to write more realistically and contravened this approach, set off polemics.

There were also efforts made to legitimate pronunciation. The pronunciations that distinguished French-Canadian from standard modern French were traced back to the French of the seventeenth century or to provincial dialects, as Tardivel had already done at the very beginning of the century:

The premise of this article [by Monseigneur Desranleau] is that the pronunciation of the vernacular – when it has not been affected by the proximity of English – has remained what it was in France, in the seventeenth and eighteenth centuries. [. . .] but what is particularly original about his work is the analysis of the old registers of his parish, especially those dating from the time when French priests were recording events. [. . .] From the way the priests spelled proper names and current words, we can see how they were pronounced. [. . .] and how our *habitants* today pronounce them. [. . .] Conclusion: there is no need to impose this old pronunciation in our schools and colleges, but neither should we meet it with a contempt it does not merit, or scornfully qualify it as *Canadien*. "*It is simply the pronunciation of the grand siècle of Louis XIV*," says Monseigneur Desranleau.[19]

A few comments are in order here. Later, more scientific, studies that examine the written registers and archives of the seventeenth and eighteenth centuries from all the populated regions of Quebec, in particular a study by Juneau,[20] have shown that very diverse pronunciations coexisted among the first generations of *Canadiens*, which is apparently explained by the different origins of the French colonists. Progressively, the pronunciation became more unified though minor regional differences developed. In other words, while it was possible to trace the pronunciation of some word back to French vernacular of the seventeenth century or to some provincial dialect in France, the system of pronunciation on the whole was the result of a particular synthesis. The claim that that the French-Canadian peasants of the twentieth century pronounced French like the peasants of Normandy or Poitou, the elites of Paris, or the people of Paris in the seventeenth century was rather far-fetched.

In addition to the reservations that constantly resurfaced in regard to how the language was taught, the writers seemed determined to find nothing original in Canadian French. With the exception of a few new words that the particular environment in Quebec justified, any creative activity was deemed undesirable. This is another example of the low opinion French-Canadians had of themselves at the time. All their pride and glory boiled down to the role they played in preserving and transmitting the original culture. At the end of the nineteenth century, they had said "let's be proud of our origins;" in the 1930s, they indirectly said, "only our origins can allow us to be proud." True, in 1932, because of the massive exodus from the rural areas, the French-Canadians were going through a period for which they were most unprepared – economically, politically, and socially.

In the years from 1910 to 1920, the peasant class had been discussed as a totality. In the 1930s, regional distinctions started to be made. The countryside located near the cities or industries began to suffer the same criticism that had formerly been reserved for urban areas. Progressively, only the most distant and isolated rural areas were assigned the prestigious task of transmitting the cultural heritage in all its purity. This was the last stage in the discourse legitimating the language of the peasants. After the war, there was still some talk in this vein, but more as an anachronism left over from earlier times and slated to disappear than as the foundation of Canadian French. In a radio talk from 1939, for example, Father Saint-Pierre declared:

> There is no doubt that in your region [the lower St. Lawrence River] the French race has remained the most wholesome; the language has maintained the purest accent and a vocabulary with the most varied forms, and this is because you have never felt the need to become bilingual; the domestic traditions have been most firmly established, the faith has been preserved as a living force, and the culture as most universal.[21]

Interference from English, which affected all classes of French-Canadian society except the peasants, was the scourge. This can be read between the lines of all the texts that glorify the language of the peasants, and explains the ongoing justifications of peasant French. Yet, fifty years after the campaigns against anglicisms began, there was only small praise for the actual language, and even that was decreasing. It would not be long before this discourse came to an end, since its continuation would have meant condemning the entire society. A new strategy developed that focused on pedagogical objectives, which left the peasants to their fate, and their colourful language, a language that was not to be included in the teaching in any case, or used in literary works, but that served primarily to give the lie to the myth of patois.

Between 1910 and 1940, statements about the language of the peasants being purer, more true, or more wholesome, implied that truth and purity were French; hence the determination to discover the origins and pronunciation of each word that was not "normal" in contemporary standard French. But in regard to the French spoken in France, there were other differences that could not be checked in the dictionary of the Académie française or in handbooks for correct pronunciation. These were the specificities of popular French or French argot. The columnists had a lot to say about argot and the accent of the Parisian working class. The English habit of systematically and negatively comparing *French Canadian Patois* with *Parisian French* was part of the picture. On this topic, Abbé Étienne Blanchard, author of a "Chronique du bon langage" [Column on Good Language], wrote in *La Presse*:

> About "Parisian French": herewith a sample of the language used by young Parisians, obviously street urchins. It leads one to wonder whether this language is worth more than that of young Montrealers of the same class. True, the latter have anglicisms in their language, but the young Parisian has a slang that is no more acceptable.

There follows a passage from *La guerre des mômes* by Alfred Machaud. Blanchard's conclusion:

> If this is the kind of French we are criticized for not speaking, we say, thank God![22]

French-Canadian columnists thus did not consider French argot or slang legitimate. They saw it as corrupted language that was as disreputable as the anglicisms they criticized in the language of urban Quebec, as well as in that of French anglomaniacs. In the end, the French of the Quebec peasants was judged better than that of the French peasants who spoke patois, better than that of Quebec's urban population and French anglomaniacs since they used anglicisms, and better than that of the people of Paris, who used slang. Nonetheless, a few doubts remained. The language was legitimate, but it was not really what they aspired to, and even though there were thousands of differences between it and the language spoken in France, it was in fact the latter that remained the model, the reference, and, finally, the objective.

The quarrel over patois: 1910-1940

In 1910, the myth of *French Canadian Patois* had been in circulation for fifty years already. And in 1998, it is still around, as people who have attended my lectures have confirmed. Nothing is more tenacious than prejudice, and you can be sure that tourists in Scotland will see instances of the legendary tight-fistedness of the local population wherever they look, which they probably wouldn't notice if the prejudice didn't exist, and which they wouldn't look for in another country. Given this situation, we may well ask what it was about *French Canadian Patois* that so riled the French-Canadians that they spent the next forty years publishing dozens of articles per year on the subject. In contrast to the myth of the penny-pinching Scots, which may be unpleasant but does not put the Scots' social or political status into question, nor stigmatize their entire culture, the myth of *French Canadian Patois* implied ignorance, lack of culture, and a kind of degeneration. It cut the French-Canadians off from their roots, and denied them the prestige they drew from these roots; this, in turn, made it possible to cast aspersions on their institutions, especially their schools, and the reasons to maintain the political rights of French in Canada. When the purpose is to undermine the linguistic rights of a community, there is no more efficient method than to describe its language as a patois. In this same period, the Flemish were trying to get their language accepted in the Belgian Parliament, and they were subject to similar attacks. Flemish was qualified as a "collection of patois."[23] Beyond the displeasure that French-Canadians felt at the contempt expressed through such prejudice, the fear that it would be used as an argument to deny or curtail their linguistic rights explains their vigorous reactions. Louis-Arthur Richard, who fought the prejudice with articles and pamphlets, explains this clearly:

> Our adversaries, never short of ideas, will reply that we do not speak French but a miserable patois that has no literary value, and no practical use. It is hard to forget the hateful cry of Member of Parliament Morphy: *Beastly horrible French.* Nor can we easily forget the line from Beaverbrook's book, which every Canadian household feels the duty to own: *Others, again, switched off from English to French Canadian patois.* And how many other slanderous comments of this sort do we read periodically in work by Canadian or American journalists, some of whom are writing in good faith, but have been terribly led astray by our enemies whose power we cannot afford to ignore.[24]

Gradually, people began to lose patience. Before 1910, writers had been content to simply deny the accusations; then, with Tardivel, they began to respond: the language we speak is the language we inherited from our ancestors; it is French, and may well be marked by provincialisms and archaisms, and affected by interferences from English, especially in the cities, but it is still French.

As time went on, the prejudice seemed to have spread throughout North America, and was so solidly anchored in the minds of the English that completely extravagant interpretations arose. In the 1920s, for example, when the ambassador of France was holding a speech in Plattsburgh, and declared that he would be speaking to the French-Canadians in the audience in their language, American journalists assumed he finished off his talk speaking patois.[25] Numerous anecdotes describe similar incidents. Quebec journalists, irritated at how this notion about patois was expanding, attributed it to the ignorance of the anglophones. Because they had learnt little French in school, and retained even less, they were quick to perpetuate the prejudice which excused them from not understanding the French-Canadians and from not being understood, since they had, of course, only learnt *Parisian French!* Louis Lalande tells the following story:

I remember as though it were yesterday the bursts of laughter from one of my friends, an authentic Parisian, university-educated, a perfect conversationalist, who had come from France two years earlier to teach in one of our universities. There were four of us, on our way from Montreal to Quebec one beautiful evening in July, and we were talking on the deck of the boat. Nearby were a gentleman and a lady from Pittsburgh and their grown-up daughter. The girl had taken French courses in a High School and then finished her studies in Bordeaux [. . .] Well, that evening, as was usually the case, our Parisian was in full form. He talked and talked, he laughed, he gesticulated, he discoursed . . .

The man from Pittsburgh was curious, and relying on all the French his daughter must have acquired, he said, "So what is he talking about?" The girl listened discreetly, then raised her shoulders in a gesture of disdainful pity, "I will never be able to understand that Canadian patois!"

Come now, you dear young thing from Pittsburgh! Don't try to use your French to understand ours. It might get deflowered. In your father's mind, you are doubtless very able. And your mother must be thinking, "How pure her French must be, since she couldn't even understand that Quebecker."[26]

If we believe an article from *La Presse* from 1937, the anglophone population of America was so convinced that the French-Canadians spoke patois that it became impossible for French-Canadians to teach French in American universities and colleges unless they had a diploma from McGill University. As the author of the article said, "No French-Canadian need apply."[27] A number of articles tell of private tutors losing their jobs because they were French-Canadians and so couldn't teach *Parisian French*, and of translators' troubles with clients who suspected their work was in patois, all of which further demonstrates how much damage this myth did at a very practical level.

When we look at the articles that appeared on this question between 1910 and 1940, they express various attitudes. At the end of the nineteenth century, some authors had simply denied the accusations outright, and been scandalized by the term *patois*. Paul Lefranc, author of a column on language in *La Presse*, wrote:

Our English and American friends reproach us for not speaking "Parisian French." They are making a mistake, since "Parisian French" does not exist; it is an illusion. But that is not the only myth our friends subscribe to. There is also the myth about "Canadian patois," which doesn't hold up either.[28]

In a speech to open the first conference on the French language in 1912, Monseigneur Bruchesi stated categorically:

There is no patois here that needs to disappear. We take this solemn occasion to proudly assert this. Nowhere in Canada does patois exist, not in our countryside or in our cities. It is true that a good number of our expressions might not be understood by someone from Paris; but a peasant from Brittany or Normandy would understand them. They are relics of old French.[29]

These writers generally recognized that Canadian French had its particularities but they absolutely rejected the idea that this made their language different from French. Several of them, in turn, attacked the English spoken in Canada and the United States, which, they said, was not the English of Oxford. Étienne Blanchard wrote:

Do the English of Canada and the United States claim to speak the pure English of London or of the universities in Cambridge and Oxford?

In the USA and in Canada there are American and English Canadian neologisms that were created here on this continent, or English words that have taken on a different meaning than they had in England.[30]

A journalist from *La Patrie* adopted a more ironic tone about an article published by an Ontario paper:

In a letter to the editor published by the *Mail and Empire,* a citizen of Ontario is perturbed at the little attention paid by the English of Ontario to how they pronounce the only language they speak [. . .] We have noted other such comments in the *Mail* of Toronto and the *Standard* in Kingston. The French-Canadians have so often been reproached for speaking a patois that is essentially different from the language spoken in France, that they will not be sad to hear such confessions from our compatriots in Ontario.[31]

Nonetheless, even if these arguments helped to turn the criticism around, they did not resolve the problem of the apparently widespread prejudice. For several writers, the term *patois* was a "serious insult."[32] This reaction was clearly a hypersensitive response to the negative comments and reveals a certain linguistic insecurity in those who responded. The French-Canadians were hurt at being judged so negatively and did everything they could to convince their compatriots that Canadian patois was just a legend. Omer Héroux, for instance, reported in 1919 that a young Quebec lawyer, Louis-Arthur Richard compiled a list of statements from French people and authoritative foreigners that expressed favourable opinions on Canadian French. This text, first published in the journal of the alumni of the École polytechnique of Montreal, was then translated and distributed by *Action française*. The purpose was obviously to reach an English public and try to undermine the prejudice about patois. Héroux considered this an excellent initiative and informed his readers where they might procure a copy of the brochure entitled, "Do the French Canadians speak Patois?"[33]

Another group of writers countered the attacks with a healthier dose of irony and derision that, however, still revealed how irritated they were by the myth persisting. Some used the term *Parisian French* in the sense of "terrible Toronto translation."[34] Paul Lefranc, columnist for *La Presse* and a translator, expressed himself clearly on this topic:

> It's pretty clear that when we talk about *Parisian French* we mean the French manufactured for us in Toronto and environs. In the minds of those people, we do not speak real French, but a kind of patois, while their translators use the real French from Paris. Their absurd translations are, how-

ever, what we appropriately and derisively call *Parisian French*."[35]

The same article gave a few examples of such translations:

"Put the plates away out of the reach of children until required in another room." "Gardez les assiettes d'être atteintes par les enfants jusqu'à ce qu'on a besoin d'eux dans quelque autre chamber."

Another example that is apparently typical of many of the translations of the period:

"Smoking, spitting and loafing are not allowed in this station. Anyone violating this order will be prosecuted." "Ici on ne fume pas, ni expectore, ni flâne. Quelqu'un faisant ceci sera prosécuté."[36]

After 1938, the term *Parisian French* is no longer used to describe problematic translations, a symptom of what was happening to the French-Canadians at that moment. But there were many articles that were more or less satirical on the topic. Their authors used every possible occasion to poke fun at those who still believed in *French-Canadian Patois*. Funny anecdotes served to demonstrate how stupid the English were. Doctor Léo Parizeau, for instance, the author of many letters to the editor on the subject, demonstrated that the inventor of *Parisian French*, this admirable "patois that has the advantage of being understood by both of the main ethnic groups of the country" could only be a genius. In fact, it must be Edison since "the Edison section of the world's fair in Paris in 1889 had displayed a modest oil painting of the Master's lab with the following caption: Le nouveau laboratoire de Llewellyn Park (New Jersey) réservé pour les expériments scientifiques, le plus complète et cher laboratoire du mond entière"[37] [a caption riddled with mistakes in grammar, spelling and usage. TR].

The twenty or so anecdotes of this sort that appeared between 1910 and 1939 can be summed up quite simply. They try to show that the English Canadians and the Americans do not understand French, or that they cannot distinguish so-called Parisian French from other forms of French, and that the French-Canadians do not speak patois.

A series of anecdotes for example presented people from France, preferably Parisians, who were mistaken by the English-speaking interlocutors for French-Canadians speaking patois, just because they could not understand them.[38] Omer Héroux, for example, tells this story:

> In this same column we told the story of the gallant American who arrived at the Department for Public Education in Quebec City asking to speak to one of the public servants in a language he firmly believed was French. The public servant who didn't understand a word of his gibberish finally said in English, "Sir, don't you speak English?" They conversed in English then, but that evening at the Chateau Frontenac, the American told his friends, "People had told me these French-Canadians only speak patois. Just imagine, this afternoon at the Department for Public Education, I couldn't get them to understand my French!" [. . .] "Do you know the name of the man you were talking to?" asked one of the Quebeckers present. "Yes, here's his card." "Paul Cazes," the Quebecker read out slowly [. . .] "Do you know you managed to find the only Parisian in the Department?"[39]

Here is another example, reported by a journalist from *Le Devoir*:

> You may remember that when the pilots from the *Bremen* [. . .] arrived at Île-Verte American journalists produced all kinds of fantastical accounts around this expedition. One

of them even described a reception held at Fitzmaurice in Clarke City at which the priest harangued the pilot in *French Canadian Patois*. At the time, we pointed out that the priest at Clarke City is a Frenchman from France, R.P.L.-M Cantin, a Eudist.[40]

French people from Bordeaux or Alsace, with pronounced provincial accents, were generally warmly congratulated by the English for their admirable *Parisian French*. France Ariel, a French woman who lived in North America during the First World War and was outraged by the prejudice, had much to say about it in her memoirs published in 1921. This anecdote was re-published in Paul Lefranc's column:

> Here's a little story that proves that the fiercest partisans of "Parisian French" do not know what they're talking about and don't know their heads from a hole in the ground. One day, a lecturer from France got off the ship in New York. He wasn't just anybody. He arrived loaded down with important sounding books and ministerial recommendations. He spoke very well, but he was from Avignon, and that could be heard clearly in his accent. We were introduced, and when he opened his mouth we knew he was from "somewhere in Provence." I had the pleasure to attend one of his lectures. On the way out, I met an American lady I knew; she was quite enthusiastic. I asked her if she had understood. "Oh, sure," she said, "he speaks such good Parisian French."[41]

Another series of anecdotes gives accounts of North American francophones travelling in France and being perfectly able to understand the French whereas English-Canadians or Americans, thinking they spoke *Parisian French*, could not make themselves understood. A journalist from *Le Devoir* told the following story:

In the last war during which many French-Americans crossed the Atlantic, a young American officer who had a certain wit, told the following story: "I know French, the French of Paris! At least that's what I'd been told. Our young Frenchies only speak patois though. The problem is the French people I met in France didn't understand a word of my French but they perfectly understood our Frenchies' patois. I think the poor fools don't really know the French spoken in Paris. Unless, of course . . . [42]

Finally a few of the anecdotes have to do with translations; some of these, written in excellent French were considered patois, while others, in terrible language, were dubbed the purest *Parisian French*. Paul Lefranc often returned to this issue in his column:

> One day when I had translated twenty-nine English words by nineteen French words, my client told me, "You must have used French Canadian patois." I replied that no such patois existed and that my sentence adequately rendered the idea expressed in his. He didn't want to believe me, and to prove that my language was bad, he said, "In Canada, you say "patate" and in France they say "pomme de terre." A brilliant demonstration![43]

The disappearance of these kinds of articles toward the end of the 1930s reveals how French-Canadians' attitudes changed. They were less and less able to joke about this tenacious and destructive prejudice, and in the end, they began to believe that their language was indeed different from standard French, even though they continued to challenge the term *Parisian French*.

Another attitude that started with Tardivel, and went on into the 1960s is obvious in the attempts made by authors to explain in minute detail why and how the reputation assigned to their language was incorrect. Newspaper columnists such as Abbé Blanchard, Paul Lefranc, the members of the Société pour le parler français au Canada, Adjutor Rivard, Louis-Philippe Geoffrion and journalists Théophile Hudon, Louis Dupire and Albert Alain participated. They used the methods Tardivel had introduced, returning to the beginnings of colonization, and explaining the differences that had developed in regard to standard French.

What is noticeable in these texts is that contrary to those who refuted the bad reputation assigned to their language or wrote ironic commentaries, these authors did not seem surprised or scandalized. Perhaps they already unwittingly shared the opinion that started around 1920 and became much more widespread after the Second World War; this opinion held that the French-Canadians gave rise to these negative judgments:

> if everyone in Canada used the same words as in France for the same objects and the same ideas, no one would accuse us of speaking patois.[44]

Writers continued to deny that French-Canadians spoke a patois – the term itself was utterly irritating – but they recognized that Canadian French was so particular (not to say so poor) that it was not surprising for strangers to make such negative comments. They agreed that the English might have difficulty understanding it. They oscillated between irony, defensiveness, and disapproval, revealing their own rather difficult positions as men of letters who were conscious of the anglicization processes, yet considered themselves morally responsible to defend their compatriots. The conclusion of such texts was often to exhort the public to correct and take care of its French, as in this example from Jacques Clément:

> The elite of the United States and the educated class of Franco-Americans have a very low opinion of the way we speak, and our compatriots suffer as a result [. . .] Dear fellow-citizens, it is time to deal with our language. It is piti-

ful to listen to our so-called educated class. In public, its language is poor; in private, its language is atrocious.[45]

Even Doctor Léo Pariseau felt dejected after awhile:

> I can keep rejecting the legend of our French-Canadian "patois," but there will always be others bemoaning the state of our French. We definitely do not speak patois, but we will soon be speaking pidgin.[46]

Still, until the Second World War, the dominant attitude of the French-Canadians, or at least of their spokespersons, was to reject the prejudice about patois, either with ironic comments or by expressing their reservations. But they continued to ask where it came from. Abbé Étienne Blanchard openly asked this question in 1918.[47] In his view, *The Habitant* by Drummond, which had appeared in 1897 and was reprinted many times, was the source of the problem. Louis-Philippe Geoffrion took up this explanation in an article that appeared in 1928.[48] He claimed that when you told people from Toronto that the language Drummond put in the mouths of his characters was not the French of the *Canadiens*, they replied:

> It has been general practice to describe the language used by Dr. Drummond as French-Canadian dialect which being interpreted means a variety of English speach [sic] used by the French- Canadians.

The broad distribution of works by Drummond, whose poems appeared regularly in the newspapers, and whose work was widely imitated, certainly contributed to the expansion of the myth of patois. Blanchard and Geoffrion's irritation is understandable. And for some English-speakers, the massacred form of English that Drummond presented was doubtless *French Canadian*

Patois. But it is hard to know whether they thought this was the only language spoken by French-Canadians. As we saw, the prejudice was already present in 1865, thirty years before *The Habitant* appeared, so the book probably just served to reinforce the notion. In any case, the first article by Blanchard resulted in a few letters to the editor, one of which claimed the French from France were the worst critics of the French spoken in Canada; as teachers of French in the schools of Ontario and the United States, they were trying to ensure their employment.[49] This opinion was shared by others, among them Léo Pariseau, who saw it as the defensive reflex of virtually illiterate Frenchmen, trying to secure their fortunes in America:

> The former chauffeur from Paname (Paris) dare not admit that he understands the language of the *Canadiens* if he dreams of becoming a translator in New York. Similarly, the former school inspector from Trou-la-Mort (in the deepest provinces) must pick out our archaisms and trace them to the Middle Ages if he wants to become a lecturer in Chicago.[50]

On the other hand, many French people living in Canada, or simply traveling through, defended the French-Canadians and their language, and refuted the myth of patois as nonsense:

> I must admit that as soon as I heard of this red herring about Canadian patois I expected one of my own numerous compatriots to take a shot at it. But much like me, they probably think it is too ridiculous to even be considered seriously.[51]

Whatever its origin, the persistence of the prejudice was attributed to the ignorance or deliberate malevolence of the English. People began to feel that this bad reputation was not only tiresome, but was causing French-Canadians real harm:

> [. . .] a legend that has caused us to lose social status in front of a crowd of uninformed people.[52]

> This legend is not only tiresome, it harms us. It serves as an excuse for those leading campaigns against French and it can paralyze those who are well-intentioned. Why fight for a patois? What are the merits of such a jargon?[53]

Doctor Léo Pariseau, who for years led a veritable campaign against the prejudice, was perhaps the most eloquent in expressing his anger at the anxieties French-Canadians felt as a result of this issue:

> The legend of French-Canadian Patois has gone on too long, and done too much damage. It serves as a pretext to justify the destructive activities of the madmen who want to kill the French language in the New World.[54]

The vocabulary

What kind of vocabulary was used to speak about *French Canadian Patois* and *Parisian French*, and what does this tell us? I have been using the expression *French Canadian Patois* because it recurs most often in these texts, among expressions such as: *Canadian French, Quebec French, Quebec Patois, patois canadien* or *canayen, patois canadien-français, langue canayenne, parler canadien, Canayen habitant* and to finish off this long list, *Indian jargon* and *Beastly horrible French*.

These expressions are more or less ironic, depending on where they come from. The term *Canayen habitant* obviously referred to Drummond, while *Indian jargon* came from a report by an American who heard that

French-Canadians spoke exactly that.[55] By using the English version of these expressions writers distanced themselves from them, both asserting that there was no French term and that the concept only existed in the minds of the English:

> Add to this the fact that "French-Canadian patois" is an ancient legend that has been refuted a hundred times and that only exists in the sick minds of a few crazy Americans who are a hopeless cause.[56]

As for *Beastly horrible French*, that expression was coined by M. Morphy, an Ontario Member of Parliament, who was evidently not enamoured of French-Canadians.

As for the adjectives: *contemptible patois, miserable patois, pidgin, incomprehensible language, vulgar patois,* they translate the stigma that the French-Canadians felt in the term *patois*, and the contempt it contained. *Vulgar, miserable, contemptible* are also adjectives that imply lack of culture and poverty, and though the French-Canadians knew that economically they were in a subordinate position, they objected to the lack of culture imputed to them. As for the word *patois* itself, it implied a kind of degeneration of the French language and culture that authorized the English to feel contempt for the brutalized descendants of a prestigious race, as a journalist from *La Patrie* clearly stated:

> It is obvious that the French who make thoughtless or incorrect comments about the activities of the French-Canadians are not aware of the wrong they do us in supplying ammunition to those who claim we belong to a degenerate race that speaks a vulgar patois.[57]

Those who had something to say on this question between 1910 and 1940 invariably qualified *French*

Canadian Patois as a *legend* or a *myth*, thus denying it any truth. They also spoke of it as a *delusion, a prejudice*, a *pretext*, and as *slander*, and the myth or legend itself was described as *laughable, tenacious,* as a *constantly repeated joke,* a *ridiculous label*, and an *old, old prejudice that can't be uprooted.* It was, in effect, very tenacious; by 1940 it had been around for almost a century and was not about to subside.

The term *Parisian French* appeared with fewer lexical variations. It was almost always cited in its English form, used in as distanced a fashion as the English *French Canadian Patois*. Occasionally, terms such as *français de Paris* or *français parisien* were used, usually in quotation marks or italics, but always to insist that this language did not exist, or if it did, it could only be *argot*, i.e., slang. In regard to pronunciation, the *accent faubourien* [working class Paris accent] was mentioned, but always qualified as vulgar and cheap. So-called *Parisian French* was described as *nonsense,* as a *prejudice*, a *legend* and a *joke*. Finally, as we have seen, between 1910 and 1940 the expression was used to poke fun at the terrible translations being produced in Toronto and New York by translators who had at most a theoretical knowledge of French, and relied entirely on bilingual dictionaries. They produced *Toronto Parisian French*, an obviously ironic label.

But the real irony lies in the fact that after decades of denying and objecting to the negative comparisons the English made between *French Canadian Patois* and *Parisian French*, the French-Canadians ended up being less and less sure that this opinion was in fact mistaken, and some even admitted that, yes, they did speak patois.

The struggle against anglicisms: 1910-1940

As we have seen, the struggle against English interferences in French was already well underway at the end of the nineteenth century. It continued during the period we are concerned with here, though the prejudice about patois forced writers to be more circumspect in order to avoid providing materials that might further nourish the myth. Nonetheless, a sizeable number of the articles on patois also referred to interferences and emphasized the connection that might exist between this and the prejudice about a bastardized language.

In the nineteenth century, men like Arthur Buies and Louis Fréchette, and others struggling against linguistic interferences, had addressed their criticisms largely to the urban middle-class, the professional men, since this segment of the population was most likely to be bilingual, and was also responsible for making texts available for the general public. It was thus important to alert the journalists, publicists, writers, legislators, and lawyers about linguistic interferences they were exposed to because they were bilingual, and which they in turn were likely to disseminate in the population. Between 1910 and 1940, the urban classes were still largely the target for such criticisms though other social classes, all except the peasants, were also being addressed, as Édouard Montpetit showed:

> *Anglicisms. They're the enemy!*: This title of a pamphlet has become a slogan the vanguard is constantly repeating. The enemy is located within the city, and it is forging ahead: it is brutally present where everything is in English, everything from the money to the brains, from the smallest piece of machinery to the tools designed for the mind, making its insidious way into social evenings and environments populated by snobbery, carelessness and habits. Distance is the only thing that still protects the countryside from this scourge.[58]

The environment

What is under attack here is the very anglicized environment in industry, commerce, and more generally, in the urban workplace. Every article on the topic mentions the frequent contact with English to explain the more or less extensive levels of interference in different segments of society. Montreal was soon designated as the city where there was most interference, with English being much more present there than in the other cities. This argument about the environment was often mobilized to emphasize how inevitable the anglicization of Canada was. With industry and commerce in the hands of the English, the French-Canadians seemed to think there was little they could do, except ask their compatriots to use French signs and labels as the ACJC had in its campaigns of the 1920s and 1930s. But though an English environment at work and on the street was perceived as inevitable and unchanging, some of the writers continued to press their fellow-citizens to demand French in advertising:

> We have to be even more demanding when it comes to announcements and advertising. People are asking us for favours; politeness normally requires that people who make requests do so on your terms. Merchants who do not respect the tastes and feelings of their clients are as impertinent as dealers trafficking goods in uncivilized territories.[59]

And they didn't much like the *Parisian French* they were often served up.

The Governments

Governments were often the objects of criticism in this period; their passive stance and even contempt for the rights of French were considered to make an already difficult situation even more so. Some distinctions were made, with the federal government perceived as the very agent of anglicization, little disposed to defend French in Canada, and even directly responsible for subjecting the constitutional rights of the French to ridicule. One letter to the editor, published in *Le Devoir* under the pseudonym Céram Versant, said:

> It is indeed questionable whether French in Canada can insist on its constitutional rights. The British North America Act may say that for the "writing of records, minutes and newspaper articles with regard to these Chambers (Parliamentary Chamber of Canada and the Legislative Chamber of Quebec) the use of the two languages (French and English) is obligatory," but the fact remains that this text may be nothing more than a scrap of paper.[60]

This type of comment is often found in work by journalists as well:

> [. . .] in Quebec, much like in the offices of Ottawa bureaucrats, French-Canadians are too often subject to problems because they do not speak the majority language. The abuse is glaring.[61]

Many issues made the federal government look suspect in the eyes of the French-Canadians who saw it as working toward their assimilation; these included the very limited bilingualism of the federal government, the fact that its bureaucrats were obliged to work in English, the slow production of translations of regulations and documentation, the lack of activity in regard to the anti-

French measures of anglophone provinces, and the fact that the military functioned only in English.

The provincial government of Quebec suffered less criticism, but people seemed to consider it incapable of efficiently defending French, a suspicion that was confirmed by the facts. The government did adopt two laws in favour of the French language before the 1960s, but one of them was repealed only a year after it was adopted in 1937. As for the Lavergne Law of 1910 that made bilingualism obligatory in the public service, its application seems to have been rather sluggish, as shown by the many articles and letters that even decades later were still airing complaints about companies. Columnists and people who wrote letters to the papers were especially vexed at provincial civil servants who did not accord French its rightful place in Quebec:

> It is high time for Mr. Taschereau to inform his clerks that they should respect the rights of French for all official documents they circulate [. . .] And the contempt displayed for French in the offices of Mr. Stavert is not an isolated example. [. . .] It is high time that he [Mr. Taschereau] set things straight with certain civil servants who behave as though Quebec were not a province where French is spoken.[62]

The ponderous and anglicized French of the municipal councilors was often held up for ridicule, and they, too, were occasionally criticized for their lack of respect for the rights of French:

> Every time our councilors go to Quebec they do so to introduce new baroque words into our charter, new mistakes in French [. . .] What's more, this servility in translation is spreading into all other areas. [. . .] Isn't it about time we told our councilors not only to speak French, but to speak good French?[63]

According to the columnists, the lack of government support for the cause of French reinforced the presence of English, while at the same time it undermined French and diminished its prestige. The government was thus held responsible for the anglicization of the francophones and of their language. Only in the 1960s did political events change this opinion.

The Anglophones

In the eyes of the columnists many of the practices of the anglophones contributed to the problem of linguistic interference: their attitude, their refusal to learn French, their tendency to impose English on their French employees, their practice of unilingual English signage and labels:

> Along with other patriotic societies, the ACJC this year decided to draw public attention to the announcements posted in our cities which, far from reflecting our French characteristics, are a manifestation of our degraded honour and pride.[64]

But even though there were demands for French-language advertising and signage, and even though writers deplored the unilingualism of the English-Canadians, they were not particularly surprised at it. After all, French was no longer a useful language. And only late in the day did these writers establish a clear link between the daily use of English at work and the demise of French. For a long time, French-Canadians seemed to expect arrogance from the English-Canadians. This was particularly evident over the course of the ACJC's "restoration of French" campaigns in the 1930s, which targeted only French-Canadian merchants and industrialists who used English for signage and labeling. Unilateral bilingualism was the rule, and English was definitely the dominant language; this surprised no one, as this anecdote told by Léon Lorrain shows:

> Canadian papers recently cited a businessman from Detroit who had just returned from South America, and who claimed that a commercial traveler who is also a French scholar has great chances of success in the countries of South America because all of the educated classes there speak French. The *Gazette* added this comment: "The merchants and industrialists of Montreal should have no trouble finding good agents to send to the south. There are many young people in our city who speak English and French with equal ease. It is hard to say which race they belong to."
>
> We know which race they belong to.[65]

Bilingualism

Rarely did any commentary address the role played by individual bilingualism in the interferences between English and French. Still, as urbanization and industrialization increased, people became more and more aware that the need to work in English had a negative effect on French. Even educated bilingual people found it hard to identify false cognates, and unwittingly used semantic borrowings, incorporating formal borrowings and calques into their language. Here is how a journalist from *Le Devoir* described an anglicized French-Canadian:

> He usually speaks French, but he knows a bit of English and at the slightest pretext, on the telephone for instance, he will mobilize his English [. . .] And what a French he speaks! It shows the effects of his English! [. . .] His vocabulary is stuffed full of anglicisms and English words. [. . .] The few French words he still has are colourless and insipid.[66]

Still, opinions were divided on this question of individual bilingualism and its effects on French. There were many who believed it was essential to learn English, and who called for more solid teaching of French in the schools in order to avoid interference. That was nothing new. Other, more alarmist, commentators were extremely critical of those who encouraged generalized bilingualism; they argued that even though people with a solid education might find it enriching to use the two languages, most people's language skills became mediocre as a result. This was the opinion of Esdras Minville, for instance:

> [...] it is surprising that under the pretext of total bilingualism, people should set themselves up as the apostles of English, which they want to disseminate with good reason and without; it is surprising that they should pretend to be appalled at the slow progress made by our intellectuals, at the increasing inability of our schoolchildren and students to organize their thoughts and express themselves clearly and precisely, and at a general weakening from generation to generation. But the one is, in fact, the consequence of the other. When we see that a few rare French-Canadians have managed to become equally proficient in the two languages, – because they were particularly talented, or because they had the advantage of being raised by capable parents, who were cultured and who supervised their education, making sure that the regular use of English would not impinge upon their young French minds – in other words, basing ourselves on such exceptional cases, we have prescribed a certain regime on an entire mass of people . . . [67]

The interferences present in the French language thus progressively led writers to reject general bilingualism, although economic and political pressure made more and more people consider it necessary.

The anglomania of the French

In regard to anglicisms, the French-Canadians soon began to compare their situation to that of the French, and by the end of the nineteenth century, they were scandalized at the many terms the French were borrowing from English. They used the pejorative term *anglomania* to describe this practice. In their eyes, the French were veritable traitors who should actually have been defending the purity and prestige of their language. They energetically refused to integrate the borrowings made in France, choosing instead to employ an equivalent word in its French form even though it might be a semantic borrowing or a calque. Most writers were irritated by such borrowings until well after the Second World War, though some, like Étienne Blanchard, Paul Le Franc, Paul Anger and Théophile Hudon, recognized that it was normal for a language to take some inspiration from other languages:

> We can accept that in France the national language will not be seriously affected by this anglomania [. . .] But it is not the same for us. Some would say, not without reason, that anglicisms [. . .] present a danger in Canada.[68]

> People have finally begun to worry about anglicisms in France. It is not a moment too soon. On this point, Canada can pride itself on being a step ahead of its former mother county.[69]

> Whatever the case may be in regard to the liberties we take with our language, the tendency to constantly graft English words and expressions onto it can only scandalize the careful *Canadien* who is on a constant lookout for anglicisms.[70]

As for English words, *Canadiens* and French are in the same boat. *Canadiens* use them because they are lazy, don't know any better, or need to do so. The French use them abusively; they have no excuse.[71]

And the columnist Jacques Clément even appealed to the Académie française:

> We beg the members of the second Congress on the French language [. . .] to present our grievances to the envoy from the Académie française, so that he exert his influence to prevent our language from being taken over by English.[72]

In the view of the columnists, France was behaving abusively in the area of word borrowings and the only explanation they could find for this was French snobbery. Despite their complaints, most writers recognized that the problem was far more serious in Canada, though at the same time, they also thought that the French in Canada was more pure because the *Canadiens* were more vigilant. Various satirical articles appeared in the papers attacking the anglomania of the Parisians, and the criticisms French writers addressed to their compatriots were happily reprinted:

> Usage can reflect rather basic instincts: a misguided taste for novelty, the silly illusion that what is *foreign* is *new* and that causes the language to accumulate almost as many vagrants as the country itself. The word "pied" is considered vulgar because it is French, whereas "foot," which comes from England, and refers to the English foot, is very fashionable! I know of people who prefer not to "walk." They do "footing" instead. Just think, everyone "walks," anyone can "walk," "footing" on the other hand is a new kind of sport for chic people.[73]

As soon as a book on the question of anglicisms appeared in France or a French writer expressed his alarm at the borrowings of his compatriots, the Quebec newspapers would pick up the story and always add their own condemnation of anglomania:

A journalist from *Le Figaro* has published a number of reasonable recommendations for those of his colleagues who use too many foreign words: "You shall not constantly use foreign words [. . .]" These recommendations apply as much to French-speaking Canadians as they do to the French in France.[74]

Some of our people justify the use of English words in their discourse by saying that the French do the same and that [. . .] we mustn't be even more French than the French. The opinions [of Hippolyte Cocherie, writer and paleographer], which were cited above, and to which numerous others could be added show that this kind of snobbery does not find approval with enlightened men or those who defend the purity of the French language.[75]

Monsieur André Thérive, distinguished philologist and great defender of the French language, has proposed that French men of letters sign the following declaration; he would be happy if French-Canadian writers and journalists did so too:

a) I voluntarily agree to privilege the use of French spelling for all the words [. . .] of foreign origin in my writing and to demand this of typesetters.
b) I voluntarily agree to privilege a French word over another of foreign origin [. . .].[76]

The impression these texts create is that Quebec was disappointed and anxious about the reluctance of the French to defend their shared heritage. In fact, the reason English was fashionable in France was because it held a dominant position, and the French-Canadians could not forgive the French for the loss of the prestige that could have been so useful to them in defending their own position. Paul Anger expressed this feeling:

> What is pushing French aside is the fact that English has become the language of business [. . .] As long as French still served for diplomatic use it held a strong position in post-secondary teaching. But now English has become its equivalent. So is it not logical to claim that the anglomania in Paris to some extent leads to the popularization of English? [. . .] And will this new French fashion not lead to a large number of our people changing their attitudes as well?[77]

The integration of a large number of English borrowings into the French language in France thus considerably undermined the efforts of the columnists and grammarians in Quebec who spent their time correcting their compatriots' anglicisms. Even though certain political and moral aspects of France had been rejected since the French Revolution, France still remained the linguistic and cultural model. But France had become a kind of delinquent mother and people were no longer sure whether to imitate or reject her, especially at a moment when she seemed to be succumbing to the dominant force that was also threatening the survival of French in Canada. French anglomania was seen as a demoralizing factor in the struggle against linguistic interference. The French-Canadians, engaged in a battle where everyone seemed in league against them, saw this French behaviour as a betrayal and bitterly criticized the fickleness and snobbery of those who should have exerted the economic and political force of the French language.

Translation

In the years from 1910 to 1940 translation was omnipresent in Quebec. It was absolutely necessary given the circumstances, and if it was poorly done, full of calques and semantic borrowings, and if it deployed language that was poor and colourless along with awkward syntax, it could be the vector for the further degradation of French. Of course not only the quality, but also the quantity of translations was at issue. Most of the texts to which people were exposed every day – advertisements, signs, newspapers, labels, etc. – were either written in English or translated from English. For a long time, the profession of translator hardly existed, and translation was done by almost anyone, with results ranging from appalling to excellent. The worst translations, those qualified derisively as *Parisian French*, were often the terrible versions produced in places like Toronto by people whose mother tongue was not French or who had only rudimentary knowledge of the language. Judging by the numerous indignant and mocking letters to the editors on this topic, many such texts must have been produced for English companies that did not consider it necessary to hire translators:

> The newspaper crammed full of hasty translations [. . .]; advertisements riddled with Americanisms or written by English who write a Parisian French that is beyond ridiculous; catalogues from New York or Toronto [. . .]; and the cinema [. . .] all of this obviously affected the habitant.[78]

In ascending order as far as quality goes, translations were also produced by francophones who had only a vague knowledge of the written language and its nuances; these were largely merchants, clerks, or employees asked to create French labels or translate certain parts of texts that companies would then post. Crammed with semantic anglicisms and calques, these texts were composed in an impoverished language that was still more acceptable than so-called *Parisian French*.

Then there were the news items published in dailies that arrived in English dispatches and were translated into French by journalists. Here too, anglicisms and awkward structures prevailed. A journalist from *La Patrie* wrote the following response to a satirical article on Quebec newspapers,[79] published by a Belgian journalist in 1920:

> There is something we need to explain to our Belgian colleague, something he is apparently unaware of, namely that the news published in our papers is hastily translated from English. He may be right in pointing out a number of headings that reveal this, and that seek only to be brief. We will definitely not make the claim that our newspapers could not be improved, although considerable progress has been made. We must simply regret the use of anglicisms. It would be ridiculous to defend certain barbarous constructions or certain comical errors. Didn't a French paper from Montreal yesterday write that when the American aviators arrived in Boston they were so moved they "crié" [shouted] [an anglicism derived from "cried." (Translator's note).][80]

These three types of translation – *Parisian French*, translations done by amateurs, and hasty translation of news items, for many years made up the bulk of the translations that French-Canadians were exposed to daily. It is, therefore, no great surprise that they were seen as a major source of interferences.

From the beginning there were excellent translators at work, some of whom became ardent defenders of the French language; one of these, Paul Lefranc, often commented on translation problems in his columns. Though this period saw pressure put on companies to hire proper translators, actual progress had to wait until after the Second World War. As long as amateurism and negligence were the rule, translations were clearly one of the main vehicles of linguistic interference, since the translated texts reached people who didn't know English and were never in touch with the language.

Individual attitudes

These were numerous: snobbery, laziness, neglect, ignorance, lack of pride, and defeatism. Snobbery was the main criticism columnists used on their compatriots who used English words in conversation. This accusation, which had also been employed against fashionable city people in the nineteenth century, applied to a larger public in the twentieth century – though for the same kind of behaviour:

> We know *Canadiens* who think they are distinguished because in English society they behave like valets. *Snobbery* has many nuances: over there [in France] the French language is contaminated when English words are slipped directly into conversations; here, we dislocate out jaws to emit the guttural Saxon sounds.[81]

Snobbery and anglomania were established concepts in Canada. A few years after the Cession journalists were already complaining about them, for English must already have acquired a certain status. French-Canadians were regularly seen talking English among themselves. Similarly, in certain social classes, the frequent use of English borrowings seemed to imply contact with anglophones and indicated that the speaker belonged to the upper class of society. Prestige that comes with the dominant class is usually associated to the language this class speaks. The members of the middle-class will imitate its speech in the hope of appropriating some of this prestige. With English the dominant language in Quebec, it is not surprising that middle-class francophones used it and imported its terms into their French in order to appear connected. These borrowings were presumably not the same as those made by the working classes, but this question has not been studied and so we will not speculate further.

The pretentiousness of the francophone bourgeoisie was criticized with considerable bitterness because its members were educated and had at their disposal a broader French vocabulary than the working classes who used English words because they needed to, or did not know the French words – a problem the journalists clearly recognized.

Clearly, the upper class of French-Canadian society soon formed two factions. On the one hand, there were those termed anglophiles and americanophiles for whom French language and culture had lost virtually all its prestige, and who often had their children educated in English ("to give them every opportunity"). They were largely part of the bourgeoisie connected to business and industry. They advocated American methods, and claimed to be practical and realistic. Adélard Desjardins, who published *Plaidoyer d'un anglicisant* [In Defence of an Anglicist], represented the most extreme views of this group:

> Let us not prevent ourselves from stepping through an open door. Those who support French [the francicists] agree with us on the topic of primary bilingualism, which leads only to confusion and muddled ideas. But while they demand bilingualism in the public service, they are contemptuous of teaching both languages in the schools. Indeed, they want to ban English from the schools, some-

thing they will never achieve, since the people will not allow this, forced as they are to earn their money in hard labour paid for by English hands.[82]

The other faction, defenders of French values, or "francicists" as Desjardins called them, was made up of members of the educated bourgeoisie and people in the liberal professions; they were the ones who wrote "letters to the editor." They were virtually "anglophobes" and accorded extraordinary importance to the French language, opposing spiritual and intellectual values to Anglo-Saxon materialism. This group included many journalists, writers, intellectuals, clergy and educators, which explains why the ideas promulgated by this group (the language as the guardian of the faith, the French mission in North America, the purity of the language, etc.) dominated public debates despite the enormous pressures exerted by the economic and political power of the anglophones on the one hand, and by the French bourgeoisie connected to business and industry on the other. Their attitude toward French anglomania can be understood as a result of feeling abandoned by those who should have disproven the arguments of the other faction and demonstrated the economic and political power of French.

The supporters of French (the francicists) accused the others of snobbery, laziness, defeatism and carelessness. On the other hand though, they couldn't help but acknowledge that ignorance was the main reason the working classes were becoming anglicized. The solutions they proposed were a direct result of their analysis of the situation: you have to be proud of your language, defend its rights, use it in all situations, take care of it, and improve its teaching. The following text by a journalist from *Le Devoir* presents this reasoning:

Anglicisms, those worms gnawing away at the French language in Canada, do not hide as they carry out their deadly work. They work in broad daylight, as we watch, indifferent, and even complicit and encouraging. [. . .] they are everywhere, in business, in the courts, in public and private life, in every profession and every workplace. How often have I heard visitors comment on the negligence and carelessness that prevent us from speaking the beautiful language of France.[83]

François Hertel, a philosopher, educator, and writer had this to say:

What if we only ever used English when we didn't know the French word! But no! A vile form of snobbery has convinced us that it is more chic to say "fun" than "plaisir" [pleasure]. [. . .] Like the schoolkids who say "c'est dry" instead of saying "c'est ennuyeux" [it's boring]. And when they're taken to task, they're the ones who claim that compared to English French is an impoverished language. [. . .] The terrible thing is that we have reached this degree of intellectual laziness and ignorance. [...] If this language were more firmly in our possession, if it were spoken with more energy and with the required precision, it would do more to conserve our ancestral heritage than any economic or political achievements.[84]

As the situation worsened the complaints and reproaches grew more virulent, and the articles and books along the lines of "let's correct our anglicisms" more numerous. All these efforts might have succeeded in limiting the progress of anglicization and increasing the dissemination of French vocabulary, but they also had a formidable secondary effect, and that was to make the French-Canadians feel very uncertain about the language they spoke and wrote. As a result of tracking down the anglicisms and especially the semantic borrowings which were already in French form, and therefore that much more difficult to discern, people felt more and more hesitant about almost everything, and afraid that the least little thing that came to their minds might be incorrect. Paul Anger described this paralyzing anxiety:

> This phobia of the anglicism is probably one of the main reasons why our language is so anemic. The poor writer who has to produce text on a daily basis is often left hesitating [. . .] May I, he wonders, use that expression [. . .]? He is tortured by anxiety: I bet that's something I remember from English. I was about to – oh horror – commit an anglicism. Five times out of ten he has no reason to worry. Sweating, moaning, constantly amputating and narrowing his language, using his pen as a scalpel, for fear of anglicisms, the poor guy puts down on paper a veneered language, a colourless language that has no taste, no juice, and that doesn't have a single anglicism but not a single red blood cell either, a language that dies of chlorosis the moment it is born.[85]

This perverse effect of the hunt for anglicisms, together with the humiliation set off by the myth of *French Canadian Patois*, gradually made the French Canadians very dismissive of the language they spoke, an opinion that became quite audible in the 1940s and 1950s. Forced to live in permanent contact with English, subject to the economic and political domination of the anglophones, and with little if any support from the French who were themselves succumbing to the English language, the French-Canadians considered themselves at least partly responsible for the degradation of their language, and for decades they felt guilty about their weakness in the face of pressure from outside. Victor Barbeau described this situation perfectly:

> We can counter those who confront us with talk of patois by referring to historians of the French language. But how

can we answer those who say we speak a jargon? That is in effect what we do: we speak a jargon. And why is that? Because we are a primitive people, an illiterate people. When I say illiterate I do not mean that we can't read or write, but I refer to all those, and it is the majority of our population, who have not received or accepted intellectual discipline, who have no way to organize or express their ideas.[86]

Types of anglicisms

A language can borrow all kinds of things from another language: lexical items, which is termed formal borrowing, as well as semantic borrowing, which consists of assigning new meaning to a word that already exists in the language. Interferences can also show up in the morphology, when prefixes or suffixes are borrowed, for example. The syntax can be influenced when syntactic structures or expressions are copied; these are called *calques*. And pronunciation, spelling, and typographic conventions are also subject to interference.

Late twentieth century writers have the same reactions to these borrowings as did writers in the nineteenth century. Formal borrowings are most often criticized, which is understandable, since these are most apparent. However, semantic borrowings and calques are considered more pernicious for the language on the receiving end, as they make changes to the very structure of the language, while formal borrowings are much more superficial.

In the nineteenth century the phonetic assimilation of formal borrowings occurred quite naturally. It was agreed in Quebec and in France that this was the most desirable solution, the advantage being that the foreign words simply melted into the language and could be made to conform to its phonetics, its morphology and its spelling. Such assimilation had already produced a size-able number of words in Quebec, words such as *bécosse* (back house), *drave* (drive), *mitaine* (meeting), *empailleur* (umpire), as well as numerous place names that added a few unlikely saints to the existing litany: *Sainte-Folle* (Stanfold), *Sainte-Morissette* (Somerset), and even *Sainte-à-R'brousse-Poil* (Sandy Brook's Pond).[87] However, toward the end of the nineteenth century, phonetic assimilation became less current. Abbé Étienne Blanchard, for one, objected to it, and thought necessary borrowings should be given French pronunciations and spellings:

> I think the French are right to use French spelling and pronunciation for English words they take into their language [. . .] These English words are detrimental to the orthography and harmony of our spoken language.[88]

In the same article Blanchard suggested making a whole series of words French, for example, *groume* (groom), *stoque* (stock) or *vaterprouffe* (waterproof). The tendency to pronounce such words *in English* grew stronger over the course of the twentieth century, to such an extent that in the 1940s, journalists remarked that in Quebec any word that appeared foreign, whatever its origin, was automatically pronounced in English:

> Many young guys and girls [. . .] just as competent in their mother tongue as they are in English in which they chatter easily, seem to think that any new word they encounter must be English and therefore pronounced with a Yankee accent.[89]

Yet semantic borrowings were more energetically criticized than formal borrowings:

We are rich enough to use our own funds and not go running after foreign products. It is really the last straw when these products originate with us, and have only gone abroad in order to change their dress. You could say they are émigrés that come home. If they come home without our habits, morals, practices, and without French dress, we could say they are not wanted.[90]

In response to a reader's letter about semantic borrowings, Blanchard cites Adjutor Rivard, who was very intolerant of interferences:

These are the prodigal sons of the French language. They return to us deformed, shredded, mutilated; they inspire pity, for their journey has been tedious, their exile hard, and their unhappiness great [. . .] If their contacts with the barbarians have not killed the Latin core within them, they can become French again.[91]

Semantic borrowings cause ambiguity because people are unsure about whether to interpret them according to their French or their English meanings. Their French form makes them less apparent, and this causes more uncertainty. This is the type of anglicism that demands the greatest vigilance, and one of its effects is to impoverish the language (as described by Paul Anger earlier). Writers often applied metaphors to such borrowings that turned them into enemy infiltrators, who have slipped past sentinels in disguise. The battle was becoming exhausting.

On the other hand, the question of morphological borrowings was seldom addressed. Contrary to phonetic assimilation, this advanced form of absorption of foreign elements did not attract writers' praises. Instead, it was considered troubling, since it indicated that English had penetrated more deeply into linguistic structures:

Anglicisms include any word that is dressed in French. A powerful example is the English root of a word to which is added a French suffix (. . .) The suffixes that are attached to verbs are usually "er," and to nouns "eur" or "euse." For example: pitch – pitchER, pitchEUR, pitchEUSE [. . .]. All verbs get first conjugation endings: slackER, crankER, switchER. [. . .] The imperfect subjunctive of these verbs is particularly elegant: "que je slackasse, qu'il slackât."[92]

The calque, sometimes referred to as a conceptual, phrasal, or syntactic anglicism was certainly the form most vehemently criticized. It was rarely discussed, however, although Arthur Buies had already pointed it out at the end of the nineteenth century. By the 1920s people were much more aware of the problem:

[. . .] anglomania here slips from vocabulary to syntax and gnaws away at the language; it will destroy it if we don't pay attention.[93]

There were certain forms of influence that English exerted on French that seemed to completely escape the notice of the columnists and writers. Only one article in the entire corpus referred to the abusive use of capital letters, and none discussed imitated punctuation, false cognates in spelling, the conventions of writing addresses, or forms of politeness.

The vocabulary around anglicisms

The vocabulary in the articles addressing anglicisms can be classified in six categories. This phenomenon makes for an interesting study since it reveals the deepest feelings of those writing on the subject. Three categories are different types of metaphors: the vocabulary of conflict that sees French and English as enemies at war; the biological vocabulary which turns French into an organism under threat from a foreign body; and the spiritual vocabulary that links anglicisms with immorality and makes the defence of French a virtue. The other categories simply describe the different linguistic variations: aesthetic vocabulary, vocabulary that expresses value judgments, and finally the vocabulary of strangeness.

1. The vocabulary of war

Many articles and columns used the following metaphor: anglicisms are a *destructive, underhanded enemy* that *infiltrates and invades* French. The authors called upon their readers to *fight* this *invasion*, to *repulse the attacks, be tenacious* in this *battle, to rush the enemy, organize the defence* against this *peril* that was causing French *to lose ground*. Semantic borrowings were described as *pernicious, sneaky intruders,* who were *infiltrating* and entering *without a passport*, and some texts hovered on the verge of accusing francophones who used borrowed terms from English of betraying their language and making room for the enemy to take its place. It is like watching the battle on the Plains of Abraham, lost through treason.

This metaphor of war was illustrative of the French-Canadians' feeling of being under siege by a hostile culture that wanted to annihilate their language. As though it were a real war, the writers and conference speakers constantly appealed to patriotic feeling, to combative spirit, and to resistance. The titles of their articles sounded the alarm: *Beware! Anglicisms: they're the enemy!* This image also revealed the French-Canadians' feeling that their most precious belongings, their identity and their culture, were under attack and threat. They obviously took a defensive position, typical of all their policies since the Cession. Although the term *struggle* remained in use until the 1960s, the war metaphor was most popular from the late nineteenth century until the 1930s. Why did the image change? Perhaps it seemed inappropriate at the time of the very real Second World War to call upon people to wage war on the influence of English. Perhaps too, the emphasis was becoming a little outmoded. Although the struggle against interference from English carried on, the terms were depersonalized, and the comparison was to a disease rather than an enemy. Like war, a disease, can be deadly.

2. Biological vocabulary

The biological metaphor was also in use from the end of the nineteenth century until the 1970s, and it became much more frequent as the war image was abandoned. Here, French was described as *a sick, anemic organism* struggling to *survive* in an *unhealthy environment* which had been *contaminated, razed, or gnawed away at* by some *microbe* or *tenacious and prolific parasite.* These creatures could be *worms that overran* everything, or a *cancerous tumour*, a *virulent scourge*, even a *pathology that was carrying out its deadly work*. Words such as *wound, epidemic, atrophy*, and *great disease* were used.

What is expressed by this terminology, beyond the mortal effects of interferences, is the feeling of powerlessness in the face of evil. It is no accident that most of the references were to tiny pathogenic agents – worms, parasites, microbes – whose action may seem limited, but whose proliferation within the organism that harbours them is lethal. This is, in effect, how the writers concerned with anglicisms saw their gradual effect; each one taken individually was not particularly important, but as they multiplied out of control they would end up destroying French.

3. Spiritual vocabulary

In this case, the writers saw anglicisms as a *sin against the language*. They used the verb *to commit* an anglicism, and the *apostles* of French asked their readers to *examine their consciences,* to trim such *blemishes* and *degradations* from their language; they reminded them that they had to *have faith in the mission* of their *sacred* French language, but they often had the impression of *preaching in the desert.* Warlike vocabulary and spiritual vocabulary often met in the term *Crusade* against anglicisms and the *Crusaders* who led these expeditions.

Oddly enough, this metaphor occurred less frequently than the other two, even though one of the main themes in the defence of French was "the language as guardian of the faith," and the question of language was always part of the religious issues, at least until the 1950s. After 1960, the image was no longer used at all, reflecting Quebec's social development during this period.

4. The vocabulary of aesthetics

Adjectives and qualifiers that express aesthetic qualities were generally applied to the French language, *the most beautiful language in the world,* whose *unstained splendour,* whose cachet, whose *lovely* nouns, and *good French syllables* must be preserved. Anglicisms, on the other hand, with their *guttural sounds,* transform the language into *frightful, vulgar gibberish*. This *frightful mix disfigures, deteriorates, deforms* and *ravages* the *beautiful face of French*, and *makes your hair stand on end.*

The notion of ugliness was applied to anglicisms throughout the period under examination; that is, from the mid-nineteenth century to 1970. This chauvinism is one further manifestation of French-Canadians' intolerance toward a cultural influence they had not sought out, but been subjected to. Such discourse is hardly found in European writers who use the term "destructuring" rather than ugliness when they warn of linguistic borrowings.

5. The vocabulary of strangeness

The effects of anglicisms included *bastardizing* French, and changing it into a language that was *barbarous, bizarre, a jargon, a lingo, or an extravagant gobbledygook* that defied comprehension, was *very worrying* and that people *jabbered on in,* a language that *flabbergasted,* and *astounded* due to its *dizzying number of aberrations.*

The idea of strangeness was often associated to that of ugliness and contrasted with notions of clarity and precision, qualities generally ascribed to French, as well as to the notion of purity. It is noteworthy that while writers willingly used pejorative terms to describe the French used in Canada (terms such as *jargon, lingo, gobbledygook,* as well as *franglais, frenglish, américançais*) they systematically rejected the term *patois,* which the English used as late as 1950. This vocabulary of strangeness translated the writers' fear that the interferences might end up transforming the language to the point where it would no longer be French, which would, in turn, break the links to France, its traditions, prestige, and condemn them forever to isolation and extinction.

6. *The vocabulary of value judgments*

This category is anything but homogeneous. The positive terms tended to assign to French a national and cultural value that should be preserved: *the majesty of the French language* is an *inheritance*, a *family memory* that is the responsibility of the French-Canadians; they owe it to their *national dignity*, their *patriotism*, to their *national feeling* to *preserve* it, and to *purify* it by accepting only legitimate borrowings.

The negative terms, on the other hand, referred to French as a *humiliated language,* with an *impoverished vocabulary,* a language that was the *victim of a tragedy.* The abuse of the language through *useless* anglicisms, was a *destructive mania* that *harmed* the language, *mistreated* it, *did it wrong,* at the very moment the language was *in decline, suffering a veritable degeneration,* and becoming the language of *servility.* The poor results of the battles waged against anglicisms were considered *scandalous* and *disgusting.* The writers found it *shocking, ridiculous, stupid,* and *hateful* to use borrowings.

This vocabulary reveals one clear phenomenon: the homeland of the French-Canadians was, in fact, seen to be their language. Certain authors used the term *compatriots* to name the French-Canadians, while they referred to the English-Canadians as mere "concitoyens" [fellow citizens] – an important difference. It shows to what extent the writers felt they were part of a nation, while their ties to English-Canadians were only contractual or administrative. Further, all expressions of *patriotism, national feeling, national dignity, nationality,* applied only to the French-Canadians, to their institutions, culture and language, and completely excluded English-Canadians. The French-Canadians felt they were a nation distinct from any others, and that this was central to their identity. The difference between *compatriot* and *fellow-citizen* expresses a very different relationship with the other. The compatriot belongs to the same fatherland (ancestral lands), the same culture, speaks the same language, has the same values and aspirations, is linked to the other through ties of blood and history; this is the person with whom one can construct the nation, or at least struggle for its survival. The fellow-citizen is a person with whom one has a contract, who lives according to the same laws, in the same country, in the same town; it is a relationship ruled by conventions. Not all the writers make this distinction, far from it, but those who do thereby underline the indissoluble bonds to the nation and the contingent relations to the state.

The French-Canadians' anxiety over identity, in all its torment and intolerance, was clearly demonstrated in these texts on linguistic interference. And the period between 1910 and 1940 was absolutely crucial in this regard, since during these years the traditional ways of life disappeared rapidly. The profound social changes that occurred, bringing French-Canadians and English-Canadians closer together in urban agglomerations and destroying wide swaths of traditional lifestyles, raised further fears about the absorption of the culture into the "abyss of great big Anglo-America." Linguistic interference was one of the most obvious effects of cultural influence being rejected for ideological reasons; it was a symptom of the French-Canadians' incapacity to master their social, economic and political life. Thus the relentless battle against anglicisms was also a manifestation of French-Canadians' resistance against English domination. Added to this was the fear that French-Canadians would no longer be able to claim they were part of prestigious French culture, an argument they had always used to counter the assimilation efforts by English Canada. Every possible argument was mobilized to convince people to fend off the invasions of English: there were moral, historical, practical, and aesthetic reasons. But although the calls for individual effort remained constant, no concrete collective measures were undertaken. The campaigns to restore the French language, the distribution of lexica, and a few other such operations did nothing to stop the influx of borrowings and even less to re-establish a balance where all the prestigious aspects would be on the same side. The Second World War interrupted these operations for a few years. Its various consequences on the social balances at play in Quebec were to have considerable repercussions, whose reverberations are still felt today.

CHAPTER VII

Post-War Years: 1940-1960

Maria Chapdelaine's daughter worked in a munitions fac-
tory in Valcartier during the war and now lives with her
family of five children in the Rosemont neighbourhood of
Montreal. Her married brothers went to work for the pulp
and paper mill in Jonquière, but are now employed by the
Aluminium Company of Arvida and Shipshaw... This is a
fictional epilogue for Louis Hémon's novel that tells the
actual story of thousands of working class families.[1]

This is how the sociologist Jean-Charles Falardeau, writing in 1953, summarized the social changes of the twenty or thirty preceding years. The declaration of war in
1940 had put French-Canadian linguistic and nationalist
preoccupations on hold, and also caused a clear break
between anglophones and francophones, with the latter
strictly opposed to conscription, as they had been in the
First World War. The French-Canadians did not like to
be under orders from the English, and the disaster of the
Dieppe landing proved they were right to be distrustful
of an army in which they played the role of footsoldiers
and whose upper command structures they could not
influence. Betrayed by the Liberal Party, to whose elec-
tion they had contributed because it promised not to
institute conscription, they once again felt how their
minority position weakened them politically. Moreover,
the occupation of France in 1940 had tarnished the prestige of the culture on which the opinion leaders had
once based their defense of the French-Canadian cause.

Some French-Canadians complied with the exhortations of poet Alain Grandbois,[2] and like Olivar Asselin in 1916, they signed up in the hope of helping to liberate the mother country. Others, who were more left-leaning, volunteered in order to fight Nazi ideology. Many young people saw the war as an opportunity to escape from the confines of Quebec society and travel the world. For most Quebecois, however, the war simply brought a profound change in the conditions of life.

At first these changes manifested themselves on the economic level. As all of Europe's resources were taken up by the war, the North American economy as a whole entered an exceptional phase of development and productivity. Quebec was part of this and its industrial development was brutally fast. The peasant economy as well, which was stalled before the war forcing most farmers to supplement their incomes by working in the lumber industry, suddenly improved its profitability. For a few years farmers saw their lives improve substantially.[3] Certain sectors of the culture industries, and especially book publishing, benefited from the very favourable conditions. For the duration of the occupation of France and a few years afterward, an agreement between Canada and the French publishing industry gave Quebec publishers the right to publish authors who were under contract to French publishers as well as books listed in the catalogues of French houses. This led to a considerable development of the Quebec publishing industry, providing a basis it had never had before. This state of affairs also contributed to the development of cultural activity in general, benefiting the generation growing up at that particular time.

This new prosperity brought various other changes with it as well. In rural areas, when agricultural incomes dropped again once the conflict was over, a large number of farmers became lumber workers in order to maintain their lifestyles. The sociologist Gerald Fortin claims that the prosperity of the war years restructured values and the social hierarchy according to income. People moved from an economy of production to an economy of consumption:

> [. . .] the criteria for social stratification was no longer how you made your money; what became important was how you spent your money.[4]

In larger numbers than ever, peasants began to abandon the land and move to the cities and into industry, which ended up rendering the system of values taught by the traditional elites and the clergy quite obsolete. Indeed, their position began to weaken seriously. The new system of values developed in contradiction to and conflict with the old one so that for a time there was a period of uncomfortable co-existence, which made it very difficult for the French-Canadians to define themselves as a collective.

Although the clergy appeared to maintain its power, allied as it was with Prime Minister Duplessis whose rule continued until 1959, its authority did begin to slip. The workers' movements with their union politics began to shake up the control that had held them in its grip. The educated class, whose members were descendants of the first urbanized generations and had been born in the towns, expanded. The universities, which had largely been engaged in training men for the liberal professions – doctors, pharmacists, dentists, lawyers – began to turn to other fields of study, in particular social sciences: economics, sociology, political science. Numerous young people who began post-secondary studies in Quebec completed their work in Europe or the United States, initiating an intake of new ideas into the still very isolated French-Canadian society. This was the generation that would make the Quiet Revolution, which seemed so brusque and sudden because the social changes leading up to it had developed more or less secretly without appearing as part of the official or public discourse.

Identity

From the beginning of the twentieth century onward the French-Canadians had felt they were a dominated national group with minority status. While their traditional elites continued to define the French-Canadian as a peasant, and to celebrate this peasant's moral virtues, an ever-increasing proportion of each generation escaped the strictures of this definition and found itself exposed to both the social obstacles imposed by the English and stigmatization by the elite in its own community. From the beginning of the Second World War, less than 20% of the working population of Quebec was located in the agricultural sector.[5] The traditional discourse therefore no longer had any basis in reality. A negative identity, which had been gestating for decades, surfaced quite painfully. The French-Canadian was, in fact, no longer a peasant but a worker or employee of the English bosses; he was uneducated and had no prospects for social improvement. Although he was still a Catholic, his ties to the Church were weakening, with the priest of an urban parish holding neither the power of the priest of a country parish, nor playing the role of leader that the latter had exercised. The French-Canadian still held to family values, but the clan had dispersed and the ties were being reduced to the immediate family. The size of the families was decreasing too – to four or five children – due to urbanization. Contacts with the English had become much more important than in the past, because of work and city life, and the French-Canadians had grown more aware of both the dominant role the English played and their own social inferiority. Finally, if they spoke French, some accused them of speaking patois, and others said it was a very poor French full of anglicisms. They were encouraged and pressed to feel proud, but found fewer and fewer reasons to do so.

The post-war period thus rang in a much more severe identity crisis. In its early stages, until 1940, reactions to the threats against French-Canadian identity had ranged from strategies to suppress the resulting anxiety which ignored the reality of the situation (the French-Canadian "mission" in North America) to the revalorization and idealization of the unique character of the group (the noble nature of the *habitant* and the language of the "Grand Siècle." As the crisis grew more intense in the post-war period, reactions changed. Many French-Canadians began to show signs of internalizing the negative image, and displayed submissive, guilt-ridden behaviour. Some simply assimilated, and gave up their identities in an effort to escape the stigma that marked their people as "small earners" and "porteurs d'eau" [drawers of water]. Most of these chose to become English, but among the more educated population, there was also a wave of "Parisianism" that proceeded from a similar rejection of the stigma, valorizing intellectual values rather than the pragmatic ones implied by assimilating to English culture.

The two points of view are laid out by Adelard Desjardins, who supported anglicization, and Lucien Parizeau, for whom "only Paris counted." Desjardins wrote:

Basically, we have three different regimes confronting each other. The supporters of French, aware of the dangers of ethnic bilingualism and deliberately blind to the predominance of English, loudly demand French unilingualism.

178

The masses, for whom the whole issue of bilingualism is quite opaque, support both languages because on the one hand our chauvinists keep on extolling the instinctive love they feel for the French language, and on the other because these masses have learnt the painful daily lesson that they need English. We, on the other hand, advocate English unilingualism, thus taking into account the serious drawbacks of bilingualism and the practical necessity of English for our race of "small earners."[6]

Parizeau's point of view is expressed as follows:

Those who are surprised that we assign as much importance to France and things French as we do to our own things have not realized that the only salvation for our people, who are indecisive and domesticated from above – just like a fish who rots from the head downward – lies in a return to the French nationalism of the great Fournier. By this I mean that our hybrid people, who think in Anglo-French and express themselves in a mixed language, will otherwise gradually decline, becoming completely Americanized, and never recover their unity.[7]

These positions stem from identical premises: on the one hand, the dominated situation of the French-Canadians, and on the other the bilingualism that this situation imposed on them and that was causing their language, culture, and creativity to deteriorate. One position advocated simply giving up the stigmatized language, while the other one argued for a return to roots by associating with a prestigious nation, a strategy that would erase the stigma as well as three centuries of shared history. Few people in Quebec fully supported either of these radical positions, whose greatest merit was to clearly present the issues. Most were content to put up with the situation, a situation that engendered so much anxiety, however, that when the reaction came in the 1960s, it was very sharp. This would have been the case even if the Quebecois had chosen a third option: ridding themselves of the stigma by restoring their culture from within; in other words, by collectively giving themselves good reason to be proud of what they were. To do so they would have had to acquire characteristics they did not yet have: material comforts, the control/ownership of the means of production, high levels of education, dynamism, audacity and ambition. All of these characteristics except education were considered part of English-Protestant culture and its inherent materialism by their elites, and could not be acquired unless the value system was completely restructured. This restructuring process began in the post-war period, and threw the French-Canadians into a state of great agitation. Jean-Charles Falardeau wrote in 1953:

> In the past, French-Canadians had the reputation of being less ambitious and less mobile than other North Americans. Nowadays, they are at the other extreme: in a state that could be qualified as social agitation.[8]

But all these upheavals, and the questioning of the old system of values before a new one was solidly in place, plunged the collective into ambiguity and uncertainty. Never had the French-Canadians, who were getting ready to give themselves another name, thus "de-baptising" themselves, had such difficulty defining themselves. The sociologists Fernand Dumont and Guy Rocher put it this way:

> We are suffering enormously from having lost the ability to tell others and ourselves what we are.[9]

The language situation, 1945-1960

On the social level, French had made no progress for decades. On the contrary, the massive movement of the rural population toward the cities, where English remained absolutely dominant, placed an even larger number of French-Canadians into a bilingual situation. French thus found itself relegated to the private sphere. Moreover, the largest part of these new urbanites, most of whom had very little education, could not resist the linguistic interference caused by bilingualism. Finally, the prestige and dynamism of the American culture exerted an influence that was no longer as effectively opposed as it once was, since the discourse celebrating traditional values no longer held.

The campaigns of the ACJC in the 1920s and 1930s may have had little effect in restoring French, but they did alert a large number of young people who continued to apply its tenets to be vigilant, even militant, long after the movement died down. In the 1940s and 1950s, the JEC (Jeunesse étudiante catholique [Young Catholic Students]) and the JOC (Jeunesse ouvrière catholique [Young Catholic Workers]) were part of a generation dedicated to social action. Even though these associations were the Quebec branches of international organizations, their members were motivated by the desire to bring social progress as well as economic and political improvement to the French-Canadians. A number of those who were instrumental in the Quiet Revolution and in the *French Power* initiative in Ottawa, got their first experiences in these youth movements.

With the exception of the second Congress on the French language in 1952 and the third Congress in 1953, appropriately named Congrès de la refrancisation [Congress on the Restoration of French], where increasingly alarmist reports were presented, both on usage and on the quality of the language, the post-war years saw little collective action in favour of French. But a number of institutions were founded to develop the cultural bases of the French-Canadian collective: the Académie canadienne-française was founded in 1944 under the aegis of Victor Barbeau; the Institut d'histoire de l'Amérique française under Lionel Groulx in 1946; the *Revue de l'Amérique française* published its first issue in 1947; the Association canadienne des éducateurs de langue française was established in 1948. Similarly, studies of French Canada began to be undertaken in Quebec universities. On the whole, this period was particularly fruitful for intellectual activity. The development of post-secondary studies, to which larger numbers of students had access, allowed a new middle class to take shape, which played a crucial role in the subsequent evolution of Quebec.

The discourse on language

If we were to look only at the discourse on language in the years from 1940 to 1960, we would have to conclude that the French-Canadians of this period suffered a full collective depression. Never before were the commentaries so pessimistic, the image of the language so negative, or the self-criticism so severe. And the newspaper columns on language were never so numerous. There is a striking difference in tone between the sometimes reserved praise heaped on the French-Canadians in the years between 1920 and 1930, and the virulent criticisms hurled at them between 1940 and 1960. A brief selection of texts from *La Presse, Le Devoir*, and *La Patrie* published between 1947 and 1958 gives some idea of the tone:

In a word, French is dying in Canada![10]

When you pay even the slightest attention to the daily language of the majority of our people, either a completely slack and sloppy language, or a strained language full of all kinds of mistakes [. . .] when you hear or read the either baroque or impoverished language that former students of the colleges and reputable schools use to express themselves, then you have to acknowledge the courage of those who publish work that specifically criticizes this state of affairs.[11]

In other words, even though we may write proper French, we are often content to speak a terrible gibberish.[12]

Right across the social spectrum, though to differing degrees, the language spoken by French-Canadians is unbelievably destitute and vulgar.[13]

According to the speaker [Victor Barbeau], the language we speak is increasingly wretched. Its relationship to the language we try to write is more and more uncertain, and it is dangerously far from living French. I say French, and not Parisian French; only a few snobs continue to criticize us for using flavourful regionalisms as they do in Lac-Saint-Jean or in the Bas-du-Fleuve area [. . .]? But how can we defend the language we are destroying in Montreal? [. . .] It has taken on forms that are increasingly spineless, whose countless flaws we hardly notice because our ears have grown accustomed to them but whose mistakes, heavy structures, and vulgarity cannot be denied.[14]

Pierre Baillargeon, a columnist writing on language in *La Patrie* was correct in asserting:

Some travelers who are misinformed or prejudiced against us can be too severe in their criticism of us. But they are not alone, nor are they particularly unjust. However, our most aggressive critics are, in fact, among us.[15]

183

How can we explain this change in the discourse? First, we need to realize that up to 1940 any praise that was uttered was for the French of the peasants. The language of the urbanized class, both working and middle classes, was already stigmatized because of its anglicization. After 1940, the peasant was no longer typical of the French-Canadian; indeed he seemed to disappear from the collective consciousness. As a result, the negative discourse about the urban population took up all the space. In the post-war period occasional commentaries in fact showed that the rural language was no longer considered superior to that of other groups:

> In his "Étude sur le parler populaire au pays des bleuets" [Study on popular language in blueberry country], Father André Laliberté says the spoken language is similar to that used in Quebec City; [. . .] "We don't speak as well as you [Quebec City], but we believe we speak as well as they do in Montreal and elsewhere," the lecturer said.[16]

> Our language is no longer that of the peasants of the seventeenth century. Only in the most distant parts of our countryside does Jacques Bonhomme still speak his patois.[17]

> It is true that country people speak a good old version of French enhanced with regionalisms and dialect forms [. . .] But it is also true that the good old words are quickly disappearing, replaced by anglicisms (in the negative sense), and are worn-out, disfigured, truncated, and mutilated by lazy articulation.[18]

> The destruction of French in peasant language is in line with what has happened in the cities. [. . .] anglicisms are not only found in individual words, but even – and this is much more serious – in idiomatic expressions.[19]

It was generally recognized that despite his isolation the peasant had also ended up being affected by anglicisms, the "evil" that had long plagued the urban population. On the other hand, the archaisms and regionalisms that were characteristic of this peasant language and that had been celebrated for their quality and flavour by the Société du parler français au Canada were not considered pleasing by the new commentators, who almost all advocated a rapprochement with standard French. For example, in the remainder of the article cited above, Jean-Marie Laurence wrote:

Let us resuscitate the good old words.

Oh, no, Simplicie; only if there is no equivalent in modern French. Would we go back to the French of three centuries ago? Sometimes archaisms can be charming but often they are as illegitimate as anglicisms or barbarisms.

The regionalisms that were considered so praiseworthy in the 1930s came under attack from all sides:

We have some healthy regionalisms here, and good regional authors, such as Claude-Henri Grignon and Alfred Desrochers. Describing a part of the country is a legitimate undertaking. But a certain form of regionalism can also serve poor writers to construct books full of anglicisms under the pretext of maintaining local colour.

I have never before been so aware that this type of regionalism, which I find so irritating, may, in fact, further *anglicization* when it is used by unwitting authors. It is an indirect way of isolating the French-Canadians, and condemning them to live among normal folks like a herd of deaf-mutes.[20]

There was clearly a refusal to withdraw from society, and much more of a desire to open up to the outside world, especially to France, even though sentiments in this regard remained rather ambivalent. French-Canadians were feeling more and more surrounded by Anglo-

American culture, and restricted to the territory of Quebec; an opening toward France and other francophone countries seemed a way to prevent their own culture from suffocating. Under these circumstances, the condition of the French language became crucial; if the language spoken in Quebec diverged too radically from standard French, communication would become more difficult and the regeneration that such revived contacts might bring with them would have no effect. This analysis of the situation resulted in a movement for mass education that became a veritable broadcasting and press campaign, and included books and competitions around good language use, a campaign that sought to standardize the language of the masses. As always, it waged war on anglicisms, but also questioned the legitimacy of archaisms and regionalisms that had previously been considered precious. Further, and quite innovatively, it sought to standardize pronunciation. One of the slogans of the third Congress on the French language in 1956 expressed this as "guerre aux bouches molles!" [war on limp lips]. Columnists such as Roger Duhamel and Jean-Marie Laurence, who wrote on language issues in the papers, advocated neutralizing pronunciation:

> Pronunciation is one of our greatest sins. We enunciate poorly; we don't attack the words, and are content to just mouth them. In general, we have *"limp lips,"* just as R.P. Lalande recently charged.[21]

> Three great dangers threaten the integrity of French in Canada: sloppy pronunciation, impoverished vocabulary, and anglicisms of all kinds.[22]

The ideological changes that took place during the postwar years, as well as the continued movement into the cities, caused the French-Canadians to re-evaluate their linguistic situation from the perspective of new social structures. And the conclusions they drew were disquieting. Although some claimed there had been progress in regard to the quality of language, this was ascribed to a small elite group of educated people while the masses were undergoing a flagrant deterioration of their language. Jean-Marie Laurence wrote a language column in *La Presse*, ran a language program on the radio, and later on television as well, and described the situation in 1957 as follows:

> Spoken language has become more refined among *language professionals* – thanks largely to radio – and our elites, whose composition has changed due to our evolving social structures.
>
> The most striking phenomenon, however, is the progressive anglicization of the masses, currently visible in the mixing of French and English. Authentic French is becoming the "language of culture" (or of ostentation) while English is gradually infiltrating our "contact language," our everyday language.
>
> What we have is, in effect, a split – on the one hand, an elite that is becoming "intellectualized," and on the other, the general public tending towards "Americanization."[23]

In sum, the greater the influence of English, the more it was rejected by the educated class that was turning more and more toward French culture. Questions about whether French had any chance of surviving in Quebec arose:

> Many are discouraged by the amount of effort that is required and they claim that with a certain realistic optimism we might envisage the creation of a new language called "canayen," a language that is full of anglicisms and local expressions. This would mean just accepting the catastrophe. [. . .] But is there any hope of constructing something lasting with such miserable fragments when we are in fact besieged by assimilation. We need to react vig-

orously, which is possible. It can be done by connecting with contemporary French, with the international francophone community.[24]

People wondered what language they would be speaking in twenty years. And the attempts to answer this distressing question always took the same tack: if we want this language to be French then we have to react immediately and energetically. This was the reason for the massive efforts to standardize the language by educating the population, and the constant reminders that people make every effort to use their language well. By the late 1950s, however, certain members of the new class of intellectuals began to question how effective these efforts actually were. First of all, they couldn't help but see that despite decades of work the results were not forthcoming. They became aware of a certain paralysis, as well as complexes that took hold of people who were afraid to "commit" an anglicism, and of the language progressively deteriorating across the entire population. A discourse that was still rare in the 1930s began to show up with much greater regularity in the daily papers:

> Anglicisms that corrupt the vocabulary and especially the syntax [of French] have forced us into a defensive stance. We are being admirably zealous in hunting them down. But in being too concerned with correcting ourselves, there is a danger of going too far and emptying our language of its picturesque expressions and its flavour.[25]

However, from the end of the war, it became more and more apparent that the changes affecting the language of the French-Canadians were directly and closely linked to the changes affecting their society. Factors such as urbanization, proletarization, economic and social domination, imposed bilingualism, omnipresence of English in the cities, brought with them worsening linguistic contamination and interference, and the impoverishment of French. And so people began to see that the solution to this problem lay in correcting the socio-economic situation of the francophones and enhancing the prestige and the use of French, and not only through education and the efforts of individuals. This new type of discourse came from young intellectuals educated after the war in various social science disciplines. Even their more scientific style of writing marks a change:

> When a minority group is forced to use a second language for many of its social activities, its field of experience, the conceptual content of its language, and its skill in using the symbols of the language are restricted [. . .] Faced with such advice [taking care with your language, etc.], I wonder whether the thesis that Sapir developed about language being the result of experience, has not been forgotten. It is doubtful that a population can come up with sufficient effort to compensate for the deficiencies in a social system that does not ensure that language and experience come together.[26]

Patois: 1940-1960

In these two decades, in which French-Canadians began to realize that their language problems had socio-economic causes, the old idea that their language was a patois – a notion the English were happy to entertain – was constantly present. The occasional article on this topic in the English-Canadian or American press would remind them of it; for instance, in 1946, a Montreal paper announced that Monsieur Paul Toupin would be going to France to study philology, "The youthful student is preparing what will be the first scientific study of Quebec Patois." The journalist reporting this fact added that: "This word makes a very unpleasant impression."[27] Jacques Clément also commented on the subject mentioning an article in an Ontario paper entitled, "Québec parle une nouvelle langue et a beaucoup du fun" [Quebec speaks a new language and has a lots (sic) of fun].[28] The following year Jean-Marc Léger recounted the request made by an English-Canadian linguist in regard to "the everyday patois spoken in Montreal."[29] And even though an article from the *New York Times* on how French had improved in Quebec allowed an optimistic journalist for *Le Devoir* to assert that the legend of Quebec patois had now been abolished,[30] the spectre is still around, fifty years later.

And so there was hardly any change in North American public opinion on the language of the French-Canadians. What did change considerably, however, was the reaction of the French-Canadians themselves to this bad reputation. Up until the Second World War, all of the commentaries on this issue revealed that the French-Canadians absolutely refused to admit, or recognize, that their language was anything other than French. A regional form of French, perhaps, that was doubtless flawed, but was still French. Little by little writers began to develop a new attitude that continued to deny that their compatriots spoke patois (in fact, they found the term itself particularly objectionable), but also gave some credence to the negative assessments. Canadian French was so special (i.e., so bad) that it was hardly surprising strangers didn't understand much, and made such negative comments:

> The lesson we have to learn from all this is that we have to take care of our language – wherever we are – in the street, on the streetcar, in the car. This journalist's article shows just what kind of reputation we are acquiring abroad because we are so negligent with our language.[31]

We are scandalized by the impertinent and stupid criticisms of certain English-Canadians who celebrate the virtues of Parisian French and think that in our province we speak a patois, derived from French. This is a gross exaggeration, to say the least; however, we have to admit that our language now has only the most distant connections to real French.[32]

Every day we get upset that the French consider us simpleminded. It would be wise to ensure this legend is not perpetuated, and that instead of blaming our critics we take measures to stop these criticisms from developing. We owe it to ourselves to try in every possible way to raise ourselves to a level that doesn't give anyone the occasion to make such negative observations [. . .][33]

The fear of negative criticism from strangers clearly grew more intense as the contact with strangers increased. The reiteration of this fear at this particular time may be partly explained by the rapid development of international communications. But it also shows that the French-Canadians had begun to internalize the negative remarks coming from the *other*, which may explain why there were so many warnings of the kind, "If we don't make the effort to improve our language, *the others* will continue to judge us negatively." Sub-text: and they will be right. It was not long before this sub-text came to the surface and was made explicit. In fact, the association between quality of language and intellectual level was being made more and more often, as this last quote shows. Already at the beginning of the century, Jules Fournier had attributed language problems to intellectual laziness, which, in his opinion, affected the entire nation. This idea, later taken up by Victor Barbeau and François Hertel, was often repeated in the twenty years we are dealing with here:

Daily language is characterized by ignorance of or contempt for syntax which often makes it even more unintelligible than the sloppy pronunciation that drops syllables or runs them together. The impoverished vocabulary that some people use and the way others are careless with language ends up affecting our minds.[34]

The traditional language of the countryside may be too simple to further intellectual development, but anglicized language is corrupted language, and as we have seen, such a language destroys the relationship between creativity and communication. Neither of these forms of language possesses any aspect of a language of culture.[35]

Faced with this relationship between language and thought, means of expression and intellectual level, the myth of patois remained a serious insult and a danger. The French-Canadians did not appreciate being viewed as a collective of ignoramuses. Still, the criticisms uttered by their own elites were so severe with regard to language that some ended up believing that they did in fact speak a vulgar, unstructured patois:

Six years ago I founded a magazine. It was supposed to be a magazine in which Canadiens could treat subjects of interest to everybody, in *French*, i.e., in a language spoken by a hundred million people. I did not allow any patois. My collaborators and I opposed the reigning regionalist forms which we considered deleterious.[36]

The question whether there is a Canadian language is a topic for discussion. We have a certain patois, expressions from the countryside.[37]

These last two citations, early examples of the term *patois* being given new use, show that it was applied to the language of the countryside; it was rejected, essentially because of the move to have French-Canadian culture become part of the international French-speaking communities, which required the use of a relatively standardized language.

The newspapers often raised the question of regional language in literature. It was advocated by writers such as Claude-Henri Grignon, and later by Roger Lemelin, who defended it in the name of the originality of French-Canadian literature, truthfulness and realism in the descriptions, spontaneity and creativity of the authors, whose work would be rendered sterile and dry by too much puritanism in language. Such arguments were systematically refuted by all the columnists – Baillargeon, Laurence, Daviault, and more occasional writers. They all agreed to reject the idea of creating a "Canadian language" which, besides being quite impoverished and contaminated with English, would condemn the French-Canadians to isolation, and, in the end, to assimilation. That at least was the opinion of Rex Desmarchais:

> The French language, which is our mother tongue, has proven itself in the world for more than three centuries. It has powerfully contributed to the knowledge of the human spirit, to the progress of science and the arts; it has shown itself to be a precise instrument for the exchange of ideas and communication between people. It has given rise to one of the most beautiful literatures. In sum, it has been a wonderful agent of civilization.
>
> I find it unbelievable that a Canadian writer should want to give up this language or think of deforming it, massacring it in the hope that a new language might be born as though by magic from the massacre. A writer worthy of this appellation should not lend his authority to support the mistakes, slips, gaps, degradations in popular everyday language – whether it be rural or urban. On the contrary, he must make every effort to correct popular language, and make his writing a model of precision and linguistic purity.[38]

While Desmarchais apparently rejected every deviation from standard French, seeing this as a *mistake* or *gap*, Jean-Marie Laurence allowed a certain "character" in the language but insisted that it must have style:

> At the lunch yesterday Monsieur Jean-Marie Laurence took up the comments of Claude-Henri Grignon (Valdombre) on the literary quality of Canadian "parlure," and expressed his opposition. He rejected the "exaggerated realism" that Valdombre demands, and proclaimed the need for a certain "stylistics" so that the work become real art [. . .]
>
> As for the language itself, Monsieur Laurence compared *Maria Chapdelaine* and an imaginary modern novel he entitled *Les Souffles* (!) In the first work, he said, the language is indeed regional but it is skillfully presented and is therefore part of the standard language. Whereas in the second case . . . [39]

In the following year, Pierre de Grandpré took up the same argument, emphasizing that "linguistic indigenism" would condemn literary, theatrical, and cinematographic work produced in Quebec to stay within the limits of the province:

> If, after the creation of such a language, our writers would like to occasionally proffer a few examples of our local talk, our rural or popular language, for the admiration or amused curiosity of strangers, this would require a stylistics for which we still have to acquire the necessary finesse and taste (at least as much as writing in standard French requires). [. . .] Some of our novelists, Germaine Guèvremont or Félix-Antoine Savard (in some way renewing Ramuz' work on Swiss Romande speech), have already shown us the aesthetic uses of a reasonable dose of these qualities. [40]

In any case, as time went by, the rural language, whether it was transcribed literally or stylized, seemed less and less appropriate to describe the reality of Quebec. Thus, a university professor, interviewed by *Le Devoir* in 1957, had this to say when asked the question:

> Do you believe in the actual or future existence of a Canadian language?
>
> Henri – Unfortunately not. [. . .] We have a certain patois, expressions from the countryside, a clearly rich vocabulary that is deliciously archaic and that we created. But this language – however beautiful it is – only goes with the countryside where it came into existence. It condemns anyone who uses it [...] to paint only the country and its people. You cannot require young writers to give up the demands of current society, or their own concerns, in order to create an image of the values that no longer even exist in some faraway little village, as television, newspapers, industrialism, urban clothing styles and ways of thinking – basically from New York – make their appearance.[41]

Exit the peasant, and the countryside. But the disputes around the topic of literary language did not end there. Far from it. They started up again around the subject of *joual*, with hardly a transition.

And what about Parisian French?

The question of patois, on the one hand, and the possibility of developing a Canadian language based on people's usage, on the other, were issues that both sharply re-focused the question about the relationship that French-Canadians had, or wished to have, with France. For over a century, the English had been claiming that the language the French-Canadians used was not French, and couldn't be French unless it was "Parisian." The French-Canadian men of letters, who had long fought off the English remarks, now began to admit in more and more anguished tones that the gaps between the language of Quebec and standard French were indeed growing wider, and that even if people were still speaking French, it wouldn't last much longer unless there were an immediate reversal of these tendencies. Others insisted that the total adoption of standard French would mean renouncing their own identity.

Most of the population, caught between those who were constantly demanding that they correct their language and the others, who tried to valorize it the way it was, were living a contradiction. They wanted the constant criticism to stop, but were not so sure they wanted to identify with a stigmatized version of their language, and they clung to their links with a prestigious culture. Given this situation, it is not surprising that the relations with France and the French spoken there were very ambiguous; this was even more the case with regard to Paris. Further, people kept hearing that the famous *Parisian French* the English brandished as the model of prestige was full of English words, a capital sin in their eyes. Readers' letters began to show a reaction against the stiff puritanism in language and the "parisianism" advocated by certain columnists, especially Pierre Daviault, whose attacks were quite categorical.

On the whole, the discourse on language from the years 1940-1960 reveals several important breaks with the pre-war years. The language columnists expressed extremely negative views on the language of the French-Canadians in general, and condemned any form of regionalism. The concern about anglicisms and assimilation became acute, and great pessimism was expressed about the future of French-Canada. People were, in fact, no longer sure they actually spoke French. The new class of young intellectuals began to reject the traditional solutions the educated class had resorted to, advocating that the socio-economic situation be revamped instead. The identity crisis demanded quick transformations without which French-Canadian society in Quebec was in danger of disintegrating. This crisis led to the central object around which collective identity was structured being subjected to a critical discourse that had never been as virulent. The direction in which the French-Canadians took their subsequent collective action was strongly determined by the feelings of dispossession and alienation expressed in these nonetheless prosperous post-war years.

CHAPTER VIII

The Language Columnists and the Linguistic Norm: 1817-1970

Our ideas about language in Quebec are inextricably linked to history.[1] Any linguistic norm is a product of society that, like many other institutions, undergoes a lengthy development, and involves tensions between various sub-groups within a collective which may cause changes, that in their turn may have an effect on the collective. It is not necessary to rehearse the history of how the French norm developed, or how it evolved between the fifteenth and the eighteenth centuries, but it is wise to acknowledge that the ideas that people in Quebec have developed about this norm are intertwined with its history. It is impossible to know what the francophones of America felt about their language until the first metalinguistic text appeared around 1817, the date of the first newspaper columns on language published by Michel Bibeau in *L'Aurore*. At that point, nearly sixty years had passed since Canada was ceded to England thus severing the contacts with France, sixty years during which linguistic evolution was no longer directly ruled by the dominant class from the home country or its institutions. Even if these institutions survived the turmoil of the French Revolution – like the Académie française did, though with a few years of intermittent operation – they had come under the control of the bourgeoisie, the new dominant class. It took some time for the Académie to consider and approve the resulting changes in the hierarchy of linguistic variants, but it finally did.

So, what authoritative source does Michel Bibeau refer to when he condemns a certain French usage? He refers to *Essais de grammaire* written by Abbé d'Olivet[2] and published in 1732, almost a century earlier. Clearly, no reference books published in Canada existed at that time, and recent works from France were doubtless extremely rare given the very limited contact with France.

The discourse on language really developed a few decades later. In 1841, the publication of Thomas Maguire's *Manuel des difficultés les plus communes de la langue française* rung in a tradition of corrective texts that would go on for many years. Maguire's book set off a controversy because he refused to recognize as legitimate any usage that did not appear in the dictionaries of France, a point of view that Abbé Jérôme Demers and Michel Bibeau strongly contested.[3] Indeed, from that date onward the language columnists would represent two opposing views: those who supported the French norm as defined in French grammar books and dictionaries, and those who defended the legitimacy of certain particularities of Canadian French. Depending on the era and the circumstances, one group or the other would have the upperhand, and many of the columnists wavered uneasily between the two poles.

People's relationship with the linguistic norm is revealed by what they recognize as the linguistic authority, and what they consider legitimate. In Quebec, the different aspects of language did not get the same treatment. One point that most of the columnists agreed on was syntax. From the nineteenth century onward, they considered that French in Quebec should conform to the grammar of standard French. The debates that did arise centered on pronunciation, and even more, on vocabulary.

When they wrote about grammar, the columnists made few explicit references to grammar books, claiming simply that certain expressions conformed to grammatical usage while others did not, without citing sources. But only a few of the columnists writing since the late nineteenth century regularly addressed questions of grammar. Louis Fréchette was one who did. His column was published in *La Patrie* from 1880 to 1883 under the pen name of Cyprien, then under his own name from 1893 to 1896, and subsequently in *La Presse* from 1897 to 1900. He rarely gave explicit references but it is clear that his judgments were based on normative grammars, and specifically, contemporary grammars. On the topic of whether to use *au Canada* or *en Canada*, Fréchette responded to a letter writer:

> As M. Decelles claims that the antiquated forms of Richelet give him more authority than more modern lexicographers such as the Académie, Larousse and Littré, he will permit me to tell him how very wrong he is [. . .] Only *au Canada* conforms to grammar and usage.[4]

In a column published in 1895 he took on a novel published in Quebec by Père Lacasse and severely criticized its many grammatical errors:

> The fact is that more often than not Père Lacasse says white when he should say black, and black when it should be white.[5]

Abbé Étienne Blanchard, one of the most prolific writers of columns on language in the history of Quebec, published under various pen names in *La Presse* between 1918 and 1950, and in one of his first pieces on "Bon langage" [good language] referred to E. Ragon's *Gram-*

maire française, cours supérieur.[6] Blanchard himself went on to publish thirteen works on "good language," with a central focus on vocabulary, and had a distribution of 270,000 copies in 1938, a considerable number for early twentieth century Quebec. The columns he wrote for *La Presse* from 1934 to 1952 under the pen name of Jacques Clément, often had things to say about grammar, though never citing sources either.

Columnist Jean-Marie Laurence focused most on grammar, publishing his texts in *Le Devoir* from 1932 to 1947. He was one of the rare writers, if not the only one who was also a linguist, and he published reviews of the *Grammaire de l'Académie, Syntaxe du français moderne* by Georges and Robert Le Bidois, and the *Grammaire historique de la langue française* by Nyrop; Laurence himself wrote a grammar book that was widely distributed in Quebec schools.

Lastly, René de Chantal writing in *Le Droit* from 1953 to 1963, and Gérard Dagenais in *Le Devoir, La Patrie,* and *La Presse* from 1959 to 1968 also looked at questions of syntax and grammar, always from a normative perspective. And finally, in the 1950s and 1960s, Quebec newspapers published columns on language written by French grammarians. *Le Devoir* reprinted work by Robert Le Bidois from *Le Monde,* while *La Patrie* reproduced texts by André Thérive. The metadiscourse on the topic of grammar was thus quite constant from the nineteenth century onward, and in Quebec it advocated conformity with the norms established in France.

In regard to pronunciation, the question of legitimacy is much less clear. Columnists occasionally mentioned the topic. In his earliest texts Michel Bibeau criticized the fact that what was written "oi" should be pronounced as "oué," and some authors turned their articles into lessons on pronunciation. Eugène Lassalle, for example, published a series of articles entitled "Parlons bien" [Let's speak well] in *La Presse* for several months in 1908. In the early years of the twentieth century, there is feeling of uncertainty, however, as though the columnists had few sources to refer to and did not dare be too categorical. In 1901 Jules-Paul Tardivel gave a talk entitled "La langue française au Canada" that was reprinted June 22, 1912 in *Le Devoir*.[7] The talk included a detailed study of eighteenth century grammars, specifically Buffier's *Grammaire française* (1741), Mauvillon's *Cours complet de la langue française* (1758) and the work by Restaut (1730-1774) and argued that many of the pronunciations held to be wrong or "canayen" by his contemporaries were in fact upperclass pronunciations of the eighteenth century. While he did not recommend perpetuating them, he hoped that critics would stop denigrating these forms. This argument was often repeated, notably by Louis-Philippe Geoffrion,[8] who also referred to Richelet and Vaugelas. At this juncture the point was to mobilize as much energy as possible to combat the bias about *French Canadian Patois* which most French-Canadians viewed as a serious attack. But the columnists of the 1920s and 1930s also took on their compatriots' "bouches molles" [limp lips] and sloppy speech, and never missed an opportunity to applaud the creation of public-speaking competitions and elocution courses, which were developing in the schools. Finally, in the 1940s and 1950s, the Quebec population got access to real courses in normative phonetics – in the *Le Devoir* columns and the radio programs of Jean-Marie Laurence. At this point, archaic pronunciation could claim a certain air of nobility, but it was no longer considered legitimate.

This leaves the question of vocabulary, an area where the relationship to the French norm becomes very clear. To simplify the matter, the columnists of the nineteenth and twentieth centuries were concerned with two big classes of words and expressions: anglicisms and canadianisms. The term canadianism included archaic terms, provincialisms, and neologisms, whether in regard to form or meaning. The term anglicism referred to all types of borrowing from English. Anglicisms were systematically criticized by the columnists ranging from Michel Bibeau, Arthur Buies, Louis Fréchette, Jules-Paul Tardivel, Étienne Blanchard to a large group of writers such as Olivar Asselin, Jules Fournier, Louvigny de Montigny – too numerous to list. Very soon, borrowing from English came to be seen as a threat to the integrity of the French language and became the subject of campaigns in the newspapers, other publications, and in corrective lexica. A serious problem arose, however, when the writers and columnists noticed that the early twentieth century French dictionaries were beginning to accept a sizeable number of borrowings from English. In the columnists this triggered increasingly strong reactions; some even went as far as to contest the legitimacy of the dictionaries. In his speech upon being accepted in Belgium's Royal Academy in 1924, Édouard Montpetit gave a succinct overview of the problem:

> We no longer know where anglicisms stop, not even if they do so at the doors of the Académie française, and we dare not use words that are perhaps better value than those the authorities will consecrate tomorrow. Archaisms have been condemned by usage and remaining faithful to them relegates us to not being heard; canadianisms do not reach beyond the limits of our horizons, and it is too much to hope that they will enter a language whose home is located in distant Paris: usage itself is hesitant about our imposing ourselves as the norm [. . .][9]

Today, the same kinds of reactions persist. The fact that the linguistic norm is defined elsewhere is still perceived as a problem, which becomes acute when this norm accepts interferences from English without any resistance, taking in what has come to be seen as the "greatest danger," the primary source of linguistic insecurity. One possible solution to the anxiety generated by these interferences was to adopt everything the French dictionaries accepted, without further discussion, and to reject all the rest. In the 1950s and 1960s, this was the much-contested position of one Dagenais, a position that was adopted with a few nuances by Laurence and Daviault as well.

In regard to canadianisms: the appearance of Thomas Maguire's book caused voices to be raised in defence of certain exclusively Canadian usages. Such controversies would erupt regularly. We have seen that Louis Fréchette did not support what he called "canayen" and referred to the dictionaries of the Académie, the *Larouuse*, and the *Littré* to condemn certain archaic or provincial terms. Alphonse Lusignan, who also wrote a column on language entitled "Fautes à corriger" [Mistakes to correct] from 1884-1885 in *La Patrie*, published a response to another columnist, called Rapin in the same paper in 1880. Rapin had criticized expressions such as "jeune fille ricaneuse" (for "rieuse") [girl who laughs a lot] and "chaise empaillée" (for "de paille") [chair with a straw seat]. Lusignan wrote:

> I don't know which dictionary Rapin consults and he should keep in mind that Littré exists and is worth something as far as lexicographers are concerned. But even if not a single dictionary formally authorized the expression, I would still use it. It is in general use in the country, it is logical, and we *Canadiens* have the same right to have our words, our expressions, our proverbs as anybody from Limousin, Auvergne or Paris [. . .]. Dictionaries do not give the whole language.[10]

This more nuanced position reappeared from time to time in the columns on language, especially from the moment the Société du parler français au Canada began to disseminate its findings, and writers such as Adjutor Rivard and Louis-Philippe Geoffrion published regularly. More and more declarations about the legitimacy of Canadian expressions as well as calls to have them included in dictionaries appeared. Paul LeFranc, alias Blanchard, commented on a 1921 publication by France Ariel[11] as follows:

> Madame Ariel is right to demand that French dictionaries ought to include our Canadian words the way they include certain words from Brittany that have a particular meaning. Future makers of dictionaries take note.[12]

Nonetheless, many people continued to view canadianisms as suspect, as the following report from a conference on pedagogy held at the University of Montreal's Faculty of Arts in 1927 shows:

> A third way of speaking well is to carefully avoid canadianisms. By canadianism we mean old words from the fifteenth, sixteenth and seventeenth centuries that are no longer in use in France but have survived in our language. A canadianism is also a word created from this and that to express new things. We must ban the former, though we respect their source and age, from our written language, and even our spoken language, though less severely. In their struggles for survival, our fathers were not able to bring their vocabulary up-to-date. We can do so, and it is our duty to rid our language of terms the dictionary of the Académie does not accept.

Blanchard cited this report in an article he published in 1950, entitled, "Que le mot dise partout la même chose; sinon ce serait Babel" [May each word mean the same everywhere, otherwise it would be Babel]. In other words, he supported this position, though he also said that dictionaries tended to be behind the times, especially in regard to technical vocabulary, and that they should not be too rigidly adhered to.[13]

Toward the end of the 1950s, when the feeling that the language had seriously deteriorated was very strong, some of the most visible columnists began to reject anything that did not correspond to the French norm. For Jean-Marie Laurence, archaic usage was no more acceptable than anglicisms. And Gérard Dagenais wrote:

> Provincialisms that have acquired status through usage and that show up in dictionaries are not just substitutions of words. As long as Robert, and Larousse and Quillet and the Académie do not remove the word "cuisinière" from French vocabulary and assign its meaning of "stove in the kitchen" to the term "poêle," I will refuse to allow anyone who claims to express themselves in French the right to use "poêle" instead of "cuisinière" [. . .] No harm meant to our supporters of canadianisms, but there cannot be ten French languages, or even two.[14]

As the 1960s and 1970s approached, the years that would be shaken up by the struggles over *joual* and the reforms of so many aspects and institutions of Quebec society, it seems that the linguistic insecurity in regard to canadianisms reached a high point, which made the option of referring to a reliable norm that much more reassuring. If benefiting from this advantage meant discarding everything the reference books did not mention, in this case the specific aspects of Quebec French, then so be it! For Quebec society to give up the reassuring certainty that French dictionaries provided, it had to acquire a positive view of itself, a self-esteem that, in 1960, was still a chimera.

CHAPTER IX

The Quiet Revolution and Joual on the Move: 1960-1970

In September 1959, Maurice Duplessis, Premier of Quebec, died suddenly of a heart attack during a trip to Shefferville. Paul Sauvé, his successor, began a speech that was re-broadcast on radio the day he was nominated, by saying, "From this point onward . . ."

The new premier was apparently not the only one who experienced the last years of Maurice Duplessis' reign as a restrictive era that had cramped a social development then in full swing. The upcoming generation of more educated young people could no longer accept the ultra-conservative Quebec government, which, allied as it was to the clergy and large English-owned industries, had been trying to perpetuate a social structure that no longer responded to peoples' needs or offered room for the young. The same applied to the working class that was trying to organize and kept being confronted by repressive political forces. This situation led to the great strikes of the period in which young intellectuals and workers came together to struggle against a public order that had become intolerable.

On October 21 of that same year, André Laurendeau, the editor-in-chief of *Le Devoir* wrote a small piece entitled "La langue que nous parlons" [the language we speak], in which he deplored the kind of French spoken by adolescents: "I have four children in the school system as well as nephews, nieces, their friends [. . .] almost all of them speak *joual*." Two weeks later a priest working as a teacher answered in a letter to the editor: "I agree with you. Our students speak *joual* [. . .], they write *joual* [. . .]. *Joual* is their language."[1] The letter was signed by Frère Untel [Brother Somebody] (the pen name of Jean-Paul Desbiens) and its title was a line taken from the body of the text, "Je trouve désespérant d'enseigner le français" [Teaching French drives me to despair]. These two texts, which addressed the usual well-established concerns reiterated in every generation at least from the beginning of the twentieth century, set off a reaction that can be described as quite extraordinary. Dozens of letters poured into *Le Devoir*, most of them supporting Frère Untel and joining him in his criticism of what was perceived as the radical decline of language and culture in Quebec. *Les insolences du frère Untel*,[2] the book he published a few months later with a preface by André Laurendeau, kept the debate going, which became increasingly emotional. While adolescents were the main targets at first, people soon began to say, as Desbiens did, that *joual* is "truly our language."[3] A broad campaign of self-criticism set in, to the extent that few other peoples in history have experienced. For the next fifteen years *joual* was at the centre of people's preoccupations and public debates. Paul Daoust, a linguist, who wrote his doctoral thesis on the debates around *joual* as expressed in various kinds of publications, found that an average of three articles per week was published on the question between 1959 and 1975. He located 2523 articles and works written by 1303 different authors.[4] These figures alone translate the intensity of the crisis. Further, Daoust found that 90% of these texts expressed negative views on *joual*, and were even violently opposed to *joual*. This provides some measure of the collective anxiety that crystallized around the term André Laurendeau had almost accidentally assigned to the language spoken by his children and their friends.

Many of the readers of *Le Devoir*, like Frère Untel himself, attributed the origin of the word *joual* to Laurendeau. But Laurendeau corrected this a few months later saying that the expression was a "working class term" already in circulation when he was young.[5] Daoust found that the first written use of the word, in the sense it was given in 1959, occurred in 1938, appearing in *Les pamphlets de Valdombre* by Claude-Henri Grignon.[6] The actual origin of the word is relatively unimportant; it doesn't really matter whether it was originally a working class expression of limited use, since so many people attributed its invention to Laurendeau or Frère Untel in 1960, or if it was created by Grignon and derived from a stereotyped version of the working class pronunciation of the word *cheval* [horse]. What is important is that the exchange of letters between Laurendeau and Untel in *Le Devoir* allowed the word *joual*, meaning a type of language, to make its entry, and literally its fortune.

At first sight, the debate around this word seems to be little more than the prolongation of the debate that had moved Quebec society over *French Canadian Patois*. Still, even though people seemed to slip from one term to the other with hardly any transition, there is a fundamental difference between them, and in the rapport that people had with them. The term *patois* was used by the English to describe, or rather denigrate, the French of Quebec, and to contrast it with *Parisian French*. Further, even if the word was rejected, it seemed to refer to a somewhat archaic, provincial language that was rough and unrefined. In the eyes of the French-Canadians, these characteristics of archaism, provincialism, and lack of refinement at least had the advantage of evoking their relationship with the French colonists of the seventeenth century and the heroic conditions under which the nation had survived. *Joual,* on the other hand, was negatively connoted from the very beginning. About fifteen months after his first article appeared, and feeling rather perturbed by the depth of the Pandora's box he had apparently opened, André Laurendeau returned to the issue in an article where he tried to temper his judgment: "Qu'est-ce que parler *joual*?" [What does it mean to speak *joual*?] (*Le Devoir*, January 20, 1961):

> Where does the phenomenon come from? Frère Untel says it comes from flaws in the mind and the soul. Doubtless. But we are looking for more immediate causes that are more easily discerned: influences in daily life that have acted upon defenceless minds. It seems that *joual* comes from Montreal; it has to do with the massive industrialization that took place in a social environment where English is the language of industry that urbanizes and uproots people. This industrialization subjected us to a certain vocabulary where the co-existence of two languages – the one being the language of the rich, and the other the language of the poor – has contaminated the latter. [. . .] Canon Groulx has already described the history of this degeneration of our language. And he said something very important: let us not look at our people as though they were guilty when they are actually the victims.[7]

This text uses the word "degeneration," which is, in effect, what the word *joual* symbolized. It was not only a question of the French language degenerating, but also of the culture and the entire nation in decline. The degeneration and decline of an enslaved people; flawed in mind and soul, as Desbiens wrote; people who had lost the spirit of their language and were alienated. Such negative opinions filled the texts about *joual*. Because language is the first and most fundamental mode of expression of a culture and a collective identity, these cries of alarm about the state of the language, emitted at the beginning of the 1960s, made the French-Canadians call into question every aspect of their collective social and political organization. This is what made the crisis around *joual* so different from everything that had come earlier. People had long been worried about the French spoken in Quebec; for years writers had accused people of being ignorant or lazy or inappropriately snobbish, or lacking in pride. But this was the first time a collective will developed to correct the situation by targeting the socio-economic and political causes of the problem.

Once again, anglicization lay at its heart, but this time, and despite the explanations and exhortations of Groulx, Laurendeau and a few others who related *joual* to the French-Canadians' inferior social position, the self-flagellation was intense, and grew worse. The feelings expressed by very many texts in the first years of the decade were summarized by Germaine Bernier, who wrote a women's column in *Le Devoir* at the time:

> With time [. . .] English opinion has changed somewhat and the legend of French patois in Quebec has been disappearing. But over the course of the past year [. . .] we have learnt that our people, and especially the young people in our schools, colleges, factories, and on the street speak *joual*, a popular term to designate deteriorated French [. . .] Now we no longer need others to shame us by claiming we speak poor French, a French that has lost its elegance, is dismembered, devalued, and degraded.[8]

Shame is one of the words that came up often in articles on *joual*. Shame for the language being spoken, shame for what French Canadians had become. The feeling that culture and language in Quebec had suffered generalized deterioration seems to have been very intense. This was not new, but it was intense. Even when the writers of articles or letters denounced the socio-economic position of the French-Canadians and used it to explain the state of the culture, they were no less worried by this state, and all of them deemed it necessary to react. There was a clear sense of urgency. At this point, one could speak of the collective interiorization of the negative image that had been developing for some time. And although *joual* was often described as patois, the term progressively acquired its own definition. For example, in a TV series entitled *En haut de la pente douce*, broadcast on January 4, 1961, Roger Lemelin had his character Gédéon say that he prefers *joual* to prissy language, for one thing, because it is more natural. Many people promptly wrote letters to the papers attacking Lemelin:

> If the "rough accent," the original language that once existed here hadn't been replaced over the past fifty years by a jargon that cannot be understood by any person who has preserved French thinking, then we would not be facing such a monumental problem today: patois and argot may contribute to preserving the spirit of a language. But we must get it into our heads that this spoken version has not survived.[9]

The positive connotations still attached to the term *patois* soon became obsolete. The polemics around the language used in TV series continued for some time, with many criticizing Lemelin and sometimes Claude-Henri Grignon for the language their characters used. What the writers of these letters seemed to be afraid of was that television viewers would give up all efforts to speak a more careful French. The fear was that series broadcast in "popular" language on television, or on radio, would lead to such language becoming legitimate, and this is what most of the people writing on the subject rejected. Such a phenomenon would block the efforts to standardize the language, then referred to as "refrancisation" [restoring French]. One response to André Laurendeau's article of January 20, 1961 read as follows:

We are in the middle of a campaign to restore our French, a campaign your paper has strongly supported, a campaign that our educators and most enlightened politicians strongly support after they recognized and declared a state of emergency. Moreover, there are finally extremely wholesome reactions from the masses, all of which augurs well. The impression that one gets from your articles, however, is that you are hindering the process, taking steps backward, reversing your views to the benefit of a certain language you describe as picturesque, to which you assign a value of folklore, a language that you are trying to dissociate from *joual* though you admit you cannot define, circumscribe or establish the limits of this term, and all the while recognizing that this so-called picturesque language has been the soil in which *joual* prospered.[10]

The intense anxiety displayed in these years triggered various social reactions. In 1960, the Association canadienne des éducateurs de langue française (ACELF) [Canadian Association of French-language Educators] ran an extensive survey on the quality of students' French and made the results public at the conference in Rimouski in August. They were alarming:

All of the reports that were presented, at least the best among them, gave the impression that urgent and concerted action is required to save the French language. It is hard to see how such action can be undertaken without the support of the government of Quebec.[11]

The ACELF used the occasion to found a permanent commission on oral French which was assigned the task of making recommendations on how to improve teaching. At the same conference, Paul Gérin-Lajoie, the Minister for Youth in the Quebec government, declared a state of emergency for French and promised his government's support. The ACELF announced it would also undertake what was necessary to create an Office de la langue française [Office of the French Language], and this occurred in March 1961, along with the establishment of a Ministry of Cultural Affairs.

The first institution born of the Quiet Revolution

The Office de la langue française, which was the inspiration of Georges-Emile Lapalme, who also became its first director, appears to have been founded as a response by the government of Quebec to the ever-increasing demands of the population, demands that can be traced back to about 1937.[12] At the second Congress on the French language the Société du parler français au Canada, noting the deterioration of the language, had recommended the creation of such an organism in order to improve the situation. But only after the Second World War, in the 1950s, did the francophones of Quebec begin to think about using the state of Quebec as an instrument in the service of their language and culture. For this to happen, the feelings of dispossession and linguistic alienation had arrived at an unprecedented level, and set off a crisis culminating in 1960 with the quarrel around *joual*.

The third Congress on the French language in 1952 again noted the inexorable deterioration of the language, with the remedies proposed so far, essentially individual effort and language teaching, appearing to be as futile as the efforts of the groups acting to defend French against its deterioration. In retrospect, the year 1956 seems to have been decisive in changing the leadership's attitude. The recommendations made by the fourth Congress, held that year, which was entitled the Congress on the restoration of French, had included the establishment of an Office du vocabulaire [Vocabulary Office] within the department of public instruction. The report of the Tremblay Commission on constitutional problems, published in 1956, recommended the creation of an Office de la langue française as well. The Académie canadienne-française would do the same.[13] From that day on, the discourse of congresses, colloquia, reports, lectures, newspaper and magazine articles, and language columns became more and more insistent and impatient: people wanted the state of Quebec to take decisive action in support of French. This movement was much stronger in Montreal than anywhere else, which can probably be explained by the fact that the effects of domination by the anglophones were felt most strongly there. People thus turned toward the state, and demanded that it intervene. The inertia of Maurice Duplessis' government was, however, a serious obstacle that exasperated the generation of young intellectuals educated in the 1940s and 1950s, who were less and less willing to accept the social hurdles confronting francophones in Canada, and saw the provincial state as the only political instrument able to impose their collective will.

Thus, in a commentary on the fact that a large proportion of businesses had signs that were only in English, published in *Le Devoir* in July 1959, Gérard Filion, director of the paper, stated that it would be necessary to create an information service to supply the population with the French terms it did not know:

[. . .] a Vocabulary Office within Quebec's department of public instruction [. . .] would be able to profoundly influence the teaching of the spoken and written language in the public schools of Quebec. The restoration of French is a labor that will take a long time and must be indefatigably pursued.[14]

The following month the Conseil de la vie française en Amérique [Council for French Life in America] announced an extensive campaign to correct the language in French Canada. Pierre Laporte commented, "This campaign on behalf of good language should mark the beginning of a vast offensive that will bring with it a provincial Office of Linguistics. Politics should be set aside for a project like this because it is in the interests of our ethnic group and of Canada as a whole."[15]

When Maurice Duplessis died in September 1959 new perspectives immediately opened up. A few weeks later, Frère Untel's first letter to André Laurendeau, also expressed support for such a measure:

> There is talk of a provincial Office of linguistics. I'm for it. LANGUAGE IS A SHARED RESOURCE, and the state must protect it.[16]

The animated discussions about *joual* continued over the entire year 1960, and the letters and articles that dealt with it, or that addressed the language issue more generally, would regularly demand the intervention of the Quebec state. Maurice Lebel, for instance, Dean of the Faculty of Arts of Laval University gave a talk in which he described the catastrophic condition of French, and made a case for "the establishment of an Office of Translation, an Office of Linguistics."[17]

In June 1960, the Liberal Party was voted into power, with Jean Lesage at its head. The population in general, and the intellectuals in particular, saw this government as being more sensitive to the cultural and linguistic problems; they increased the pressure, as did the ACELF at the Rimouski conference.

The ACELF actually created a permanent Commission de la langue parlée [Commission on the spoken language] at this event, giving it the task to prepare a report for the government on the measures that should be taken. Submitted in early 1961, this report proposed various ways of improving the spoken language in Quebec, and recommended, among other things, that an Office canadien de la langue française [Canadian Office of the French Language] be established.[18]

In an article published in *Vie et langage*, the magazine of the Office du vocabulaire français, and reprinted in *Le Devoir* in September 1960, Gérard Dagenais wrote:

> The political leaders of the state of Quebec, regardless of which party they belong to, are now aware of the need to take over the direction of the country and they are getting ready to carry out the duties this imposes upon them. It is now certain that we will soon have a public office for language. We do not yet know what its powers will be [. . .]. But our political leaders did not make this decision spontaneously. It is the result of a national re-awakening, and responds to the demands of the population. The *Canadiens* of French origin want to preserve their language. Under pressure from English and American influences on all sides, they demand that the state assume the necessary directing role.[19]

Toward the end of 1960, the government of Jean Lesage announced the imminent creation of a Ministry of Cultural Affairs. Gérard Filion commented as follows on the project:

> The Ministry of Youth proclaimed a state of emergency for French in Rimouski. The government has just announced the creation of a Ministry of Cultural Affairs. That is very good. But what concrete measures will the government of Quebec propose to protect the French language in the same way it must end the demolition of the forests and the pollution of the waters? We are eager to find out. And the government should know in advance that the measures it adopts, however strict they are, will find a profound echo

from the people in general and from the intellectual class.[20]

On March 24, 1961, the government of Quebec created the Ministère des affaires culturelles [Ministry of Cultural Affairs] and the Office de la langue française [Office of the French Language]. The many actions undertaken on behalf of French by various groups and movements within civil society since the beginning of the century had apparently not been able to put a stop to what was perceived as the degradation of the condition of the language, to the point where people had begun to doubt that it was still French. In 1960, Gérard Dagenais said, "It is certain that our people no longer express themselves in French. The exceptions simply confirm the rule."[21] Under these conditions, the state of Quebec seemed to be the only instrument powerful enough to correct the situation. The first step was to "define the linguistic model" – the term was created somewhat later. This was the mandate of the Office de la langue française. Public pressure however continued, wanting the state to also take an interest in the status of the language; since there was clearly a relationship of cause and effect between the condition of the language and the low social and economic position of the French-Canadians, the state had a decisive role to play in this area. "Establishing status" was as important as and indissociable from language planning. The various language laws adopted in the 1970s were the result. In sum, the Office de la langue française was the first linguistic institution born of the Quiet Revolution and the often reiterated will of the Quebecois to reappropriate their language. It was a birth people had long awaited.

Joual, the symbol of degeneration

In the wake of the Rimouski conference, the Lesage government set up the Parent Commission on the teaching of French. The rather feverish atmosphere in which people were focusing on reconquering public space for French probably did not allow much room for nuance. *Joual*, at least early on, served as the symbol of everything French-Canadians rejected about themselves: their colonized condition (anglicized language), the feeling of being culturally backward (archaisms), lack of education (no knowledge of syntax or French vocabulary), lack of refinement (vulgarity), cultural isolation (a language that strangers could not understand), loss of roots and identity (deconstruction, fragmentation, degeneration, decomposition of language). From that point on, it was only a small step to say that *joual* also meant intellectual and spiritual impoverishment, a step that Frère Untel took, as many had before him, and many would after him.

In sum, when André Laurendeau used the word *joual* to name the language used by the adolescents around him, he provided Quebec society with the signifier that had been missing and that designated a state of the language and culture the society perceived as distinct and new. While earlier terms had included *canayen, parlure, parler*, and even *patois*, these no longer covered the variety of languages developing in the cities. Of course, *joual*, whose main characteristic was strong anglicization, had developed over time, but by 1960 the urbanized population was in its second and third generations and more numerous than ever before. Further, the postwar wave of American culture had reached the most distant parts of the countryside, and been translated into a new crop of linguistic and cultural borrowings. At the level of language, there was no difference or discontinuity between the popular language used before the war and the *joual* of 1960. The break was at the level of collective perception. Small wonder that columnists, journalists and readers attributed different values to the term *joual* and found it hard to define. For Laurendeau, *joual* was first and foremost from Montreal and characterized by anglicisms. For others, there was more to it:

> The characteristics of vulgar language are well-known: corrupted words, a mixture of canadianisms and anglicisms, incoherent syntax, etc. A metaphor has forever named this lingo *joual*.[22]

This reader made a difference between *joual* and familiar language which, he said, "has nothing exaggerated about it [. . .]. As for the syntax, it is a language that wants to be correct. And in regard to vocabulary, familiar language uses words recommended by "le bon usage" [proper usage]."

Others saw *joual* as representing the spoken French of most Quebecois:

> Most French-Canadians speak *joual* [. . .]; secretly, in their hearts, most of them regret this.[23]

The lower classes, whether in the cities or the countryside, were sometimes identified with *joual* as a group:

> The working people, those who speak *joual* because a certain class of society has had an interest in keeping them ignorant, pay taxes and have the right to programs within their reach.[24]

Then, at a conference held at Laval University in 1962 by *Recherches sociographiques,* Gilles Lefebvre, a linguist, provided the following sociolinguistic definition:

Joual is a form of speech that is much less widespread than people would have us believe [. . .] the urban working class, especially in Montreal, has integrated many elements of the English language used by its masters into its French.[25]

Other, scientific, definitions of *joual* followed. It is, in fact, quite easy to define the phonetic characteristics of a certain variety of a language, collect samples of lexical items, analyze the syntactic structures current in a particular form, describe what characterizes each sub-group in a certain society, and define the sociolects and the regional variations. But such analyses rarely reach the general public nor do they have much effect on the opinion that this public has of its language. On the other hand, when a new word emerges in a society it always brings a new concept into the collective consciousness. In the case in point, the fact that the word *joual* entered the vocabulary of French-Canadians in a matter of months shows that there was a new collective perception of the language. But which language exactly? For a long time, this remained rather vague, but in the minds of those discussing *joual* in 1960-62, it was clearly no longer French, or was in danger of no longer being French. And that was a huge issue. Language, the element upon which a collectivity most strongly bases its identity, was itself losing its identity. Subsequently, some would advocate the adoption of *joual* as the language of the Quebecois, in the name of Quebec identity, arguing that the language of France could not express the specificity of Quebec culture. This proposal was not successful because it ignored the linguistic reality of Quebec, just as those did who dreamed of erasing every possible regionalism from French.

There is no such thing as linguistic uniformity. All societies, even the ideologically most egalitarian, divide into sub-groups, whether these are social classes or strata, whether the sub-divisions are due to socio-economic hierarchies or to geography. But in all societies, one version of the language functions as the model, as the norm, is codified and used in the education system. This is normally the version used by the dominant subgroup. In the case of French, the language used by the upper class of the Paris region has held this status since the Middle Ages, because political and economic power was located in Paris. This remains the case to this day.

We saw earlier that it was quite natural for the French language established in North America in the seventeenth century to evolve differently from that of France, and for this development to be exacerbated when the contacts were severed around 1760. Toward the end of the nineteenth century when these connections began to be re-established, educated people became aware of the gulf between the two varieties of French. French-Canadian society theoretically had two options: do whatever was necessary to keep the language within the French sphere of influence, and continue to accept the form of the language codified as the norm by grammar books and dictionaries, or allow it to detach itself from its source, evolve differently, and then formulate a new norm based on local usage. For historical as well as political reasons, the French-Canadian elites opted for the first solution (in fact, the second one was never seriously considered), which is why the campaigns for good French were waged, the wars on anglicisms were declared, the reproaches were formulated and the actions to "restore French" were undertaken.

By 1960, however, people were dismayed to see that none of these efforts had prevented contemporary language from moving even farther away from the norms of France. It had become obvious that the objectives could not be attained unless direct action were taken against the causes of this divergent development, of which anglicization was the most apparent feature.

Political reactions

Very early on, therefore, journalistic texts on the topic of *joual* addressed political demands to the governments. It is no accident that the independence movement, which had existed on a very marginal basis since the 1930s, began to organize more systematically and attract numerous young people who no longer accepted the status quo. André Laurendeau, who played a decisive role as an opinion maker in those years, wrote the following on the subject of separatism:

> A large part of the new generation refuses to have to anglicize itself in order to serve its country. It feels that this obligation transforms the central state into a foreign – and often a hostile – state. [. . .] It is unacceptable that a bilingual, English-French state, should be one of the main agents in francophone de-nationalization. [...] It is especially intolerable that no serious reform has even been considered.[26]

A few weeks later, on January 20, 1962, he launched the idea of a governmental enquiry on bilingualism in Canada, an idea that was taken up by the Pearson government, which set up the Royal Commission on bilingualism and bi-culturalism in 1963 and made André Laurendeau and Davidson Dunton its joint presidents. Only with the Trudeau government, at the end of the decade, did this enquiry lead to the adoption of the Official Languages Act. In the meantime, pressure from the Quebec population on the provincial government grew stronger. The newspapers *Le Devoir* and *La Presse* held their own enquiries, for example, into the use of French in the big stores on the west side of Montreal. One reader wrote in *La Presse:*

> If the majority of Quebecois want French to be respected, I would suggest that a more or less direct campaign be waged to declare French the first language in Quebec [. . .] There is only one way to force respect, and that is as a group, at the level of the provincial government. At the individual level: zero.[27]

The problems around using French, or rather the difficulties experienced in getting served in French, especially in Montreal, led many writers to demand that the provincial state proclaim Quebec unilingual, and thus force the anglophones of Quebec to become bilingual:

> The solution should soon come from our Quebec government, which would proclaim French unilingualism. It would be desirable not to have to take measures that are so radical as to force our anglophone compatriots to practice bilingualism; but unfortunately, after almost two centuries of co-existence, there is not much that can be described as encouraging in the offing.[28]

It is noteworthy that the authors of these last two extracts are rather hesitant when they call for strong measures, an attitude that is visible in the use of the conditional tense ("I would suggest," "the Quebec government would proclaim") and all kinds of attenuated language ("more or less direct campaign," "It would be desirable," etc.) They seem to regret having reached this point, but there is also a feeling that their patience is definitely being strained.

It is also clear that people wanted to make the provincial state, already under considerable pressure, a more active, and much stronger, political instrument. Many thought that this state, as the only political body under the control of the French-Canadian nation, should carry out its political will. Depending on whether or not people hoped to see the federal government install actual equality between French and English-Canadians, they looked around for options. Those who believed this would never occur began to define themselves as Quebecois, and not French-Canadians. For example, readers supported independence as the only way to prevent the anglicization of Quebec:

> The further you get away from Quebec the greater the effects of anglicization and protestantization. The reason we cannot save these French minorities is because we do not control our culture, and because Ottawa, with its grip on Quebec, stops us from fully expanding it. Is it because we want to save these French minorities in the English province that we do not have the right to self-determination, or total independence?[29]

> We are not French-CANADIANS; we are QUEBECOIS. We have never thought CANADIAN, and we never will, because "CANADA" is synonymous with England and we are not English. Canada is doing everything it can to anglicize us, but we are winning (somewhat weakly) and we will always win, even if we are affected by this anglicization.[30]

On the whole the earliest texts that used the word *Québécois* and more or less explicitly rejected the term *French-Canadian* also expressed their support for independence, often linking this notion of taking over power with the condition of the language. Indeed, only a few years later, the term *Québécois* completely replaced *French-Canadian* in general usage, and this quite separately from people's political views. In the same way that a euphemism allows you to refer to a taboo, by concealing the stigma attached to it, the act of giving oneself a new name gets rid of the negative connotations attached to the old name. Over the past thirty years, we have seen Black Americans exchange the term *Negro* for *Black,* and more recently, for *African-American.* The reference to skin colour has changed to a reference to origins while demands about nationality have been maintained with the element *American.* In the change from *French-Canadian* to *Québécois,* the purpose was clearly to get rid of the negative connotations of the first term, and at the same time modify the identity factor by introducing the territorial aspect – Quebec – where francophones controlled the government. At the same time, however, this caused a break with the francophones in other provinces of Canada, and this was not painless. However, before Ottawa adopted the Official Languages Act, there was little hope of these francophone minorities surviving. In certain provinces their level of assimilation was alarming. In December 1961, *L'Actualité* published the following figures for the Canadian West: in Manitoba, 21.1% of francophones had assimilated to English; in Saskatchewan and Alberta the number was 31.9% and in British Columbia it was 54.6%. In 1964, an article on bilingualism published in *Liberté* by Fernand Ouellette gave the following figures: rate of assimilation of French-Canadians in New Brunswick was 9.4%, in Newfoundland 81.6%, in British Columbia 62%. Ouellette made a direct link between the level of bilingualism and the level of assimilation, and judged that "bilingualism is the channel for assimilation."[31] The number of francophones in Canada was thus in danger of shriveling up to a point where only Quebecois would be left, for a more or less limited time. Finally, the change in name had the effect of transforming the francophone collective in Quebec into a majority, allowing it to perceive itself as such and to act accordingly at the political level. A major change.

In a chain reaction of sorts the name change brought with it a series of new labels or new usages, such as the word *francophone*, which had been rare up to that point, and which, in Canada, is used to designate a person whose mother tongue is French. Dictionaries, on the other hand, use it for "any person who usually speaks French." Further, the French language minorities in the other Canadian provinces slowly acquired new names as well; all except the *Acadiens* [Acadians] in the Maritimes, who already had a distinct name. Terms such as *Franco-Manitobain*, *Franco-Ontarien*, and *Fransaskois* came into use, and the strange collective term *Francophone hors-Quebec* [Francophone outside Quebec] arrived at the end of the 1970s to complete the list and consecrate the fragmentation of the French-Canadian nation.

Similarly, the adjective form *canadien(ne)-français(e)* was generally replaced by *québécois(e)* in most names of institutions such as unions, associations, groups of various kinds, the names of journals, and even the Académie canadienne-française which, in 1992, was renamed Académie des lettres du Québec.

Other, more discreet, transformations also marked the change in identity occurring in the 1960s. When people wrote about Quebec in the 1950s, they usually used the expression *the province of Quebec*. From the mid-1960s onward, the tendency to simply write *Quebec* and drop the reference to the province became almost systematic. Further, where events once took place *dans le Québec*, this changed to *au Québec* in the 1960s, subtly, and syntactically, seeming to change the province into a national state.

The Official Languages Act, and other measures taken by the Trudeau government to create a better position for French in Canada and slow down the anglicization of francophone groups clearly came too late to prevent the restructuring of identity as illustrated by the name change.

In cutting off their ties with the weakened branches of French-Canadians that had settled in the West and been prevented from flourishing by Canadian politics, the Quebecois also had to give up on the dream to truly share Canada with the English-Canadians. What they gained as result was cohesion at home, and with this cohesion they were able to craft a more efficient instrument to exert political pressure on the federal government, even in regard to support for the francophone minorities. After all, the Official Languages Act was adopted largely in response to threats of separation from Quebec.

Joual as a literary language: misrepresentation or faithful reflection

In the history of Quebec literature, the language question has always played a central role. As Marie-Andrée Beaudet argues in her essay on this point, the linguistic insecurity that French-Canadian authors and critics felt in the early twentieth century made it difficult to create a literary domain in Quebec that was separate from France, and especially from Paris:

> As "language and literature" seemed indissociable at that time, the directors of the Société du parler français [Society for spoken French] used the example of provincial French to validate the idea of "ethical" literature, i.e., a literature that pays more attention to the markers of national or provincial identity than to formal perfection, a perfection that seemed out of reach because of the linguistic situation, or more precisely due to the negative perception of French in Quebec. [. . .] National literature was assigned the mission to preserve and illustrate the values of identity and religion which contemporary French literature no longer did for the Quebecois, either because of its physical distance or its ideological differences.[32]

Regionalist literature developed as a prolongation of this ideology about "ethical" literature, and it dominated the literary domain for a few decades, contributing to the maintenance of the stereotype of the French-Canadian as a Catholic peasant. A survey of writers at the second conference of *Recherches sociographiques* in the early 1960s showed how outdated this stereotype was:

> For male writers the first urban novels, those of Gabrielle Roy and Roger Lemelin, for example, demonstrated that a French-Canadian literature was possible. They recognized themselves in these urban novels. They found a world they knew, different from the traditional rural world that had been dominant in the ideological conception of French-Canadian literature.[33]

It was important for the writers to get into step with the society they lived in, and so the stylized language of peasants found in regionalist literature was no longer suitable. It was time for the question of language to be raised again. The publication in 1964 of Jacques Renaud's *Le Cassé* set off a new polemics over the relationship between language, literature, and society. Renaud and writers from the *Parti pris* group such as Gérald Godin, André Major, Paul Chamberland and Laurent Girouard wanted to use *joual*, which they considered a fragmented and impoverished language, to expose the conditions of domination and alienation that the Quebecois lived in. For these authors it was not a question of legitimizing the language but rather of triggering a healthy reaction against it, against a language they saw as a symptom of inferiority. They hoped this reaction would have a revolutionary effect, and would change the social order. A few months earlier, the writers around *Liberté* had discussed the language question in Quebec and come out against unilateral bilingualism and the linguistic alienation it caused. In his well-documented analysis of the topic, Fernand Ouellette came to the conclusion that "the problem of language in Quebec *must be politicized immediately.*"[34] But there was no unanimity on the use of *joual* as a literary language, even in order to expose and attack the conditions underlying this language. In October 1965, *Le Devoir* published a series of articles on the subject. Jacques Brault wrote:

> *Joual* certainly does not carry our cultural future within it, and at the moment, the best thing to do is to tear it out of our bodies, root out this suffocating gangrene [. . .] If the revolution (and especially the literary revolution) is to be channeled through *joual*, it must move beyond *joual*, and move us beyond it too, as quickly as possible.[35]

Jacques Godbout criticized the apparent gap between literature and social reality in Quebec, and saw the more or less temporary use of *joual* as possibly leading toward slow rapprochement:

> Quebec writers are quite aware: ideally we should be writing in a French that the greatest number of francophones in the world can understand, *but without ever sacrificing the exact description of our society.* Which is why spending a few years carefully transcribing Quebec reality (in *joual*) could bring a reconciliation between literary writing and actual social reality, i.e. a reason for writing.[36]

Godbout thus wanted to find a way of writing in Quebec that would remain within the scope of French. In Jacques Ferron's view, "*joual* was not something you write. Its only dignified use would be to serve as the jargon for a conspiracy."[37] And Gilles Lefèbvre, the linguist who defined *joual* as the anglicized language of the urban working class, responded as follows to the question "Should we count on *joual*?"

Some of our writers [. . .] thought they could take on this search for an identity, a justified escape from ethnic alienation, a more or less reasonable revolt against a shameful past and the perpetual condition of being in a minority without failing in their duty to set an example. [. . .] But what exactly is the object that is so despised: do we feel contempt for our language, or for ourselves? And do we truly wish to further humiliate ourselves by choosing as a symbol of our identity a language we despise? [. . .] We should not confuse the reasonable "canadianization" of French [. . .] with *joualization,* in other words with a form of creolization through massive and poorly digested borrowings, and cultural isolation in a marginal sub-language.[38]

The problem of cultural isolation was a very real one for these writers who, for the most part, wanted to reach beyond the narrow limits of Quebec and were afraid of losing access to an international readership by using a language that had become too specific. Others, like Claude Jasmin, took hold of joual in the name of identity and authenticity: "Shout and yell using a real language, full of mistakes, but real . . ."[39]

But it was in the theatre rather than the novel that the question of *joual* would crop up again at the end of the decade. Popular language had long been used in the theatre, but basically for bedroom farces and comic effect. The staging of Michel Tremblay's *Les Belles-soeurs* in 1968 produced shock waves, probably because the play, which was a realistic comedy, had far more to do with social theatre than with bedroom farce. Shortly after the box-office success of *Belles-soeurs,* Marcel Dubé, the dramaturge, responded as follows to a question on the language of the theatre:

I don't agree with people who query the use of *joual* as a language. Comments along those lines came up again recently in regard to Michel Tremblay's *Belles-soeurs*. In terms of literature, *joual* doesn't go anywhere, but it is necessary in *Belles-soeurs,* as an element whose poverty, ridiculousness, and even distress are closely tied to the theme of the play. Which doesn't mean we have to make it a general law for social theatre in Quebec. It is not a necessity or a mark of language that represents us. In fact, we would be poorly represented. Exceptionally, *joual* can be used as a way to protest against colonization and deficiency.[40]

Despite reservations and rejections on the part of some critics, *Les Belles-soeurs* was successful. Many young authors took up *joual* as a result; theatre pieces by Jean-Claude Germain, Jacqueline Barrette and many others appeared on Quebec stages and for a few years, they dominated Quebec theatre. Still, little by little, nuances appeared in the way linguistic realities were portrayed in the theatre, and although the polemics around *joual* did not impose this form as the only version of Quebec French in the theatre, it seems to have given dramatists access to the whole range of language and sociolects as possible means with which to represent society.

Parisian and international French

The old, and much challenged, opposition between *canadien patois* and *Parisian French*, was paralleled in the 1960s by a comparison between *joual* and normalized language, though this norm no longer had a specific location. It was termed international French. Gérard Dagenais, for example, wrote in 1960:

How can we ever expect our English-language compatriots to take our demands for bilingualism seriously if we do not speak an international French that those among them who speak French can understand?[41]

This notion of *international French* which is highly abstract since no specific group of French-speakers uses the language, quickly gained recognition. Many articles written over the course of the 1960s used it as a reference. It makes sense to ask why.

In the preceding years, the notion of Parisian French had been contested, on the one hand because people felt it was an English invention, and on the other, because they thought the French spoken in Paris could be divided into two basic types: argot [slang] which was rejected as vulgar, and plain French, spoken by all educated people across France. This simplified a linguistic situation that was considerably more complex, but simplification is the norm in public debates. So why did the adjective *international* become necessary? One reason is that after the war people had become much more aware that French was spoken in many countries, and this allowed them to envisage access to a larger and more diversified world. The government of Quebec established its first international contacts at this time, set up delegations abroad, and became very active in creating networks of cooperation and developing international relations between francophone countries, all of which was seen as a counter-balance to Anglo-American influence. But that is not the whole explanation. Intellectuals, artists, and writers of this period were also rejecting Paris as a cultural reference. Several different factors played into this but their respective importance is hard to assess. Some writers were concerned about adequate and authentic representations of Quebec society, and the literary language in common use no longer served that purpose. In an interview in *Le Devoir* on the polemics around his TV series, Roger Lemelin said, "To authentically be ourselves, we cannot follow the path the French take."[42]

Writers were also trying to create real Quebec literature that was more than just an add-on to French literature, and could be an autonomous literary field. This search for their own literary identity mirrors what was going on everywhere in the society. In regard to language, the various newspaper texts of the period give the impression that people were searching for a linguistic norm that would come from Quebec but could also be viewed positively. In 1961 a woman reader wrote to *La Presse* on this topic:

> There is a golden mean in everything. We owe it to ourselves to speak well, but also and especially to not "talk like the French." We do not want a French dialect, but a French-Canadian dialect. Speaking well does not mean speaking with affectation. It means banning anglicisms and poorly or half-pronounced words from our conversation.[43]

It was indeed perceived as an affectation or as snobbery if people adopted "French" pronunciation, though on the other hand, radio and television announcers often suffered criticism from their audiences if, by chance, they used "Quebec" pronunciation. This was considered lax. In fact, "French" pronunciation continued to be the reference in official situations and as the language of representation, and politicians continued to be criticized for using language that was too familiar. But it is clear that many readers were irritated by the position that a number of columnists such as Pierre Beaudry, Gérard Dagenais, or Jean-Marie Laurence took, who were quick to attack any linguistic phenomenon typical of Quebec (pronunciation, vocabulary, archaisms, neologisms created to replace anglicisms). The readers understood these attacks as the servile acceptance of a foreign norm, as a refusal or rejection of Quebec identity, and finally as contempt for the Quebecois. What was seen as anglomania and snobism on the part of Parisians, who were borrowing all kinds of words from English – and different words than those borrowed in Quebec – was also supremely irritating for many Quebecois, including columnists such as Empédocle, a pen name, who wrote in 1961-1962:

Monsieur Gérard Dagenais' taste for Paris is not always convincing. He is basically right that our French should come as close as possible to what is called international French these days [...] Where he gets it wrong though is when he wants this principle to apply to warts and all. He rejects the term *gomme à mâcher*, for instance, on the pretext that they say "chewing gum" in France. That's really a bit much![44]

The Quebecois seemed to feel the constraints of this norm which they could not influence more strongly than ever, and reacted against certain columnists who wanted them to adopt it completely and without question. The feeling was widespread at the time, and was clearly expressed by the reader below:

We French-Canadians have reached a dead-end with our language. We are forced to follow the development of the language according to the whims and decrees of the French. We try to clean all the anglicisms out of our language while they adopt them every which way, and then impose them on us. They pride themselves on this, and think it is intellectual.[45]

These kinds of texts often referred to the Americans, who had no problem transforming English every which way without worrying about British reactions, and generally commented that their enviable economic and political power allowed them this freedom. Still, it is quite clear that anglomania in Paris is what pushed people to look for a norm that was not defined in or by

Paris, but was developed multilaterally by all francophones of the world: in other words international French. When *Parlez-vous franglais*, the famous book by René Étiemble came out in 1964, Quebec newspapers paid it a lot of attention, lending unanimous support to the French writer in his attack on Anglo-American influence. Jean-Éthier Blais wrote:

> You cannot read *Parlez-vous franglais?* without becoming quite anti-American. They are barbarians, there's nothing else to say, and it is hard to understand why the French government doesn't kick them out along with their henchmen [. . .] Meanwhile, our people have created a thousand French words from English, as the recent work of Victor Barbeau shows. What are the French waiting for?[46]

Every new appearance of a French dictionary also set off reactions. Readers would scour it for new borrowings from English, and ask what use such a dictionary served; and the columnists would generally add their tirade on the useful or useless aspects of these borrowings, often agreeing with their readers that the French were indeed being abusive about how they proceeded.

The notion of *international French* was replaced by *universal French* at the end of the decade, when it appeared in 1967 at the Second Biennial on the French Language in Quebec City. The Biennial was an initiative set up by the linguist Alain Guillermou, the founder of the Office du vocabulaire français [Office of French Vocabulary] and general-secretary of the Fédération du français universel [Federation of Universal French]. Guillermou defined universal French as follows:

> I see universal French as quality French, written and spoken in the same way in all francophone countries. The adjective "universal" does not mean "concerning the whole world;" it means "concerning a whole group," and

the group is made up of all the francophones in the world.[47]

The direction being taken was to unify French by formulating a norm that would incorporate words from other francophone countries and provinces of France and would be the same for everyone. People were most interested in vocabulary, in specialized terminology, and in technical terms. The goal was to both unify French, and displace Paris as the centre, a goal that was addressed by several speakers at the Biennial as reported by the journalist Pierre Olivier:

> Everyone concerned (especially the French) should take note that French is no longer the "exclusive property of the French in France" and that the language must adapt and make room for regional realities if it truly wants to become universal.[48]

These demands came from Africans such as the Moroccan journalist Ben Ziane and Olympe Bhêly Quenum from Dahomey as well as from Quebecois. People no longer wanted to hear that "il n'est bon bec que de Paris" [only the language of Paris is French] as François Villon asserted in the fifteenth century.

The Biennial led to the establishment of the Conseil international de la langue française [International Council on the French Language] and the Fédération internationale des professeurs de français [International Federation of Teachers of French]. This expansion of the norms for all francophone domains, abstract as it was, clearly responded to wishes of Quebecois who needed to "possess" the language that seemed to be escaping them, if only symbolically. They were appropriating the right to speak. It also allowed them to break out of their isolation, and with the help of other francophone countries, establish more of a balance with the Anglo-

American masses they were facing. To re-burnish the prestige of French in Quebec, the Quebecois had to perceive it as having a place on the international scene, grasp its usefulness and modernity, and contribute to it as well, as this reader wrote:

> If we want our language to align itself with that of the other francophone groups we have to "talk" to them, and we have to want to do so. Through an intensive but honest propaganda campaign, the people of Quebec need to be shown that the francophone world is as active, modern, and attractive as the anglophone world.[49]

The idea of an international norm for French immediately met with great success in Quebec; for example, when the language committee for Radio Canada reported to the Gendron Commission in December 1969, it made the following recommendations:

> Recognize only the norms of universal French, the French used in Quebec; create closer ties with the other francophone countries; critically examine teaching methods – especially for French; revalorize culture; extend required education; encourage reading; accept bilingualism; and finally realize that France is no longer the only centre of the francophone world.[50]

International French is what the Office de langue française recommended when it took as its first task the precise definition of the linguistic model that would serve as the reference. Its very first publication, entitled *Norme du français écrit et parlé au Québec*[51] defined this model as follows:

> The Office believes that in the face of the enormous pressure that the English environment of North America puts on French in Quebec, it is essential to refer to the francophone world for support; this means aligning ourselves

with international French, all the while allowing room for North American realities to be expressed.

The linguistic norm for Quebec, which governs the French used in administration, teaching, courts, religion and the press, must match the French used in Paris, Geneva, Brussels, Dakar, and all the large French-speaking cities.

The schools question

The change of name from French-Canadian to "Québécois" had been determined in part by the desire to get rid of at least the psychological aspects of being a minority, and all the powerlessness this implied for political action. In the last years of the decade 1960-1970, people became aware of another phenomenon: the fact that while the majority position of francophones in Quebec was clear, it was quite fragile and threatened by a situation that was not new, but was growing considerably more important at this point. For a long time, the division of the school system into Catholic and Protestant sectors had brought with it the division of immigrant children into one of the two groups, depending on their denomination. Immigrants from southern Europe, Spain, Portugal, and especially Italy, had for the most part sent their children to French Catholic schools, while non-Catholic immigrants, Protestant or not, sent their children to the more tolerant English schools. An English-Catholic system had also developed to respond to the needs of the ethnic Irish population. Until the early 1930s, immigrant children divided up more or less evenly between French and English schools, with the French schools at a slight advantage, but from 1931 on, the two English systems begin taking in more students. Thirty years later, in 1961, 90% of the children of new Canadians were opting for English schools. As immigrants became more and more numerous, they began to make up a substantial percentage of the population, especially in Montreal, where they congregated.[52] This absorption of almost all immigrant children into English schools could only lead to a constant and steady increase in the anglophone population, and a reduction of the French majority as a result. Some could see the day when Montreal would become mainly English-speaking. Even so, English was over-represented in the city – in business, signposting, services, language at work, although its population was 65% French. Indeed, the increase in the proportion of anglophones could only further aggravate the marginalization of French in the public sphere. The possibility of "losing" the big city was logically perceived as a serious risk for the future of Quebec society, and for its survival. But it takes time for a population to express its anxiety. In 1961, after André Laurendeau published a commentary on a study by Jacques Henripin, a demographics specialist, that discussed the future ethnic and linguistic make-up of Quebec, a French reader wrote to *Le Devoir*, to report that since he was not a Catholic, he had been forced to send his children to English schools. He criticized this policy as one that could only do damage to the Quebecois:

> The province of Quebec finds ingenious ways to keep out authentic francophone elements that could strengthen it in the face of English.[53]

Still, it was only in 1967 that the question was debated in public and at length. One writer, for example, complained that in an English school in Saint-Henri, only 34% of the students had English as their mother tongue, while the others were all immigrants of various origins, or French-Canadians (13%). He wrote:

This situation, which we also see in other parts of Montreal, is quite unacceptable; it is a form of cultural genocide that can drown our French majority in Quebec in an anglophone ocean. [. . .] Let us open our eyes before it is too late; the French language is dying day by day in Quebec, especially in the Montreal area, because of weak policies that allow immigrants to go to school in the minority language [. . .]. We ask the government to produce legislation that will oblige all immigrants other than anglophones to attend French schools, and to promote French unilingualism in Quebec (the opposite of what is in place in the other nine provinces).[54]

At the end of 1967, several articles appeared in the newspapers around this question, and the population was quite horrified to discover the extent of the phenomenon. More and more demands were made that the Quebec government take energetic action to correct the situation. A spokesperson for the Rassemblement général pour la souveraineté nationale [General Assembly for National Sovereignty] expressed such views in *La Presse*:

While Monsieur Johnson is struggling to prevent the anglicization of French-Canadians living outside Quebec, *La Presse* recently reported on its front page that in downtown Montreal 10% of French-Canadian children and 90% of new Canadian children were enrolled in English schools. [. . .] What exactly are Monsieur Johnson and the ministers of Education and Cultural Affairs waiting for to put an end to this unacceptable situation? [55]

Faced with such anxieties, the Minister of Education ordered an interministerial committee to study the matter. This committee's report confirmed the massive anglicization of immigrant children and recommended that strong legislative measures be adopted.[56]

The controversy around the schools of Saint-Léonard erupted into this environment. The school board had decided to make French school mandatory for all new Canadians, a large proportion of whom were of Italian origin in this east Montreal neighbourhood. English-Quebeckers and immigrant associations launched a huge protest movement. The fight went on for months with groups of francophones, such as the "Mouvement pour l'intégration scolaire" [Movement for Integration in the Schools] forming to support the school board's decision and demanding that the decision be more widely applied. There were demonstrations and counter-demonstrations. Faced with these upheavals the government ended up tabling a bill that was adopted in November 1969 despite the strong opposition it triggered in the population of Quebec. Bill 63 ensured free choice in the language of instruction, and although it contained a few measures designed to improve the learning of French in English schools, it perpetuated the situation that had been under attack for several years, i.e. the massive anglicization of immigrants. Only in 1974 did Bill 22, passed by the Liberal government of Robert Bourassa, provide for concrete measures to integrate these children into francophone society, measures that were reinforced by Bill 101, adopted in 1977 by the Parti québécois under René Lévesque.

This controversy had the effect of making the Quebecois even more aware of how unable they were to assimilate new arrivals into their language; they realized to what extent economic, political, and demographic factors were playing against them and threatening their culture in America. It was becoming more and more obvious that the last remaining option was political. This realization doubtless contributed to reinforcing Quebec identity for it meant working together in collective action to oppose the will of a political majority that had never stopped eroding French-Canadian society. The schools question was doubtless also one of the main reasons why the "Union nationale" disappeared as a political force. This party, which had represented a timid and conservative kind of nationalism, and shown enormous hesitation in the face of the people's will, not adopting a single law that might regulate these issues, was swept out of the political picture in Quebec within a few years.

The Parent, Laurendeau-Dunton, Gendron Commissions

Under ever-increasing pressure from the public the decade between 1960 and 1970 saw the development of a series of reactions that took a number of years to translate into effective measures, and whose consequences profoundly changed Quebec society. They are felt to this day. Education was the first sector affected. While the question of language was not what underlay the reform of the Quebec school system by the government of Jean Lesage, elected in 1960, it did play some role.

The existing structures, almost completely in the hands of the clergy, who controlled virtually all secondary and university education, as well as a large part of the primary education, no longer suited the needs of Quebec society. Urbanization and industrialization had made a more educated workforce necessary than when most people lived off the land and the forests. Primary school alone was no longer enough. And though the small number of students who went on to study humanities at secondary level in "cours classiques," or took other kinds of secondary education such as business or professional training had increased, this did not satisfy the development needs of Quebec society. Further, education seemed to be less and less adapted to students' needs, and quite rigid both in terms of content and administration. The government of Maurice Duplessis had continuously supported the virtual monopoly of the religious communities in education. Jean Lesage, as head of the Liberal Party, based his electoral campaign on the modernization of Quebec and made the reform of the school system a key element. One of his slogans was "Grade 7 for everybody," which gives some idea of the extent of the problem. Access to secondary and higher education was thus at the centre of the measures his government adopted.

The teaching of French was a major concern. In 1960, the polemics around *joual* erupted; from the start people found the language used by teenagers a cause for concern, and the education they were getting did not seem to stop the language from deteriorating. This question was the main topic of *Insolences du frère Untel*. The Association canadienne des éducateurs de langue française, the ACELF, also expressed its concerns over this, and the newspapers picked these up. When the Royal Commission on education was formed by the Lesage government in 1961, it was assigned the task to examine the structures as well as the contents and methods of the education system, and to formulate recommendations in view of a reform that would increase and ensure students' access to the best education, which included linguistic education.

The Parent Commission report, submitted in Spring 1966, was largely concerned with school textbooks, the virtual monopoly of the Christian Brothers publisher [Frères des écoles chrétiennes], whose language the Commission considered mediocre. The Commission also judged it necessary to improve teacher training in order to present students with linguistic models that conformed to the norms of standard French. Finally, the work of the Commission led to the Quebec government setting up a system of public primary and secondary schools throughout the province, and creating Cégeps, colleges for general and professional education, that offered pre-university education in the sciences, humanities, arts, literature, and in professional training. Since these colleges charged no tuition, they were much more accessible than the private colleges had been. The education level of the general population increased rapidly, with all kinds of consequences, even in regard to spoken language.

Observers, including sociolinguists, agree that spoken language in Quebec has become more standardized over the last thirty years; for example, the pronunciation that was most stigmatized because it was the least standard has diminished; vocabulary has grown richer, and anglicisms, especially formal borrowings, have decreased. Education has obviously had some effect, though it is not the only factor in this development.

The Commission on Bilingualism and Biculturalism

Except for a few symbolic, almost derisory gestures, such as bilingual checks, the French-Canadians did not make much headway with the federal government under Conservative John Diefenbaker. Their demands and recriminations were largely met with royal indifference. When the independence movement started to organize and make itself heard in the early 1960s, the federal politicians were taken aback by what was actually a secessionist movement they had not seen coming. In November 1961 André Laurendeau wrote:

> Separatism as an oppositional movement is establishing its usefulness: it is forcing federal politicians to address topics they generally ignore. They can now tell English Canadians that the most active sector of French Canada is no longer satisfied with the position it has been assigned in Canada. Mr. Dorion, for example, says, "It is inconceivable that we cannot demand equal treatment for the two

ethnic groups that participated in establishing the Canadian Constitution without exposing ourselves to the subtle contempt of an active, and too influential, minority of the Canadian population." The person speaking is a federal cabinet minister.[57]

Laurendeau himself suggested that a pan-Canadian enquiry be held to evaluate the linguistic situation and propose reforms that would correct this imbalance. The Liberal government under Lester B. Pearson, elected in 1963, took up this idea and less than four months later set up the Royal Commission on Bilingualism and Biculturalism. The situation indeed seemed critical. For several months the Front de libération du Québec (FLQ) [Quebec Liberation Front] had engaged in terrorist activities, inspired by various anti-colonialist movements such as the National Liberation Front in Algeria, and various revolutionary groups in Latin America. The FLQ was part of a vast international ideological movement for the liberation of oppressed peoples and social classes that translated into the Civil Rights movement in the United States, with the Black Panthers and other groups, guerrilla fighters in Cuba and in South America, and so on. The threat of political instability that the FLQ posed was taken seriously, making the Pearson government move rapidly to find solutions for the crisis. According to Guy Bouthillier and Jean Meynaud, the government set out to "undermine the Quebec independence movement by reinforcing the feeling of belonging to the Canadian collective, thus giving the federal government a new vocation to defend the French-Canadians and promote the rights of French across Canada."[58] The Laurendeau-Dunton Commission confirmed the dissatisfaction and anxiety of the Quebecois who no longer accepted the position of inferiority into which their French language had placed them.

Nonetheless, over the course of its work, the Commission encountered a certain skepticism. A sizeable number of Quebecois no longer believed that the French-speaking communities in the other provinces could survive, let alone develop, as the following letter stated:

> We can therefore assume that the question of French surviving in northern Ontario is not even being asked anymore. At one point, 70% of the population was of French-Canadian origin, but since our people had to use English at work, they had to assimilate in order to survive. [. . .] So there is no point trying to make us believe that French secondary schools in Ontario will improve anything; after they finish school people will still have to live and work in the language of Shakespeare. It is obvious that unilingualism should be imposed in Quebec to allow the French culture to survive in Canada, especially as English unilingualism is the norm in all the rest of Canada, a situation that even the utopian B.B (bilingualism and biculturalism) Commission cannot change.[59]

The Commision brought down its report in 1969. On July 9 of the same year the federal government under Pierre Elliot Trudeau passed the law on the status of the official languages of Canada which was designed to make bilingualism mandatory in all federal services across Canada. Since the federal government was a big employer, these measures gave francophones preferred access to jobs as civil servants, and made it much more useful for anglophones to learn French.

There is no doubt that the Official Languages Act contributed to improving the situation of French, especially in provinces with large anglophone majorities. The Acadians in New Brunswick, who form the largest minority, drew large benefits and managed to set up various institutions to help support and develop their culture. In Quebec, the law brought real improvements to the general situation of the francophones, but these did not seem sufficient to correct a situation perceived as critical. For fifteen years, Quebec intellectuals had been returning to and reconsidering questions about how the francophones of the province had ended up in such an inferior position given the fact that they formed the majority. They wanted to know why this situation had led immigrants to assimilate to the English-speakers, how English had become the language of the workplace for huge parts of the population, how the growing presence of English in the environment had affected French. Furthermore, they noted that for the first time in the history of Quebec the birthrate was declining, and that this factor, along with all the other social phenomena, could only cause the continuous erosion of the ratio of francophones in Canada, and in Quebec. The Montreal region, in particular, was in danger of converting to English within a relatively short time.

These analyses had slowly trickled through to the public at large via newspapers, televised debates, and other media, so that by the end of the 1960s, the ideas had penetrated the general population and were conditioning the perceptions of a large sector of this population, especially the younger generations who were more educated and informed than ever before. The measures taken as a result of the Official Languages Act were viewed as having little effect on most of the problems considered responsible for the deterioration of the status and quality of French. They did not satisfy the demands of the Quebecois, nor did they undermine the independence movement, which now became part of the political platform of the Parti québécois, founded in October 1968.

The Commission on the condition of French and language rights in Quebec

In December 1968, a few months after Daniel Johnson died, Jean-Jacques Bertrand, leader of the Union nationale party, was in power in Quebec. There was considerable social unrest over language issues, and the scandal around the schools in Saint-Léonard was in full swing; anxiety about the survival of French was acute, making people, who were more and more irritated by the prevalence of English in the workplace, demand action from the Quebec government. But that particular government, under the influence of old Duplessis supporters, was indecisive and unaware of the extent of the movement. True, the whole era was one of unrest. In 1968 young people all over the West were protesting: in the United States the protests were against the Vietnam war; in France, where the events of May 1968 had shaken up the power structures, the protests were for a more just society. In Quebec, young people focused their particular battle on demands about language. Politicians doubtless attributed the unrest to the idealism of youth that would subside with age, but the government of Daniel Johnson had made a few promises, including the establishment of French as the "language of everyday use" in Quebec. But nothing really changed. In July 1968 a letter to the editor commented:

> It has been almost a year since the government of Quebec announced its project to make French the language of everyday use. Monsieur Jean-Noël Tremblay asked all Quebecois to act on their responsibilities, demand French everywhere, and refuse to "bow down like servants before a demanding master." The purpose of all this was to make it clear that the majority in Quebec would no longer let a minority push it around. I noted that some of the means to make French "a language of everyday use" included a) giv-

ing Quebec a French face through posting French signs and advertising, b) presenting the promotional materials on Quebec in such a way that immigrants, including those in Saint-Léonard, would know they will have to integrate into a French-speaking Quebec; c) demanding that corporations align their language policies with those of the government of Quebec. Another recommendation was that unions be pressured to include clauses about respect for the workers' language in their collective agreements. I do not see even one of these measures anywhere near being implemented.[60]

Faced with all the unrest over the schools question, the government tabled Bill 85 in December, which was to ensure the right to choose one's language of education. More unrest ensued. The government withdrew the bill and set up the Gendron Commission to enquire into the situation of French and language rights in Quebec. The idea was that this would allow the government to base its language policies on objective data. But in actual fact, Jean-Jacques Bertrand did not wait for the Commission's report in order to table his Law 63 that declared French to be the language of education in Quebec yet at the same time provided the option to attend English schools, and included no concrete measures to ensure that immigrant children be integrated into francophone society. This bill became law in November 1969, and was strongly resisted by teachers, students, unions, and nationalist milieus in general. It was not until 1974 that the government of Robert Bourassa brought in Law 22, and with it concrete measures on education, on language in the workplace, signage, labeling, and the establishment of French as the only official language of Quebec.

The Gendron Commission submitted its report in 1972, and the Bourassa government used at least some of its conclusions to develop Law 22, which defined the first real language policies in Quebec, adopting a whole series of concrete measures to respond to the demands the Quebecois had been expressing over the course of the 1960s, specifically, to make French the official language of Quebec, the language of the workplace, and the language of education. Law 22 also contained measures regarding signage and labeling, making French mandatory where English unilingualism had been the rule. Law 101, adopted in 1977 by the Lévesque government, went even further in the direction of unilingualism and contained more coercive measures in every area, some of which were later contested and had to be repealed or weakened.

Language policies in Quebec in the 1970s – via Law 22 and Law 101 – were developed under constant public pressure. Once Quebec society became aware of its socio-economic inferiority and the effects this had on the language as well as its own survival and development, it used the political instrument at hand – the provincial government – to profoundly change the conditions of its existence. To do so, collective identity had to go through an important change, a change that took place in a crisis situation, through questioning, protest, and unprecedented self-analysis.

"Lousy French"

Over the course of the 1960s, the Quebecois had progressively become aware of the relationship between the state of the language in Quebec and their socio-political position in Canada. One event that seemed rather anodyne at the time made this relationship very clear, and also set off lively reactions. Pierre Elliott Trudeau, then Minister of Justice in the Pearson government and a candidate for the leadership of the Liberal Party, declared in an interview he gave in English, broadcast in February 1968:

The French-Canadians should abandon their demands for more rights and use the powers they already have to improve the "lousy French" spoken in Quebec. I don't think Ottawa should give one single whit of power to the province of Quebec until it has shown the rest of Canada that it can teach better language in its schools.[61,62]

"Mauvais français" [poor French], "français bâtard" [bastard French], the translators had to look around for a translation of the famous "lousy French" which was finally rendered as "français pouilleux" [lousy, flea-ridden, verminous French]. The Quebecois were deeply shocked by this declaration, not so much because Trudeau described their French as "lousy" (they were used to that kind of judgment from decades of newspaper columns), but because Trudeau's statement *explicitly linked their political rights to the quality of their language*. The response was immediate, and it reversed the issue:

> Why do we need greater powers? In order to repair the damages done to the French-Canadian people (conquered in 1760) by two centuries of political and economic servitude.[63]

This point was, in fact, the focus of all the political action and pressure from public opinion over these years. The problem had been acknowledged, and it was serious. It was therefore appropriate to act to "repair the damages" and people got down to doing so. The Quebecois no longer accepted the idea that they were "to blame" for the situation they were in, for the condition of their language, their culture or their society; but it was their intention to accept the responsibility. In his response to the criticisms set off by his declaration, Trudeau referred to several others before him who had deplored the state of French in Quebec: Lionel Groulx, Victor Barbeau, Frère Untel, Paul Gérin-Lajoie, Marcel Masse, and Jean-Noël Tremblay. Julien Bigras' response in *Le Devoir* was as follows:

> This is the point where deception takes on the appearance of truth. Not one of the politicians and historians he cites ever formulated a proposal that would deprive the people of their right to speak the way they see fit, or demand what they consider their right.[64]

In the following years, the "language problem" in Quebec was to move well outside the framework of education, and determine much of the collective action. Despite the criticisms of Pierre Elliott Trudeau, the Quebec government, whether Liberal or Pequiste, ceaselessly pressed its demands to revise the Canadian constitution so that it could manage the development of Quebec society itself, and in its own interests.

1960-1970: A Summary

The decade between 1960 and 1970 was an eventful turning point for Quebec society. Over the course of this period a great change in the collective identity developed, triggered by the post-war identity crisis that had originated in changes in the conditions of life of the Quebecois. They did everything they could to rid themselves of the negative image that resulted from this crisis and that was particularly noticeable in the discourse on language in 1960. First, they had to understand how they had reached such a point, and realize that the state of their language was only the symptom of a complex social situation; then they had to identify the forces that were detrimental to francophones and assess those that existed in order to construct a positive image of the collective. The diagnosis was carried out progressively, the causes were identified, the methods to solve the problems were found and Quebec society began to take action. Although it cannot be said that a change in identity was completely in place by 1970, the process was well underway; the Quebecois no longer saw themselves as a small introverted and dominated people, threatened with extinction, and focused on its ever receding glorious past. They did not reject France, but demanded the right to their own culture, and in terms of language, they sought to actively participate in defining linguistic norms to be shared with all speakers of French in the world. Pierre Chantefort, a French linguist, who analyzed the socio-linguistic situation in 1970, described it as follows[65]:

A mixed form [of French] could be adopted, based on A with a sufficient number of borrowings from B. This is the solution that most of those responsible for policy and culture in Quebec seem to support. It combines the advantages of the first two solutions [adopt A as the norm, or a standardized form of B] without suffering the inconveniences of B; it responds to the demands of the former and will be a language that can serve as an efficient tool on the international level, endowed as it is with the undeniable prestige of the history and culture of the great country with which it is associated. It marks the specificity of Quebec by dissociating itself from English, which would not be possible if B were adopted. [. . .] Further, adopting such a form could have a unifying function given that B is so diverse. Choosing a mixed form includes the advantages of the possible second solution, while incorporating a sufficiently large number of B elements makes it possible to assert the autonomy and specificity of the local linguistic community in the face of France. This mixed form respects the general popular view that B is closer to the national feeling and the actual values of the community.[66]

In his conclusion, Chantefort stated his conviction that this mixed variety of French would prevail in Quebec; from the perspective of twenty-five years later, it appears that his prediction was correct. Quebec French has, to a certain extent, become more standardized though it maintains various specific characteristics, especially pronunciation and lexical items, elements that are no longer stigmatized like they once were. In other words, while the Quebecois have moved closer to standard French, they have given themselves the right to be different and have stopped thinking of their specific linguistic characteristics as signs of degeneration. Even though the Quebecois at the end of the twentieth century may not be totally satisfied with the state of their language, various socio-linguistic studies have shown that they no longer consider their French an unintelligible jargon or a symbol of the deterioration of their culture,[67] as the critics of *joual* in the 1960s did. This about-face in Quebecois' opinions about their language began as a result of the controversies in the 1960s. The change in perception was based on the actual transformation of the language and a rapprochement with norms of standard French, developments that date from the same period. Gradually, the crisis that marked the early years of the decade gave way to a somewhat disorderly search, via debates and quarrels, for a way out. The strategies that people discussed differed according to the analyses they made, but soon a kind of consensus emerged that the formerly individualistic approaches, such as being careful of the language you used, or demanding French for public commerce, should be exchanged for more collective, political action. In terms of identity, the phase of revalorizing the special aspects of Quebec language and culture, which at times idealized them, was followed by discourses that were aggressive toward other cultures perceived as abusively dominant. Such aggression was aimed mainly at Anglo-American culture, but also at the culture of France. The search for identity was to go on for many years more, and include many initiatives to define anything that might be specific to Quebec; hence, the vogue of folklore, antique Quebec furniture and objects, and traditional crafts, which lasted until the 1980s. Paradoxically, this vogue was part of a movement that swept through other countries of the West, with similar phenomena visible in Europe where movements to revive minority languages such as Breton and Occitan developed. Generally, in the West, young people of the 1970s reacted against the consumer society, valorizing pre-industrial objects and techniques, traditional lifestyles, etc. While the effect of international 1960s civil disobedience took a linguistic turn in Quebec, the "back to nature" vogue of the 1970s fit well with specifically Quebec traditions. If proof were needed that Quebec society has opened up to the outside world since the middle of the twentieth century, then the fact that it was swept by the same ideological currents as America and Europe would serve as a demonstration. This opening became particularly evident in the 1960s, with a large increase in international contacts, the foundation of francophone agencies, large congresses such as the "Biennale de la langue française," and the World's Fair Expo 1967.

Anxieties around language again manifested themselves on the occasion of this prestigious international event which brought thousands of foreign visitors to Montreal and Quebec. There was fear that foreign opinion might judge the Quebecois to be backward and uninformed. Numerous letters to the editor expressed such fears, and demanded that proper French be used to disseminate information via public address systems at the

Expo and in the subway. Insecurity around language remained very strong, and did not really begin to abate until the 1970s.

The decade of the 1960s was thus characterized by efforts to establish the conditions that would not only change the language itself but people's opinion of it as well. These conditions included the transformation of the school system and more education for the general public, an increase in the contacts with other francophone cultures, greater visibility of French in the environment and in the business world. Other factors played a role in improving the image that the Quebecois had of themselves, and which were reflected in the opinions they developed about their language. These factors included the economic progress made by francophones who took over increasingly large sectors of the economic activity in the province, which rid them of the subaltern status they had seemed condemned to. Thanks to the government of Quebec, they had acquired enough political clout to carry out their collective political will in certain important areas of social life; this had obvious consequences in the area of identity, at least partially erasing the impression of powerlessness that had hung over the population up until that point. The Quebecois of the 1960s rejected the resignation of the French-Canadians "born for a small loaf of bread," and henceforth demanded their fair share of the cake.

CONCLUSION

The history of the difficult relations the francophones of Quebec have had with their language since 1760, and even more so since 1867 is a perfect example of the role played by culture and socio-political conditions in the development and transformation of collective identity. The discourse on language reflects and translates the tiniest fluctuations in the structures underlying identity, fluctuations that respond to changes in the conditions of life of the collective, and its relations with other groups.

The French language and the Catholic religion that characterized the *Canadiens* who became British subjects in 1763, gradually changed from simply being the distinctive aspects of this people to become a source of anxiety, and then distress, until the moment when the discourse on language expressed a deep collective identity crisis. In examining this discourse on language, we have observed the progressive deterioration of the image the French-Canadians had of themselves and their culture from the middle of the nineteenth century onward. Generation after generation, despite moments of resistance and various small crises, this image grew more and more tarnished until it was no longer bearable, and triggered the complete restructuring of the framework on which people based their identities, a restructuring that was consecrated by the adoption of the name *Québécois* in the 1960s.

Collective action by the Quebecois since the Quiet Revolution has consisted of the systematic revalorization of language and culture, first in their own eyes, but also in regard to other groups that were important references: English-Canadians, North American society as a whole, as well as France and francophone countries in general.

To make progress in this direction, the Quebecois had to reject their minority status which more often than not condemned them to powerlessness. This move forced them to focus on the territory within the borders of Quebec and led to a break with the francophone minorities in the rest of Canada.

With regard to the texts on language published in Quebec in the twentieth century, it can be said that the measures adopted by the Canadian government to give francophones the same rights as English-Canadians (at least in letter) came at least one generation too late to prevent the break with the other francophone communities of Canada. The threat to identity had been developing over a considerable period, and it set off the post-war crisis which was marked by an exceedingly negative discourse on the French language. In the 1960s and 1970s there was a feverish sense of urgency in the search for solutions.

Almost thirty years later, while there are still occasional complaints in the newspapers about the teaching of French, or some other aspect of the French spoken in Quebec, it is obvious that the Quebecois have a much higher opinion of themselves than they once did; they no longer feel dispossessed of what characterizes them: their French language.

What image do young Quebecois born after 1970 have of themselves and their language? They have lived in conditions that were very different from those of their parents. They have inherited identity structures that have changed substantially, but are still somewhat unstable. Only research will be able to describe this situation more precisely, but it is clearly much more positive than that of young people in the 1950s.

The history of the relations French-Canadians have had with their language since 1760 is thus a long history of deterioration leading to the crisis of the 1950s and the reaction of the 1960s. And while the language itself has undergone constant change, the opinions people expressed about it have seen even more transformations.

There is no objective measure of what is good or bad in any language; we know this from linguistics and socio-linguistics. It is, therefore, impossible to discuss the almost obsessive focus on eradicating anglicisms, the emotional search for the origins of Canadian French expressions between 1910 and 1940, the post-war anxiety about language, or the excessive valorization of the working-class language in the 1970s, without also and at the same time studying the history of Quebec and Canada.

The history of French in Quebec is the history of a dominated language, and the discourse about language could be described as a discourse on identity. Whenever the Quebecois talked about their language, they described themselves. They produced self-portraits that could be rather somber, move toward caricature, or occasionally resemble a naive Epinal print or some other sentimental image. The sources of these somber or clear tones in the image painted of Quebec identity must be sought out in the living conditions, and the relations with other societies.

When we look at the strategies adopted by each generation, we see that, faced with the difficulty of exercising their language rights, the French-Canadian elite in the nineteenth century undertook attempts to close the gap with French from France in the hope that the prestige of France would support their cause. This is why it was important to "modernize" the language and prevent borrowings from English. However, by the turn of the century, when it was clear that the French-Canadians had the reputation of speaking a patois, it became urgent to legitimate the particularities of this spoken language – hence the attempts by the Société du parler français to make connections between these particular forms and the peasant dialects of France. The tendency to reject linguistic contamination became even stronger in this period, to the point where borrowings from France were seen as betrayals (which has remained the case), and the peasant class was set up as a national symbol although it was actually growing more and more marginal. After the Second World War, it became urgent to re-evaluate the situation in the face of new realities, that is, the fact that the French-Canadians had in the meantime internalized the negative image the English-Canadians assigned them. The feelings of dejection that marked this period set off the profound troubles that moved French-Canadian society for the next thirty years. We might say that the society used an axe to sculpt a new image for itself, and spent the last years of the twentieth century polishing its rough edges.

The series of identity crises and the restructuring projects these activities engendered made the French language the most important element in Quebecois' definition of themselves. The importance of the Catholic religion, on the other hand, diminished in terms of the collective identity, although it had once strongly marked the culture and the social organization. The new element that entered into the identity structure of the Quebecois was the territory of Quebec, an issue the "partitionists" understood very well. Paradoxically, the notion caused both territorial expansion and shrinkage. In relation to territory within Canada there was a decrease, but there was expansion in relation to local participation. The parish that was once an important aspect of a person's identity lost this importance though some regions or towns still fulfill this role. While the French-Canadians may once have seen themselves as a people that was isolated and closed in upon itself, which was probably only partly true, the Quebecois of the late twentieth century feel they belong fully and equally to the Western world, and participate actively in the development of the broader culture that might be called Euro-American.

What can we learn from this story about the relations between a society and its language? Among other things, but most importantly, we learn that when pressures and threats are applied to the most important element identifying a group and establishing its difference, these will end up being perceived as a grave threat to the survival of the community. This can apply to religion, ethnicity, or any other aspect that is fundamental to the identity of a collective. From the moment that a society feels its culture and survival under threat, it can undergo identity crises setting off strong reactions that are, in fact, attempts to restore cultural coherence. As the recent history of various post-colonial or minority societies has shown, such identity crises and subsequent reactions can bring on powerful tensions, even inter-ethnic conflicts. Any state that wants social peace must therefore manage the co-existence of various communities, ensuring that not one among them feels its identity threatened or denigrated.

Another important aspect of this story is that any one object or situation may give rise to various different interpretations, or be perceived very differently, depending on the circumstances. The enterprise that involved researching and glorifying the French origins of Canadian expressions which took place between 1910 and 1940 cannot be understood without reference to the denigration of the language as *French Canadian Patois*. Without these attacks, men of letters would probably have maintained the attitudes of Fréchette or Buies. Similarly, the virulent criticisms of French "anglomania" can be understood in terms of the Quebecois suffering the same cultural influences and struggling against them.

Over lengthy periods of time we can see the same word take on quite different meanings or contract different connotations that translate into changes in perception. The noun *habitant*, for example, which once designated someone who lived from the land, and which took on the meaning of "coarse ignoramus" around 1950, demonstrates how rural life lost prestige and the collective will pushed for the modernization of society.

As we saw in relation to borrowings from English, the analysis of metaphors, their occurrence, and the periods when they were in use, also allows us to enter more deeply into the collective unconscious that is expressed through discourse. The appearance of new words such as *joual*, new labels such as *Québécois*, new structures such as *au Québec* vs *dans le Québec*, the recurrence of certain terms such as *refranciser* [restore French], *recover*, the different choices involved in lexical pairs such as *compatriote/concitoyen* [compatriot/fellow citizen] or *Cession/Conquête* [Cession/Conquest] – to draw attention to one such pair I consciously exploited after it caught my attention in certain texts – all such uses of language can be decoded if the context of their use is well understood.

By analyzing newspaper columns on the subject of language, and studying their prescriptive and critical aspects, we can define the norms of the period in question, as well as their ideological and social foundations. Further, by tracing the reproaches or praises addressed to some sub-group in society, we can follow the fickle movement of social prestige – for instance, the views expressed on the language of the peasants before and after the Second World War –, and to some extent even the opinions the collective has of itself.

Take as an example the statement made by Emmanuel Blain de Saint-Aubin in 1862: "Every well-educated French-Canadian speaks his language as well as any man with the same education in France. The working class and the farmers in Canada, in general, speak much better French than the corresponding groups in France,"[1] and compare this to Jean-Marie Morin's from 1953: "From the very top to the very bottom of the social spectrum, though to differing degrees, the language spoken by French-Canadians is unbelievably impoverished and vulgar."[2]

The language spoken by French-Canadians in 1953 had, however, not changed to such an extent that this difference in judgment was justified. It is noteworthy that Blain de Saint-Aubin was from France, and that I have not been able to find any equally positive views on the quality of language in Quebec in any works written by French-Canadians. Even in the twentieth century, even among the most enthusiastic, there is always some reservation, revealing how the uncertainty about language has a long history, and is related to the fact that the linguistic norm, whether this is explicitly recognized or not, is an external norm, and that people are therefore never completely sure of their judgment.

The analysis of this meta-discourse on language in a dominated linguistic community thus makes it possible to grasp the relations this community has with others around it. In this regard, it would be interesting to compare what New Zealanders or Argentinians have to say, since they share the fate of the Quebecois in speaking a language whose norms are defined elsewhere. It might then be possible to distinguish more clearly how great a role this external factor plays in comparison to the fact that the Quebecois formed a dominated minority group. For the moment, these aspects are inextricably tangled in the discourse about language in Quebec.

The obsession with anglicisms is perhaps the best example of this confusion, since these are rejected both because they are the symptom and the symbol of domination, and because this interference could end up mixing-up the language to such an extent that it would no longer be recognizable as French – even though, paradoxically, the French of France borrows liberally from the same source. Under these circumstances it is not surprising to see journalists and commentators getting entangled in complex arguments that legitimate or condemn a certain borrowing according to lists of conditions that are more or less solidly supported, or to observe polemics erupt between them about whether the only legitimate form of French is the language described in the dictionaries published in France.

There are a number of other questions that an analysis of the language used to discuss language can clarify, questions I have only touched on. It would be interesting to study the role of dictionaries, for example. For a long time the French-Canadians considered them the only infallible reference, and believed that if a word could not be found in the dictionary it "did not exist," or "was not French." But since the 1920s, the Quebecois have been criticizing publishing houses like Larousse for incorporating borrowings from English in each new edition, ostensibly consecrating and legitimating them, borrowings that the Quebecois then refuse to use. Before 1970 this rejection of the dictionary's authority was not, however, accompanied by demands to also include Quebec expressions, which is something that lexicographers from France have been doing rather sketchily for the past thirty years.

A detailed analysis of what is said about dictionaries, or rather about *the* dictionary, since for years it was considered a sole reference, would give us a good idea of what French-Canadians viewed as linguistic legitimacy, and of the fluctuations this concept underwent, which must parallel the fluctuations in collective identity.

Similarly, what was written over the course of generations about the language of the newspapers, the radio, and then television, could supply us with the outlines of the ideal self-image that people would like to see reflected.

And finally, still in this perspective of examining the discourse about language in order to uncover the image a society has of itself, it would be interesting to do a systematic study of all the books published about language in Quebec, starting with the collection by Thomas Maguire in 1841, continuing with the works of Adjutor Rivard, Louis Geoffrion, Louvigny de Montigny, Jean-Marie Laurence, René de Chantal and many others, right up to the present. This is a huge task, and has only just begun, but it can contribute to a better understanding of how a collective identity is developed, and at the same time enhance our knowledge about contemporary Quebec society.

NOTES

Chapter I

1. See Michel Francard, Geneviève Geron and Régine Wilmet, "L'insécurité linguistique dans les communautés francophones périphériques," *Cahiers de l'Institut de linguistique de Louvain*, Vol. I, 19 (3-4), 1993, and Vol. II, 20 (1-2), 1994.

2. Carmel Camilleri, "La culture et l'identité culturelle: champ notionnel et devenir," in C. Camilleri and Margalit Cohen-Emerique (eds). *Chocs de culure: concepts et enjeux pratiques de l'interculturel*, Paris, Harmattan, 1989, 24.

3. Ibid.

4. Bertrand Badie, *Culture et politique*, Paris, Economica, 1983, 40.

5. C. Camilleri 1989, op.cit., 54.

6. Ibid., 44

7. Hanna Malewska-Peyre, "*Problèmes d'identité des adolescents enfants de migrants et travail social,*" in C. Camilleri and M. Cohen-Emerique, 1989, op.cit. 121.

8. Ibid., 124.

9. Ibid., 127.

10. Selim Abou, *L'identité culturelle: Relations interethniques et problèmes d'acculturation*, Paris, Éditions Anthropos, 1981, p. 33.

11. Ibid., p. 31.

12. Ibid., p. 33.

13. B. Badie, 1983, op.cit., p. 78.

14. Ibid., p. 78

15. Ibid., p. 120

16. Ibid., p. 128.

17. Ibid., p. 130.

18. Guy Rocher and Fernand Dumont, "Introduction à une sociologie du Canada français," [1961], in Marcel Rioux and Yves Martin, ed., *La société canadienne-française*, Montreal, Hurtubise HMH, 1971, p. 195.

Chapter II

1. Translator's note: The transfer of New France into the hands of the British after the battle on the Plains of Abraham is normally called "the Conquest" in English. A French term "la Conquête" also exists. However, since the author deliberately uses the term

"la Cession," I translate accordingly – sometimes using the verb "to cede" or the rarer English noun "cession."

2. Philippe Barbaud, *Le choc des patois en Nouvelle-France*, Quebec, Presses de l'Université du Québec, 1984.
3. See P. Barbaud, 1984, for a detailed discussion of these questions. Critical voices include Claire Asselin and Anne McLaughlin, "Les immigrants en Nouvelle-France au XVIIe siècle parlaient-ils français?" in Raymond Mougeon and Edouard Beniak, *Les origines du français québécois*, Sainte-Foy, Presses de l'Université Laval, 1994.
4. See Raymond Mougeon and Edouard Beniak, op.cit.
5. Yves-Charles Morin, "Les sources historiques de la prononciation du français du Quebec," in R. Mougeon and E. Beniak, 1994, op.cit., 199-236.
6. Marcel Juneau, *Contribution à l'histoire de la prononciation française au Québec. Etude des graphies des documents d'archives*, Quebec, Presses de l'Université Laval, 1972. See also Claude Poirier, Aurélien Boivin, Cécyle Trépanier and Claudette Verreault (eds.) *Langue, espace, société. Les variétés de français en Amérique du nord*, Sainte-Foy, Presses de l'Université Laval, 1994.
7. See Gaston Dulong, *Bibliographie linguistique du Canada français*, Quebec/Paris, Presses de l'Université Laval, Klincksieck, 1996, for citations from these accounts.
8. Vaugelas, *Remarques sur la langue française*, 1647.
9. See Marthe Faribault, "L'apios tubéreux d'Amérique: histoire de mots," *Recherches amérindiennes au Québec*, vol. XXI, 3, 1991, 65-75, for a detailed case study of one such point.
10. Dominique Bouchard, "La culture matérielle des Canadiens au XVIIIe siècle: analyse du niveau de vie des artisans de fer," *Revue d'histoire d'Amérique française*,vol. 47, 4, printemps 1994, 479-498.

Chapter III

1. Marcel Rioux, "Notes sur le développement socio-culturel du Canada français" (1959), in M. Rioux and Y. Martin, 1971, op.cit., 181.
2. Hubert Guindon, "Réexamen de l'évolution social au Québec" (1960), in M. Rioux and Y. Martin, 1971, op.cit., 153.
3. "Francis Masère, *Considérations sur la nécessité de faire voter un acte par le Parlement pour régler les difficultés survenues dans la*

province de Québec (1766), in G. Bouthiller and J. Meynaud, 1972, op.cit., 102.

4. Jean-Charles Falardeau, "La paroisse canadienne-française au XVIIe siècle," in M. Rioux and Y. Martin, 1971, op.cit., 42.

5. Gérald Fortin, "Les changements culturels dans une paroisse agricole"(1961), in M. Rioux and Y. Martin, 1971, op.cit., 105.

6. Alexis de Toqueville, *Voyage en Sicile et aux États-Unis* (1831), in G. Bouthiller and J. Meynaud, 1972, op.cit. 143.

7. *The Durham Report*, excerpted from *Lord Durham's Report* (3 Vols.). ed. C.P. Lucas, Oxford, 1912 at www.ola.bc.ca/online/cf/documents/1838DurhamReport.html, accessed November 28, 2005.

8. Ibid., p.154.

9. John Lambert, *Travels through Canada and the United States of America in the years 1806, 1807 and 1808,* in G. Bouthillier and J. Meynaud 1972, op.cit., 123.

10. Alexis de Toqueville, op.cit., in G. Bouthillier and J. Meynaud, 1972, 143.

11. Michel Bibeau, *Épitres, Satires, Chansons, Épigrammes et Autres Pièces en Vers* [1830], in D. Noël, 1990, op.cit., 151.

12. Emmanuel Blain de Saint-Aubin, "Quelques mots sur la littérature canadienne-française," [1871], in G. Bouthillier and J. Meynaud, 1972, op.cit., 166.

13. "Enseignement de l'anglais dans les écoles primaries," *La Semaine*, 1864, in G. Bouthillier and J. Meynaud, 1972. op.cit., 173.

14. Thomas-Aimé Chardonnet, speech for Saint-Jean-Baptiste in Quebec City, 1865, from G. Bouthiller and J. Meynaud, 1972, op.cit., p. 188-189.

Chapter IV

1. Translator's note: "scieurs de bois et porteurs d'eau" shortened to "porteurs d'eau" is the translation of a comment the English writer Anthony Trollope made about the French-Canadians when he visited Quebec in 1861. He described them as "hewers of wood and drawers of water." The term was taken up in Quebec newspapers in order to be criticized and rejected. From Claude Poirier, *Le Mot de la Semaine*, chronique linguistique du TLFQ, Vol. 1, No. 2, p.1, 1997.

2. Everett C. Hughes, "L'industrie et le système rural au Quebec," [1938], in M. Rioux and Y. Martin, 1971, op.cit., p. 94.

3. Jean-Charles Falardeau, "L'évolution de nos structures sociales," [1953], in M. Rioux and Y. Martin, 1971, op.cit., p. 125.

4. Jacques Henripin, "De la fécondité naturelle à la prevention des naissances: l'évolution démographique du Canada français depuis le XVIIe siècle," in M. Rioux and Y. martin, 1971, op.cit., p. 221.

5. Albert Faucher and Maurice Lamontagne, "L'histoire du développement industriel au Québec," in M. Rioux and Y. Martin, 1971, op.cit., p. 267.

6. Horace Miner, "Le changement dans la culture rurale canadienne-française," [1938], in M. Rioux and Y. Martin, 1971, op.cit., p. 84.

7. A. Faucher and M. Lamontagne, [1953], in M. Rioux and Y. Martin, 1971, op.cit., p. 265.

8. Hubert Guindon, "Réexamen de l'évolution sociale au Québec," [1960], in M. Rioux and Y. Martin, 1971, op.cit., p. 165.

9. Jean-Charles Falardeau, "L'évolution de nos structures sociales," [1953], in M. Rioux and Y. Martin, 1971, op.cit., p. 130.

10. Léon Guérin, "La famille canadienne-française, sa force, ses faiblesses," [1932], in M. Rioux and Y. Martin, 1971, op.cit., p. 46.

11. Mgr. Louis Laflèche, speech on Saint-Jean-Baptiste Day, [1866], in G. Bouthillier and J. Meynaud, 1972, op.cit., p. 191.

12. Oscar Dunn, speech given in Montreal, October 14, 1870, in G. Bouthiller and J. Meynaud, 1972, op.cit., p. 199.

13. Jules-Paul Tardivel, "La langue française au Canada," *Revue canadienne*, Montreal, Vol. I, 1881, in G. Bouthillier and J. Meynaud, 1972, op.cit., p. 259-267.

14. Jules-Paul Tardivel, "L'imbroglio de Fall Rivers," *La Vérité*, January 3, 1885, see G. Bouthillier and J. Meynaud, 1972. op.cit., p. 403.

15. Jules-Paul Tardivel, "La langue française au Canada," *Revue canadienne*, Montreal, 1881, in G. Bouthillier and J. Meynaud, 1972, op.cit., p. 259-267.

16. Esdras Minville, "L'éducation nationale. Le choc en retour de l'anglomanie," [1934], in G. Bouthillier and J. Meynaud, 1972, op.cit., p. 473.

17. "Enseignement de l'anglais dans les écoles primaries," *La Semaine* [1864], in G. Bouthillier and J. Meynaud, 1972, op.cit., p. 173.

18. Questionnaire of the ACJC [1922], in G. Bouthillier and J. Meynaud, 1972, op.cit, p. 431. My emphasis.

19. Adélard Desjardins, *Plaidoyer d'un anglicisant,* [1935], in G. Bouthillier and J. Meynaud, 1972, op.cit., p. 491.
20. Ibid.
21. Fulgence Charpentier, "L'Anglomanie," [1924], in G. Bouthillier and J. Meynaud, 1972, op.cit., p. 437.
22. Arthur Buies, *Anglicismes et Canadianismes,* [1881], n G. Bouthillier and J. Meynaud, 1972, op.cit., p. 231.

Chapter V

1. Ernest Gagnon, "Notre langue," [1802], reprinted in *Le Devoir,* February 12, 1916.
2. Arthur Buies, *Anglicismes et canadianismes,* [1888], in G. Bouthillier and J. Meynaud, 1972, op.cit., p. 231.
3. Ibid., p. 229.
4. Jules-Paul Tardivel, "La langue française au Canada," *La Patrie,* February 7, 1880.
5. Louis Fréchette, column entitled "A travers le dictionnaire et la grammaire" [From dictionary to grammar book], *La Patrie,* August 4, 1874.
6. Louis Tesson, "La langue française au Canada," *La Patrie,* July 18, 1893.
7. Jules-Paul Tardivel, lecture at the Union catholique of Montreal, March 10, 1901, in G. Bouthillier and J. Meynaud, 1972, op.cit., p. 91.
8. Edouard Fabre-Surveyer, "Une vieille question," *La Revue canadienne,* January 1903, in G. Bouthillier and J. Meynaud, 1972, op.cit., p. 307.
9. William Henry Drummond, *The Habitant and other French-Canadian Poems,* G. P. Putnam's Sons, New York and London, 1897, p.1.
10. D. Noël, 1990, op.cit., p. 314.
11. Etienne Parent, [1842], in D. Noël, 1990, op.cit., p. 311.
12. Jules-Paul Tardivel, "La langue française au Canada," lecture held March 10, 1901, in G. Bouthillier and J. Meynaud, 1972, op.cit., p. 294.
13. Narcisse-Henri Edouard Faucher de Saint-Maurice, *Honni soit qui mal y pense,* [1892], in G. Bouthillier and J. Meynaud, 1972, op.cit., p. 281.
14. Napoléon Legendre, *La langue française au Canada,* Quebec, Daveau, 1890.
15. J. Guéras [pseudonym of Albert Lefaivre], *La France canadienne. La question religieuse. Les races française et anglo-saxonne,*

[1877], in G. Bouthillier and J. Meynaud, 1972, op.cit., p. 203.

16. Alexis de Toqueville, *Voyages en Sicile et aux États-Unis*, [1831], in G. Bouthillier and J. Meynaud, 1972, op.cit., p. 143.

17. Mgr. Louis Laflèche, *Oeuvres oratories*, [1866], in G. Bouthillier and J. Mynaud, 1972, op.cit., p. 192.

18. Pierre-Joseph-Olivier Chauveau, *François-Xavier Garneau, sa vie, ses oeuvres*, [1883], in G. Bouthillier and J. Meynaud, 1972, op.cit., p. 218.

19. Arthur Buies, *Anglicismes et canadianismes*, [1988], in G. Bouthillier and J. Meynaud, 1972, op.cit., p. 231.

20. Jules-Paul Tardivel, *La langue française au Canada*, [1901], in G. Bouthillier and J. Meynaud, 1972, op.cit., p. 295.

21. Édouard Fabre-Surveyer, "Une vieille question," *La Revue canadienne*, January 1903, in G. Bouthillier and J. Meynaud, 1972, op.cit., p. 306.

Chapter VI

1. Albert Lévesque, *La nation canadienne-française, son existence, ses droits, ses devoirs*, [1934], in G. Bouthillier and J. Meynaud, 1972, op.cit., p. 456.

2. Lionel Groulx, "La soirée de francisation à la Palestre nationale," *Le Devoir*, April 20, 1933.

3. Philippe Ferland, "Campagne de refrancisation," *Le Devoir*, August 4, 1933.

4. Omer Héroux, *Le Devoir*, February 24, 1934.

5. Omer Héroux, "La manifestation d'hier," *Le Devoir*, January 24, 1916.

6. Henri Bourassa, "La langue gardienne de la foi," speech held November 29, 1918, in G. Bouthillier and J. Meynaud, 1972, op.cit., p. 413-414.

7. Olivar Asselin, *Pensée française*, text published in *L'Étudiant*, student newspaper at Université Laval, in 1915, in G. Bouthillier and J. Meynaud, 1972, op.cit., p. 365.

8. Ibid., p. 363.

9. Jules-Paul Tardivel, "La langue française au Canada," speech held March 10, 1901, in G. Bouthillier and J. Meynaud, 1972, op.cit., p. 294-296; *Le Devoir*, June 22, 1912.

10. See note 7.

11. Anonymous, "La langue de Corneille," *La Patrie*, November 7, 1928.

12. Léon Lorrain, " La grande pitié du français au Canada," *Le Devoir*, January 18, 1930.

13. Anonymous, "Notre langue," (*L'Évènement*, Quebec), *La Patrie*, October 31, 1927.

14. Jacques Dofny and Marcel Rioux, "Les classes sociales au Canada français," [1962], in M. Rioux and Y. Martin, 1971, op. cit., p. 317.

15. Louis Lalande, "Le patois canadien," *Le Devoir*, December 3, 1910.

16. C.-H.-P. Gauldrée-Boileau, cited from *Le Devoir*, June 22, 1912.

17. Édouard Montpetit, "La langue qui se souvient," *La Patrie*, May 15, 1924.

18. Louis-Philippe Geoffrion, "La langue de nos paysans," *Le Devoir*, February 6, 1926.

19. Anonymous. "Bloc-notes. Le parler populaire," *Le Devoir*, December 3, 1932.

20. Marcel Juneau, *Contribution à l'histoire de la pronunciation française au Québec. Étude des graphies des documents d'archives*, Quebec, Presses de l'Université Laval, 1972.

21. A. Saint-Pierre, "Le Bas-Saint-Laurent, pays historique," radio-talk reprinted in *Le Devoir*, October 14, 1939.

22. Étienne Blanchard, "Chronique du Bon Langage," *La Presse*, January 25, 1919.

23. Hélène Bourgeois-Gielen, "L'usage du français au parlement belge, évolution depuis 1830," *Actes du XIIIe congrès international de linguistique et de philologie romanes*, Université Laval 29/8 – 5/9/1976, Sainte-Foy, Presses de l'Université Laval, 1976, II: 41-59.

24. Louis-Arthur Richard, "La langue que nous parlons," *La Revue trimestrielle canadienne*, February 1919, in G. Bouthillier and J. Meynaud, 1972, op.cit., p. 427.

25. Louis Dupire, "A propos du French Canadian Patois," *Le Devoir*, August 1, 1927.

26. Louis Lalande, "Le patois canadien," *Le Devoir*, December 3, 1910.

27. Jacques Clément, column "À travers les mots," *La Presse*, April 17, 1937.

28. Paul Lefranc, column, "Autour de la langue française," *La Presse*, March 5, 1921.

29. Mgr. Bruchesi, speech, "Mgr. Bruchesi demande le respect et l'amour des Canadiens français pour leur langue maternelle, " *La Patrie*, June 27, 1912.

30. Étienne Blanchard, "Chronique du Bon Langage," *La Presse*, June 22, 1918.

31. Anonymous, "Le patois ontarien," *La Patrie*, January 20, 1921.

32. Anonymous, "Langue ou patois?" *La Patrie*, October 22, 1946.

33. Omer Héroux, *Le Devoir*, November 25, 1919. An excerpt of the French text by Louis-Arthur Richard is included in G. Bouthillier and J. Meynaud, 1972, op.cit., p. 426-428.

34. The following articles are concerned: Étienne Blanchard, "Chronique du Bon langage," *La Presse*, January 25, 1919. Paul Lefranc, column "Autour de la language française,"*La Presse*, May 25, 1920, June 12, 1920, August 2, 1920 and December 4, 1920; Alfred J. Trudel, "Parisian French torontonien," *Le Devoir*, March 15, 1922; Léo E. Pariseau, reader, "Du Parisian French… en vers," *Le Devoir*, March 15, 1922, "Découverte de l'inventeur du *Parisian French* par le docteur Léo Pariseau," *Le Devoir*, December 2, 1931; Albert Alain, "À propos de parler," *Le Devoir*, October 11, 1938.

35. Paul Lefranc, column "Autour de la langue française," *La Presse*, December 4, 1920.

36. Alfred J. Trudel, "Parisian French torontonien," *Le Devoir*, March 15, 1922.

37. Léo E. Pariseau, reader. "Découverte de l'inventeur du Parisian French par le docteur Léo Pariseau," *Le Devoir*, December 2, 1931.

38. Louis Lalande, "Le patois canadien," *Le Devoir*, December 3, 1910. Omer Héroux, "Do the French-Canadians speak patois?" *Le Devoir*, November 25, 1919. Paul Lefranc, column "Autour de la langue française," *La Presse*, March 5, 1921. Louis Dupire, "À propos du *French canadian Patois*," *Le Devoir*, August 1, 1927. G.P., "Bon à savoir," *Le Devoir*, May 22, 1928.

39. Omer Héroux, "Do the French-Canadians speak patois?" *Le Devoir*, November 25, 1919.

40. G.P., "Bon à savoir," *Le Devoir*, May 22, 1928.

41. France Ariel, *Canadiens et Americains chez eux,* Granger frères, Montreal, 1920, p. 76, cited by Paul Lefranc, column "Autour de la langue française," *La Presse*, February 26, 1921.

42. Anonymous, "Le patois," *Le Devoir*, May 24, 1939.

43. Paul Lefranc, column "Autour de la langue française," *La Presse*, March 27, 1920.

44. Anonymous, "Le bon parler à la section Notre-Dame," *La Presse*, April 17, 1937.

45. Jacques Clément, column "Autour de la langue française," *La Presse*, April 17, 1937.

46. Léo E. Pariseau, letter to the editor, "Encore le patois canadien," *Le Devoir*, January 11, 1930.

47. Étienne Blanchard, "Notre parler, pourquoi les Anglais en pensent tant de mal," *Le Devoir*, July 28, 1918.

48. Louis-Philippe Geoffrion, "Le parler populaire de chez-nous [*sic*], *Le Devoir*, June 9, 1928.

49. Étienne Blanchard, column, "Canadian Patois: quelques documents," *Le Devoir*, July 26, 1918.

50. Léo E. Pariseau, letter to the editor, "Encore le patois canadien," *Le Devoir*, June 11, 1930.

51. A savage, letter to the editor, "Ça devient en ... zutant!" *Le Devoir*, November 6, 1918.

52. Anonymous, "Parlons mieux," *La Patrie*, November 19, 1930.

53. Omer Héroux, "Do the French Canadians speak Patois?" *Le Devoir*, November 25, 1919.

54. Léo E. Pariseau, Letter to the editor, "Encore le patois canadien," *Le Devoir*, June 11, 1930.

55. Omer Héroux, "Do the French Canadians speak Patois?" *Le Devoir*, July 26, 1918.

56. Anonymous, "Thaw et le patois canadien," *La Patrie*, September 30, 1913.

57. Anonymous, "France et Canada," *La Patrie*, July 15, 1922.

58. Anonymous, "M. Montpetit à Bruxelles," speech held at the Royal Academy of Belgium, reprinted in *Le Devoir*, May 10, 1924.

59. Paul Lefranc, column, "Autour de la langue française," *La Presse*, March 20, 1920.

6059. Céram Versant, letter to the editor, "La question du français," *Le Devoir*, December 24, 1918.

61. Anonymous, "Bloc-notes: Une crise?" *Le Devoir*, May 15, 1924.

62. G.P., "Rien qu'en anglais?" *Le Devoir*, May 14, 1921.

63. Fred Pelletier, "Parlons bon français!" *Le Devoir*, March 4, 1912.

64. Philippe Ferland, "Campagne de refrancisation," *Le Devoir*, August 4, 1933.

65. Léon Lorrain, *La valeur économique du fran*çais, Montreal, *L'Action française*, [1919], in G. Bouthillier and J. Meynaud, 1972, op.cit., p. 419.

66. Noël P. Deschamps, "Anglicisé?" *Le Devoir*, December 28, 1922.

67. Esdras Minville, "L'Education nationale. Le choc en retour de l'anglomanie," *L'Action Nationale*, Vol. III, 1934, in G. Bouthillier and J. Meynaud, 1972, op.cit., p. 466.

68. Étienne Blanchard, "Chronique du Bon Langage," *La Presse*, May 10, 1919.

69. Paul Lefranc, column, "Autour de la langue française," *La Presse*, March 20, 1920.

70. Paul Anger, "Le français à Paris," *Le Devoir*, May 19, 1928.

71. Théophile Hudon, *Le Devoir*, November 26, 1934.

72. Jacques Clément, column "Ls mots sans passeport," *La Presse*, June 29, 1935.

73. E. de Saint-Auban, (*La semaine littéraire*), "Les volontés du dictionnaire," *Le Devoir*, September 21, 1912.

74. G. P., "Mots étrangers," *Le Devoir*, October 15, 1931.

75. J. Poirier, "L'invasion des mots étrangers," *La Presse*, November 10, 1934.

76. Jacques Clément, column "À travers les mots," *La Presse*, October 12, 1935.

77. Paul Anger, "Le français à Paris," *Le Devoir*, May 19, 1928.

78. Anonymous, "M. Montpetit à Bruxelles," speech published in *Le Devoir*, May 15, 1924.

79. Frans Ansel, "Le français au Canada," *La Revue générale de Bruxelles*, republished in *La Patrie*, September 9, 1924.

80. Anonymous, "Notre parler," *La Patrie*, September 9, 1924.

81. Théophile Hudon, "Le terroir," *Le Devoir*, November 26, 1934.

82. Adélard Desjardins, *Le plaidoyer d'un anglicisant*, [1934 or 1935], in G. Bouthillier and J. Meynaud, 1972, op.cit., p. 492.

83. Dick, "En garde!" *La Presse*, March 15, 1913.

84. François Hertel, L'Éducation du patriotisme par la langue, *Le Devoir*, January 14, 1941.

85. Paul Anger, "Le français à Paris," *Le Devoir*, May 19, 1928.

86. Victor Barbeau, "Notre langue," speech held on October 22, 1935, in G. Bouthillier and J. Meynaud, 1972, op.cit., p. 486.

87. Jacques Clément, column, "A travers les mots," *La Presse*, October 12, 1935.

88. Étienne Blanchard, "Chronique du Bon Langage," *La Presse*, May 24, 1919.

89. Jacques Clément, column, "Les mots sans passeport," *La Presse*, October 12, 1935.

90. G. B., "Le gout de l'anglais," *Le Devoir*, December 25, 1943.

91. Étienne Blanchard, "Chronique du Bon Langage," *La Presse*, May 10, 1919.

92. Jacques Clément, column, "Les mots sans passport," *La Presse*, October 12, 1935.

93. N. Degagné, cited in G.P., "Anglomanie," *Le Devoir*, June 30, 1927.

Chapter VII

1. Jean-Charles Falardeau, "L'évolution de nos structures sociales," *Essais sur le Québec contemporain*, Presses de l'Université Laval, 1953, in M. Rioux and Y. Martin, 1971, op.cit., 126.

2. Alain Grandbois, "N'attendons pas les veines se vident," *Bulletin des études françaises*, Montreal, Collège Stanislas, no. 18, March-April, 1944.

3. Gerald Fortin, "Les changements socio-culturels dans une paroisse agricole," [1961], in M. Rioux and Y. Martin, 1971, op.cit., p. 110.

4. Ibid., p. 112.

5. Jean-Claude Falardeau, "L'évolution de nos structures sociales," *Essais sue le Québec contemporain*, Presses de l'Université Laval, 1953, in M. Rioux and Y. Martin, 1971, op.cit., p. 124. In 1951, it was 17%.

6. Adélard Desjardins, *Le plaidoyer d'un anglicisant*, [1934 or 1935], in G. Bouthillier and J. Meynaud, 1972, op.cit., 493-494.

7. Lucien Parizeau, "Deux manières d'être des 'coloniaux.' Pour un nationalisme français." *L'Ordre*, April 26, 1934, in G. Bouthillier and J. Meyraud, 1972, op.cit., p. 480.

8. Jean-Charles Falardeau, "L'évolution de nos structures sociales," *Essais sur le Québec contemporain*, Presses de l'Université Laval, 1953, in M. Rioux and Y. Martin, 1971, op.cit., p. 129.

9. Fernand Dumont and Guy Rocher, *Le Canada français aujourd'hui et demain*," Paris, 1961, in M. Rioux and Y. Martin, 1971, op.cit., p. 189.

10. Pierre Baillargeon, column "Quelle langue parlons-nous?" *La Patrie*, October 26, 1947.

11. Germaine Bernier, "Les livres: *Écrasons le perroquet*, par Louvigny de Montigny," *Le Devoir*, July 23, 1949.

12. Roger Duhamel, column "Le français en péril," *La Patrie*, April 17, 1953.

13. Jean-Marie Morin, "Propos sur l'éducation," *La Presse*, May 23, 1953.

14. André Laurendeau, "La langue que nous parlons," *Le Devoir*, October 17, 1958.

15. Pierre Baillargeon, column "Le patrimoine français dans notre pays," *La Patrie*, June 29, 1947.

16. Anonymous, "Le parler français au Canada," *Le Devoir*, February 12, 1942.

17. Pierre Baillargeon, column "La survivance française," *La Patrie*, September 14, 1947.

18. Jean-Marie Laurence, column "Paysan, mon frère…" *Le Devoir*, February 8, 1943.

19. L. Gray, "Une forme de patriotisme, l'épuration de la langue," *La Patrie*, June 20, 1946.

20. Pierre Baillargeon, column "Mélanges; l'erreur des regionalistes," *La Patrie*, November 16, 1947.

21. Roger Duhamel, column, "Le parler français," *La Patrie*, December 22, 1944.

22. Jean-Marie Laurence, column "L'anglicisme, problème social," *La Presse*, June 22, 1957.

23. Ibid.

24. Pierre de Grandpré, "*Chroniques de français* de René de Chantal," *Le Devoir*, May 19, 1952.

25. Roger Duhamel, column "Le parler canadien," *Le Devoir*, September 19, 1942.

26. Jacques Brazeau, "Différences linguistiques et carrières," [1958], in M. Rioux and Y. Martin, 1971, op.cit., p. 308-309.

27. Anonymous, "Langue ou patois?" *La Patrie*, October 22, 1946.

28. Jacques Clément, column, "À travers les mots," *La Presse*, February 11, 1950.

29. Jean-Marc Léger, "Le parler des Canadians français reste véritablement du français," *La Presse* , February 17, 1951.

30. P.S., "Notre français," *Le Devoir*, April 27, 1954.

31. Jacques Clément, column, "À travers les mots," *La Presse*, February 11, 1950.

32. Roger Duhamel, column, "Mesure opportune," *La Patrie*, December 22, 1944.

33. A. Tousignant, "La maîtrise de notre langue," *Le Devoir*, May 30, 1959.

34. Léon Lorrain, from his acceptance speech at the Société royale, cited in P. Baillargeon, column, "Quelle langue parlons-nous?" *La Patrie*, October 26, 1947.

35. Pierre Daviault, "La langue, facteur capital du progrès intellectuel d'un people, la mauvaise qualité de notre français, une menace," *La Presse*, June 22, 1956.

36. Pierre Baillargeon, column, "L'erreur des regionalists," *La Patrie*, November 16, 1947.

37. M.P., "Remarques sur nos écrivains et la langue française," *Le Devoir*, August 21, 1957.

38. Rex Desmarchais, "Notre language," *Amérique française*, Vol. 7, No. 1 Sept.-Nov. 1948, p. 14, from G. Bouthillier and J. Meynaud, 1972, op.cit., p. 582.

39. Anonymous, "Littérature 'peuple', Jean-Marie Laurence responds to Grignon," *Le Devoir*, March 10, 1949.

40. Pierre de Grandpré, "Notre langue littéraire; accentuer l'indigénisme linguistique ou tendre à plus d'universalisme?" *Le Devoir*, April 12, 1950.

41. M.P., "Remarques sur nos écrivains et la langue française, *Le Devoir*, August 21, 1957.

Chapter VIII

1. This is the text of a conference presentation at ACFAS on the representation of norms, May 2001. It was published in the conference proceedings as "L'histoire de la norme au Québec; Les relais du métadiscours," *Langue et société*, No. 39, 2002, 25-31.
2. Pierre Joseph Thoulier d'Olivet, *Essais de grammaire*, Paris, 1732.
3. See Claude Poirier, "Une langue qui se définit dans l'adversité," in *Le Français au Québec, 400 ans d'histoire et de vie*, Michel Plourde, ed., Montreal, Fides/Les publications du Québec, 2000, 120-122.
4. Cyprien, *La Patrie*, October 14, 1882.
5. Cyprien, *La Patrie*, May 25, 1895.
6. Étienne Blanchard, *La Presse*, January 25, 1919.
7. Guy Bouthillier and Jean Meynaud, *Le choc des langues au Québec, 1760-1970*, Montreal, Presses de l'Université du Québec, 1972, p. 294-296.
8. Louis-Philippe Geoffrion, "Le parler populaire de chez nous," *Le Devoir*, June 9, 1928.
9. Anonymous, "M. Montpetit à Bruxelles," speech reprinted in *Le Devoir*, May 15, 1924.
10. Alphonse Lusignan, "Empaillée," *La Patrie*, July 17, 1880.
11. France Ariel, *Canadiens et Américains chez eux*, Granger frères, Montreal 1920.
12. Paul LeFranc, column "Autour de la langue française," *La Presse*, March 9, 1921.
13. Étienne Blanchard, *La Presse*, August 10, 1950.
14. Gérard Dagenais, column "Réflexions sur nos façons d'écrire et de parler; provincialisme et anglomanie," *Le Devoir*, April 27, 1959.

Chapter IX

1. Frère Untel (Jean-Paul Desbiens), letter to the editor, "Je trouve désespérant d'enseigner le français," *Le Devoir*, November 3, 1959.
2. Jean-Paul Desbiens, *Les insolences d'un frère Untel*, Montreal, Les Editions de l'Homme, 1960.
3. Ibid., p. 25.
4. Paul Daoust, "Les jugements sur le *joual* (1959-1975) à la lumière de la linguistique et de la sociolinguistique," doctoral thesis, Université de Montréal, Département de linguistique et philologie, 1983.

5. André Laurendeau, "Bloc-notes. On parle *joual* depuis longtemps," *Le Devoir*, September 19, 1960.

6. Paul Daoust, 1983, op.cit., p. 13-14.

7. André Laurendeau, "Qu"est-ce que parler joual?" *Le Devoir*, Jan.20,1961.

8. Germaine Bernier, "La femme au foyer et dans le monde. Le comique et le tragique de la situation ne sont pas toujours où l'on croit," *Le Devoir*, January 14, 1961.

9. André Thivierge, letter to the editor, "Un défenseur du *'joual'*," *Le Devoir*, January 13, 1961.

10. Wilfrid Martin, letter to the editor, "Du 'naturel' au *'joual'*," *Le Devoir*, January 25, 1961.

11. Jean-Marc Léger, "La situation de la langue parlée au Canada français," *Le Devoir*, August 18, 1960.

12. This text is the shortened version of my article entitled "L'Office de la langue française, une naissance tant attendue," *Terminogramme*, No. 101-102, 2001, p. 11-16.

13. For the chronology, see *Le français au Québec, 400 ans d'histoire et de vie*. Michel Plourde, ed., Montreal, Fides/Les publications du Québec, 2000.

14. Gérard Filion, "On a le français qu'on mérite," Montreal, *Le Devoir*, July 29, 1959.

15. Pierre Laporte, "Une offensive de bon langage," Montreal, *Le Devoir*, August 3, 1959.

16. Jean-Paul Desbiens (Frère Untel), letter to the editor, "Je trouve désespérant d'enseigner le français," *Le Devoir*, November 3, 1959.

17. J.P. "Dire ou ne pas dire," *La Presse*, January 16, 1960.

18. Anonymous, "L'objectif de la Commission de la langue parlée. Un langage simple et naturel: non pas celui d'un academician," *La Presse*, January 30, 1961.

19. Gérard Dagenais, "Dirigisme nécessaire," *Le Devoir*, September 13, 1960.

20. Gérard Filion, "Le règne du *joual*-vapeur," *Le Devoir*, November 23, 1960.

21. Gérard Dagenais, column "Réflexons sur nos façons d'écrire et de parler," *Le Devoir, April 18, 1960.*

22. Gaëtan Côté, letter to the editor, "Un langage parlé qui n'est point risible," *Le Devoir*, January 27, 1961.

23. W. Martin, letter to the editor, "La qualité de notre français," *La Presse*, January 25, 1961.

24. B. Longpré, letter to the editor, "Nos bons "habitants," *La Presse*, February 6, 1961.

25. Anonymous, "Définition du *"joual"*: langage du proletariat haïtien ou montréalais," *La Presse*, April 7, 1962.

26. André Laurendeau, "Les Angry young men," *Le Devoir*, November 11, 1961.

27. Jean-Louis Fortin, letter to the editor, "Le français langue prioritaire," *La Presse*, February 2, 1961.

28. G. Champagne, letter to the editor, "L'anglomanie," *Le Devoir*, August 23, 1963.

29. A.G., letter to the editor, "Anglicisation," *La Presse*, January 16, 1962.

30. Alain Bouchard, letter to the editor, "L'anglicisation du Québec," *Le Devoir*, January 15, 1964.

31. Fernand Ouellette, "Le Québec et la lutte des langues," *Liberté*, Vol. 6, No. 2, April 1964.

32. Marie-Andrée Beaudet, *Langue et littérature au Québec, 1895-1914*, Montreal, Hexagon, 1991, p. 147.

33. Fernand Dumont and Jean-Charles Falardeau (eds.) "Une enquête: le statut de l'écrivain et la diffusion de la literature," in *Littérature et société canadienne-française*, 2nd Conference of *Recherches sociographiques*, Sainte-Foy, Presses de l'Université Laval, 1964, p. 87.

34. Fernand Ouellette, "La lutte des langues et la dualité du langage," *Liberté*, Vol. 6, No. 2, April 1964.

35. Jacques Brault, "Le *joual:* moment historique ou "aliénation linguistique?" *Le Devoir*, October 30, 1965.

36. Jacques Godbout, "Une raison d'écrire," *Le Devoir*, October 30, 1965.

37. Jacques Ferron, "Le langage présomptueux," *Le Devoir*, October 30, 1965.

38. Gilles Lefèbvre, "Faut-il miser sur le *joual?*" *Le Devoir*, October 30, 1965.

39. Claude Jasmin, "Malgré les événements, nous n'irons pas en exile aux terrasses de Paris," *Le Devoir*, June 19, 1965.

40. Marcel Dubé, "La difficulté de se servir d'une langue à moitié usuelle," *La Presse*, October 5, 1968.

41. Gérard Dagenais, column, "Québec doit être une province française," *Le Devoir*, April 18, 1960.

42. Lyse Nantais, "Roger Lemelin: mon succès est intolérable à bien des gens," *Le Devoir*, March 4, 1961.

43. Monique Leblanc, letter to the editor, "Bien faire et bien dire," *La Presse*, March 2, 1961.

44. Empédocle, column, "À la fortune du mot," *Le Devoir*, January 27, 1962.

45. Étienne Charron, letter to the editor, "Notre langue un peu naïve," *La Presse*, May 4, 1960.

46. Jean-Éthier Blais, "*Parlez-vous franglais?*, *Le Devoir*, April 18, 1964.

47. Alain Pontaut, "La 2eme Biennale de la langue française. Le monde francophone vient à la rencontre du Québec," *La Presse*, September 6, 1967. The citation comes from the weekly magazine *Carrefour*.

48. Pierre Olivier, "La creation d'un Conseil international de la langue française serait annoncée à l'issue de la Biennale du Québec," *La Presse*, September 8, 1967.

49. Louis Beaupré, letter to the editor, "Pour assurer l'évolution normale de notre langue," *La Presse*, February 29, 1968.

50. François Barbeau, "Le comité linguistique de Radio-Canada: le français universel doit être la langue d'usage ici," *Le Devoir*, December 13, 1969.

51. Cahiers de l'OLF No.1, ministère des Affaires culturelles du Québec, 1965.

52. *Rapport du Comité interministériel sur l'enseignement des langues aux Néo-Canadiens*, January 27, 1967, in G. Bouthillier and J. Meynaud, 1972, op.cit., p. 700-710.

53. Georges Neroy, letter to the editor, "Anglicisation," *Le Devoir*, June 2, 1961.

54. Pierre Dupont, letter to the editor, "34% d'anglophones dans une école de langue anglaise," *La Presse*, October 27, 1967.

55. Rassemblement général pour la souveraineté nationale, letter to the editor, "Légiférer pour empêcher l'anglicisation de Montréal," *La Presse*, December 30, 1967.

56. See G. Bouthilier and J. Meynaud, 1972, op.cit., p.700-710.

57. André Laurendeau, "Les Angry young Men," *Le Devoir*, November 11, 1961.

58. G. Bouthillier and J. Meynaud, 1972, op.cit., p. 677.

59. Marcel Vaive, letter to the editor, "L'anglicisation d'un groupe de francophones," *La Presse*, January 18, 1968.

60. Gilles Proulx, letter to the editor, "Les moyens de faire du français une langue d'usage," *La Presse*, July 12, 1968.

61. Anonymous, "Trudeau: à Québec d'améliorer d'abord son "mauvais français," *Le Devoir*, February 15, 1968.

62. Translator's note: cited from *The Ottawa Citizen*, February 14, 1968

63. Albert Lévesque, "Les sophismes de M. Trudeau," *Le Devoir*, February 20, 1968.

64. Dr. Julien Bigras, "Nouvelle réponse à M. Trudeau: devons-nous nous taire, si notre français est pouilleux?" *Le Devoir*, February 20, 1968.

65. [Here A = standard Quebec French as used by radio announcers on Radio-Canada; B= the language of more working class neighbourhoods of Montreal.]
66. Pierre Chantefort, "Diglossie au Québec: limites et tendances actuelles," *Cahiers de linguistique* No. 6, La sociolinguistique au Québec, Presses de l'Uniersité du Québec, 1976, p. 23-53. The study was done in 1970.
67. See K.Lappin, "Évaluation de la pronunciation du français montréalais: etude sociolinguistique," *Revue québécoise* de linguistique, vol. 11, no. 2, 1982, p. 93-113; and L. Tremblay, "Attitudes linguistiques et perception sociale des variables phonétiques," *Revue québécois de linguistique théorique et appliqué*, vol. 9, no. 3, 1990, p. 197-222.

Conclusion

1. Emmanuel Blain de Saint-Aubin "Quelques mots sur la littérature canadienne-française," 1862, in G. Bouthillier and J. Meynaud, 1972, op.cit., p. 166.
2. Jean-Marie Morin, "Propos sur l'éducation," *La Presse*, May 23, 1953.

BIBLIOGRAPHY

Texts Studied

Ariel, France (1920), *Canadiens et Américains chez eux*, Montreal, Granger Frères.

Bouthillier, Guy et Jean Meynaud (1972), *Le choc des langues au Québec, 1760-1970*, Montreal, Presses de l'Université du Québec.

Desbiens, Jean-Paul (1960), *Les insolences d'un frère Untel*, Montreal, Les Éditions de l'Homme.

Drummond, William-Henry (1897), *The Habitant and other French Canadian Poems*, New York and London, G.P. Putnam's Sons.

Granbois, Alain (1944), "N'attendons pas que les veines se vident", in *Bulletin des études françaises*, 18, Montreal, Collège Stanislas.

Laurence, Jean-Marie (1947), *Notre français sur le vif*, Montral, Éditions Le Centre de Psychologie et de Pédagogie.

Ouellette, Fernand (1964), "Le Québec et la lutte des langues," in *Liberté*, vol.6, 2.

Tardivel, Jules-Paul (1881), "La langue française au Canada," in *Revue canadienne*, vol.1, Montreal.

Texts on the subject of language in *La Patrie*, *La Presse* et *Le Devoir*, 1876-1970, from sections on "Régionalisme et populisme," "Langue populaire," "Régionalisme au Canada," "Généralités emprunts," "Anglicismes et américanismes généralités," "Franglais," "Lutte contre les anglicismes," "Prononciation anglicismes," "Patois canadien," "Parisian French" from *Bibliographie des chroniques de langage publiées dans la presse au Canada*, vol. I and II.

Bibliographies

Clas, André, ed. (1976), *Bibliographie des chroniques de langage publiées dans la presse au Canada*, vol. I: 1950-1970; vol. II: 1876-1950, Observatoire du français moderne et contemporain, Département de linguistique et philologie, Montreal, Université de Montréal.

Dublong, Gaston (1966), *Bibliographie linguistique du Canada français*, Québec/Paris, Presses de l'Université Laval/Klincksieck.

Quebec Language and Society

Asselin, Claire et Anne McLaughlin (1994), "Les immigrants en Nouvelle-France au XVIIe siècle parlaient-ils français?," in R. Mougeon and E. Beniak.

Barbaud, Philippe (1984), *Le choc des patois en Nouvelle-France*, Sillery, Presses de l'Université du Québec.

Beauchemin, Normand (1984), "La langue des francophones du Québec," in René Dionne, ed., *Le Québécois et sa littérature*, Sherbrooke/Paris, Naaman/ACCT, pp. 364-377.

Beaudet, Marie-Andrée (1991), *Langue et littérature au Québec, 1895-1914*, Montréal, L'Hexagone.

Bookless, Catherine D. (1983), "Statut de la langue française au Canada 1840-1867," Montréal, Université McGill, M.A.

Bouchard, Chantal (2002), "L'histoire de la norme au Québec (1817-1970): Les relais du métadiscours," *Langue et sociétés*, 39, pp. 25-31.

———. (2001), "L'Office de la langue française; une naissance tant attendue," *Terminogramme*, 101-102 , pp. 25-31.

———. (2000), "Anglicisation et autodépréciation" in Michel Plourde, ed., *Le français au Québec, 400 ans d'histoire et de vie*, Montreal, Fides/Les publications du Québec.

———. (1999), *On n'emprunte qu'aux riches; la valeur sociolinguistique et symbolique des emprunts*, coll. Grandes conférences, Montreal, Fides.

———. (1990), "Conte et légendes du Canada: le mythe du *French Canadian Patois*," in *Bulletin de l'ACLA*, vol. 12, 1.

———. (1989), "Une obsession nationale: l'anglicisme," in *Recherches sociographiques*, vol. XXX, 1.

———. (1988), "De la langue du Grand Siècle à la langue humiliée; les Canadiens français et la langue populaire, 1879-1970," in *Recherches sociographiques*, vol. XXIX, 1.

Bouchard, Dominique (1994), "La culture matérielle des Canadiens au XVIIIe siècle: analyse du niveau de vie des artisans du fer," in *Revue d'histoire de l'Amérique française*, vol. 47, 4, pp. 479-498.

Brazeau, Jacques (1971), "Différences linguistiques et carrières," [1958], in M. Rioux and Y. Martin.

Brillant, Jacques (1968), *L'impossible Québec: essai d'une sociologie de la culture*, Montréal, Éditions du Jour.

Brisset, Annie (1990), *Sociocritique de la traduction. Théâtre et altérité au Québec (1968-1988)*, Longueuil, Le Préambule.

Cajolet-Laganière, Hélène et Pierre Martel (1995), *La qualité de la langue au Québec, Québec*, Institut québécois de recherche sur la culture.

Chantefort, Pierre (1976), "Diglossie au Québec ; limites et tendances actuelles," in *Cahiers linguistiques*, 6, La sociolinguistique au Québec, Montréal, Presses de l'Université du Québec, pp. 23-53.

Corbeil, Jean-Claude (1980), "Aspects sociolinguistiques de la langue française au Québec," in *The French Review*, vol. 53, 6, pp. 834-838.

Coulombe, Pierre A. (1995), *Language Rights in French Canada*, New York, Peter Lang.

Daoust, Paul (1983), *Les jugements sur le joual (1959-1975) à la lumière de la linguistique et de la sociolinguistique*, Ph.D., Département de linguistique et philologie, Université de Montréal.

———. Vues et aperçus sur le français au Canada, Observatoire du français contemporain et moderne, Département de linguistique et philologie, Montréal, Université de Montréal, eds.

Deffontaines, Pierre (1971), "Le rang, type de peuplement rural au Canada français," in M. Rioux and Y. Martin.

Dofny, Jacques et Marcel Rioux (1971), "Les classes sociales au Canada français," [1962], in M. Rioux and Y. Martin.

Dumont, Fernand (1993), *Genèse de la société québécoise*, Montreal, Boréal.

Dumont, Fernand et Jean-Charles Falardeau, eds., (1964), *Littérature et société canadienne-française*, Conference proceedings, *Recherches sociographiques*, Québec, Presses de l'Université Laval.

———. (1964), "Une enquête: le statut de l'écrivain et de la diffusion de la littérature," F. Dumont and J.-Ch. Falardeau.

Falardeau, Jean-Charles (1971), "La paroisse canadienne-française au XVIIᵉ siècle," in M. Rioux and Y. Martin.

———. (1964), "Les milieux sociaux dans le roman canadien-français contemporain," in F. Dumont and J.-Ch. Falardeau.

Faribault, Marthe (1991), "L'apios tubéreux d'Amérique: histoire de mots," in *Recherches amérindiennes au Québec*, vol. XXI, 3, pp. 65-75.

Faucher, Albert et Maurice Lamontagne (1971), *L'histoire du développement industriel au Québec*, [1953], in M.Rioux and Y. Martin.

Fortin, Gérald (1971), "Les changements socio-culturels dans une paroisse agricole," [1961], in M. Rioux and Y. Martin.

Garigue, Philippe (1971), "Évolution et continuité dans la société rurale canadienne-française," [1957], in M. Rioux and Y. Martin.

Gauvin, Lise in collaboration with Rainier Grutman, Alexandra Jarque and Suzanne Martin (1997), *Langues et Littératures*, Dossier bibliographique, Montreal, Centre d'études québécoises.

Gérin, Léon (1971), "La famille canadienne-française, sa force, ses faiblesses," [1932], in M. Rioux and Y. Martin.

Grutman, Rainier (1997), *Des langues qui résonnent. L'hétérolinguisme au XIXe siècle québécois*, Montreal, Fides-CÉTUQ.

Guindon, Hubert (1971), "Réexamen de l'évolution sociale du Québec, [1960] in M. Rioux and Y. Martin, eds.

Haig, Stirling (1980), "Notes. Parlez-vous québécois? Petite mise au point de la langue française au Québec," in *The French Review*, vol. 53, 6, 914-920.

Halford, Peter W. (1994), *Le français des Canadiens à la veille de la Conquête. Témoignage du père Pierre Philippe Potier, s.j.*, Ottawa, Presses de l'Université d'Ottawa.

Henripin, Jacques (1971), "De la fécondité naturelle à la prévention des naissances; l'évolution démographique du Canada français depuis le XVIIe siècle," [1957], in M. Rioux and Y. Martin, eds.

Hughes, Everett C. (1971), "L'industrie et le système rural au Québec," [1938], in M. Rioux and Y. Martin, eds.

Juneau, Marcel (1972), *Contribution à l'histoire de la prononciation française au Québec. Étude des graphies des documents d'archives*, Sainte-Foy, Presse de l'Université Laval.

Keyfitz, Nathan (1971), "Développement démographique au Québec," [1953], in M. Rioux and Y. Martin, eds.

Lamontagne, Léopold (1964), "Les courants idéologiques dans la littérature canadienne-française contemporaine," in F. Dumont and J.-Ch. Falardeau, eds.

Kappin, Kerry (1982), "Évaluation de la prononciation du français montréalais: étude sociolinguistique," in *Revue québécoise de linguistique*, vol. 11, 2, 93-113.

Laurendeau, Paul (1985), "La langue québécoise: un vernaculaire du français," in *Itinéraires et contacts de cultures*, 6, 91-106.

Lemieux, Monique and Henrietta Cedergreen, eds. (1985), *Les tendances dynamiques du français parlé à Montréal*, vol. I and II, Montreal, Office de la langue française.

Marcel, Jean (1973), *Le joual de Troie*, Montreal, Éditions du Jour.

Martel, Pierre and Hélène Cajolet-Laganière, eds. (1997), *Le français québécois. Usages standards et aménagement*, Québec, Institut québécois de la recherche sur la culture/Presses de l'Université Laval.

Martin, Yves (1971), "Les études urbaines au Canada français," [1962], in M. Rioux and Y. Martin, eds.

Miner, Horace (1971), "Le changement dans la culture rurale canadienne-française," [1938], in M. Rioux and Y. Martin, eds.

Morin, Yves-Charles (1994), "Les sources historiques de la prononciation du français au Québec," in R. Mougeon and E. Beniak, eds.

Mougeon, Raymond and Édouard Beniak, eds. (1994), *Les origines du français québécois*, Sainte-Foy, Presses de l'Université Laval.

Noël, Danièle (1990), *Les questions de langue au Québec, 1759-1850*, Conseil de la langue française, Éditeur officiel du Québec.

Parizeau, Gérard (1975), *La société canadienne-française au XIXe siècle*, Montreal, Fides.

Péloquin-Faré, Louise (1983), *L'identité culturelle des Franco-Américains de la Nouvelle-Angleterre*, Paris, Centre de recherche et d'étude pour la diffusion du français, Didier.

Plourde, Michel, ed. (2000), *Le français au Québec, 400 ans d'histoire et de vie*, Montreal, Fides/Les Publications du Québec.

Poirier, Claude (1980), "Le lexique québécois: son évolution, ses composantes," in *Culture populaire et littératures au Québec*, René Bouchard, ed., Saratoga (CA), 43-80.

Poirier, Claude *et al*, eds. (1994), *Langue, espace, société. Les variétés de français en Amérique du Nord*, Sainte-Foy, Presses de l'Université Laval.

Redfield, Robert (1971), "La culture canadienne-française à Saint-Denis," [1939], in M. Rioux and Y. Martin, eds.

Rioux, Marcel (1964), "Commentaire: aliénation culturelle et roman canadien," in F. Dumont and J.Ch. Falardeau.

———. (1971) "Notes sur le développement socio-culturel du Canada français," [1959], in M. Rioux and Y. Martin, eds.

Rioux, Marcel and Yves Martin, eds. (1971), *La société canadienne-française*, Montreal, Hurtubise HMH.

Rocher, Guy (1971), "Les recherches sur les occupations et la stratification sociale," [1962], in M. Rioux and Y. Martin, eds.

Rocher, Guy and Fernand Dumont, eds. (1971), "Introduction à une sociologie du Canada français," [1961], in M. Rioux and Y. Martin, eds.

Simon, Sherry (1994), *Le trafic des langues. Traduction et culture dans la littérature québécoise*, Montreal, Boréal.

———. (1989), *L'inscription sociale de la traduction au Québec*, Montreal, Office de la langue française, coll. "Langues et société."

Taylor, Norman (1971), "L'industriel canadien-français et son milieu," [1961], in M. Rioux and Y. Martin, eds.

Tremblay, L. (1990), "Attitudes linguistiques et perception sociale des variables phonétiques," in *Revue québécoise de linguistique théorique et appliquée*, vol. 9, 3, 197-222.

Sociology

Abou, Selim (1981), *L'identité culturelle: relations interethniques et problèmes d'acculturation*, Paris, Édition Anthropos.

Badie, Bertrand (1983), *Culture politique*, Paris, Economica.

Badie, Bertrand and Jacques Gerstlé, eds. (1979), *Sociologie politique*, Paris, Presses universitaires de France.

Camilleri, Carmel (1989), "La communication dans la perspective interculturelle," in C.Camilleri and M. Cohen-Emerique, eds.

——. (1989). "La culture et l'identité culturelle: champ notionnel et devenir," in C.Camilleri and M. Cohen-Emerique, eds.

Couillaud, Xavier (1984). "Le cas du Royaume-Uni," in *Diversité culturelle, société industrielle, État national,* Actes du colloque, Paris, L'Harmattan.

Gallet, Dominique, ed. (1982), *Dialogue pour l'identité culturelle; 1re conférence internationale pour l'identité culturelle,* Institut France-Tiers Monde, Paris, Éditions Anthropos.

Liégeois, Jean-Pierre (1984), "Une minorité entre l'image et la réalité: l'expérience tsigane," in *Diversité culturelle, société industrielle, État national.*

Malewska-Peyre, Hanna (1989), "Problèmes d'identité des adolescents enfants de migrants et travail social," in C. Camilleri and M. Cohen-Emerique.

Linguistics: History of the language

Bédard, Édith and Jacques Maurais, eds. (1983), *La norme linguistique,* Paris/Québec, Le Robert/Conseil de la langue française.

Bourdieu, Pierre (1972), *Ce que parler veut dire,* Paris, Fayard.

——. (1982), "L'économie des échanges linguistiques," in *Langue française,* 34, Paris, Larousse.

Bourgeois-Gielen, Hélène (1976), "L'usage du flamand au Parlement belge, évolution depuis 1830," in *Actes du XIIIe Congrès international de linguistique et de philologie romanes,* Québec, Presses de l'Université Laval, 51-59.

Francard, Michel in collaboration with Geneviève Geron and Régine Wilmet (1994), "L'insécurité linguistique dans les communautés francophones périphériques," *Cahiers de l'Institut de Linguistique de Louvain,* vol. I, 19, 3-4, 1993 and vol. II, 20, 1-2, 1994.

Picoche, Jacqueline and Christiane Marchello-Nizia, eds. (1989), *Histoire de la langue française,* Paris, Nathan.

Robin, Régine (1993), *Le deuil de l'origine: une langue en trop, la langue en moins,* Saint-Denis, Presses de l'Université de Vincennes.

Trudeau, Danielle (1992), *Les inventeurs du Bon Usage (1529-1647),* Paris, Les éditions de Minuit.

Vaugelas (1647), *Remarques sur la langue française,* Paris.